Shakespeare at the Cineplex

AT THE *Shakespeare* CINEPLEX

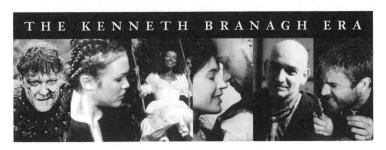

THE KENNETH BRANAGH ERA

Samuel Crowl

OHIO UNIVERSITY PRESS ■ *Athens*

Ohio University Press, Athens, Ohio 45701
© 2003 by Samuel Crowl

Ohio University Press books are printed on acid-free paper ⊚ ™

11 10 09 08 07 06 05 04 03 5 4 3 2 1

Earlier versions of four chapters of the book were previously published as journal articles or chapters in collections of essays devoted to Shakespeare on Film. In all four cases the book versions were substantially rewritten and enlarged. Those articles and chapters are as follows:

"Changing Colors Like the Chameleon: Ian McKellen's *Richard III* from Stage to Film," *Post Script* 17, no. 1 (fall 1997): 53–63.

"Zeffirelli's *Hamlet:* The Golden Girl and a Fistful of Dust," *Cineaste* 24, no. 1 (1998): 56–61.

"Flamboyant Realist: Kenneth Branagh," *The Cambridge Companion to Shakespeare on Film*, ed. Russell Jackson, pp. 222–40 (Cambridge: Cambridge University Press, 2000).

"The Marriage of Shakespeare and Hollywood: Kenneth Branagh's *Much Ado About Nothing,*" *Spectacular Shakespeare: Critical Theory and Popular Cinema*, ed. Courtney Lehmann and Lisa S. Starks (Madison, N.J.: Fairleigh Dickinson University Press, 2002).

Library of Congress Cataloging-in-Publication Data

Crowl, Samuel.
　　Shakespeare at the cineplex: the Kenneth Branagh era / Samuel Crowl.
　　　p. cm.
　　Includes bibliographical references and index.
　　ISBN 0-8214-1494-1 (acid-free paper)
　　1. Shakespeare, William, 1564–1616—Film and video adaptations. 2. English
　drama—Film and video adaptations. 3. Film adaptations. 4. Branagh, Kenneth. I.
Title.

PR3093.C75 2003
822.3'3—dc21   2002193038

For Susan

"If this be magic, let it be an art
Lawful as eating."

Contents

Illustrations

Acknowledgments

I owe a great debt of gratitude to James Lusardi and June Schlueter, the editors of *Shakespeare Bulletin*, for allowing me a "first take" in the pages of their journal on most of the films explored in this book. Several of those reviews were subsequently worked up into more mature essays to be contributed to film and performance seminars at the Shakespeare Association of America, the International Shakespeare Association Conference, and the World Shakespeare Congress. Some of those essays eventually found their way into print. A version of chapter 3 was published in *Cineaste*; a shorter version of chapter 4 appeared in *Spectacular Shakespeare: Critical Theory and Popular Cinema*, edited by Courtney Lehmann and Lisa Starks; an early version of chapter 7 was published in *Post Script*; and excerpts from the material scattered through the chapters on Kenneth Branagh's Shakespeare films originally appeared in my essay on his work in *The Cambridge Companion to Shakespeare on Film*, edited by Russell Jackson.

Similarly, early versions of some of this material were also presented to college and conference audiences. I am grateful to the organizers of the Columbia University Shakespeare Seminar, the Shakespeare Institute Lecture Series, the Shakespeare on Screen Centenary Conference, the literature faculty at the University of Toulouse–Le Mirail, the *Hamlet* on Film Conference sponsored by the new Globe Theatre, and the trustees of the Shakespeare Association of America (SAA) for inviting me to present my emerging ideas about these films to their audiences.

For twenty-five years, the film and performance seminars at the Shakespeare Association of America meetings have nourished and nurtured the remarkable growth and development of this important area in Shakespeare studies. At last count, those seminars have contributed to the publication of at least twenty books (including this one) largely devoted to issues related to Shakespeare on stage and screen. I am deeply indebted, for their critical generosity and personal friendship, to the core group of scholars who have made those seminars flourish: James Bulman, H. R. Coursen, Anthony Davies, Anthony Dawson, Peter S. Donaldson, Miriam Gilbert, Robert Hapgood, Barbara Hodgdon, Russell Jackson, Jack Jorgens, Harry Keyishian, Bernice Kliman, James Lake, Michael Manheim, Thomas Pendleton, Kenneth Rothwell, Carol Rutter, and Robert Willson. That group has expanded over the years to include new voices and fresh perspectives, particularly those of Stephen Buhler, Mark Thornton Burnett, Katherine Eggert, John Ford, Kathy Howlett, Douglas Lanier, Courtney Lehmann, Patricia Lennox, Laurie Osborne, and Lisa Starks. These colleagues have made working in this particularly rich vein of Shakespeare in performance a "playing holiday" as well as an intellectually rewarding experience.

I want to thank all the members of the three film seminars on the work of Kenneth Branagh and his contemporaries that I led at the SAA in 1997 and 2002 for enriching my understanding of these films as they raised my spirits about our common enterprise. They join with students at Ohio University, particularly those in my freshman and senior undergraduate seminars and graduate courses, who have explored this material with me in various formats over the last decade. I have stolen ideas from all of them as if our exchanges took place as it approached dawn at Gadshill; I fully expect my thefts to be repaid in kind. I want to recognize several of these young scholars and enthusiasts, with the understanding that their names must stand for many: Lindsey Day, Erin Doppes, Tony Eufinger, Colleen Glenn, Taylor Hagood, Scott Henkel, Amadeo Lupi, Jim Orrick, Piper Perabo, Imad Rahman, Gary Steinberg, Christine Veladota, James Wells, and Jennifer Porter Wiswell.

I have been blessed with a warm and congenial group of colleagues and friends who have shared their ideas with me about many of these films and who have selflessly provided support and encouragement as *Shakespeare at the Cineplex* took shape. It is a pleasure to acknowledge their long participation in a conversation about our common enterprise: Alan and Peggy Booth, Tom Carpenter and Lynne Lancaster, Ken and Devorah Daley, John Gaddis and Toni Dorfman, Lewis and Susan Greenstein, Tim and Sophie Holm, Dean and Alvi McWilliams, Charles and Claire Ping, Ed and Carolyn Quattrocki, Stuart and Anne Scott, and Duane Schneider and Crystal Gips. My thinking, particularly about Branagh's *Hamlet,* was enriched by the response of the Ohio University English Department's faculty colloquium, ably founded and led by Andrew Escobedo, to an early draft of my chapter on that film. I want to thank the former chair of the department, Betty Pytlik, for arranging for a quarter's research leave when my work on the book was gathering momentum; and thanks, too, to the current chair, Ken Daley, for keeping one of the old guys in the loop. Mike Kaiser and David Skal were both helpful in keeping me alert to the Shakespeare beat in Hollywood. An Ohio University Faculty Fellowship Leave supplemented by a Baker Fund Award helped to support six months of uninterrupted writing in an Edwardian flat in Bloomsbury in the winter and spring of 2001. It was there that the first draft of the manuscript was completed. And I want to offer a special thanks to Kenneth Branagh, Christine Edzard, and Adrian Noble for graciously stealing time from busy production schedules to talk with me about their films.

A crowning moment in the critical development of the Shakespeare on film movement came at the Shakespeare on Screen Centenary Conference, brilliantly organized and led by Professor José Ramón Díaz Fernández, held in Benalmádena, Spain, in September 1999. As part of the festivities, Professor Díaz arranged for the participants to visit Ronda, the historic bull-fighting capital of Spain. We journeyed to Ronda not just to enjoy its natural beauty but also to visit the quinta of the great midcentury matador Antonio Ordóñez whose epic battles with his brother-in-law and rival Luis Miguel Dominguín in the summer of 1959 were chronicled by Hemingway in *The Dangerous Summer*. We did so to pay honor and homage to another giant of the mid-twentieth century, Orson Welles—for, little known to the world, his ashes are buried at Ordóñez's ranch. The great man's remains are interred in a little ivy-covered well surrounded by olive trees in the hacienda's front garden. As Russell Jackson, Ken Rothwell, Tony Davies, and I gathered around this sweet, obscure shrine ("Master of the Masters," the inscription reads) to pay our respects to Welles—whose body, when it "did contain a spirit, / A kingdom for it was too small a bound"—we could not resist quipping on a variety of versions of "all's well that ends well." Those jests, however lame, were fitting, for the conference that had taken us to that remote and incongruous site was celebrating what Orson Welles and Laurence Olivier had made possible: the mature, successful Shakespeare film. That legacy and the twentieth century's long fascination with Shakespeare as material for film was indeed ending well in the work of Branagh and his contemporaries.

Patty Pyle graciously came out of retirement to prepare the manuscript for submission, courageously working from handwritten chapters mailed in from London. Once again, I have been generously treated by the Ohio University Press. Special thanks are due to its director, David Sanders, for the personal interest he has taken in this project, to my copy-editor, Dennis Marshall, for his care with the manuscript, and to Nancy Basmajian, managing editor, who was quick to respond positively to all my big and little requests.

Finally, one of the glories of working with Shakespeare in perform-ance is the opportunity to share our responses to productions on stage and screen with others. For me, that begins with family, and I want to thank Miranda Crowl and Bill Pistner and Samuel Crowl and Terry Kelleher for joining in so many good Shakespearean moments over the last decade. Now they have brought a new generation of Shakespeareans (Charlie and Theo and Aidan and Audrey) tumbling into the world to join our revels. Finally, to Professor Susan Crowl, who has shared and en-riched my experiences of these films from first take to final cut, deep thanks for making the journey of this book such a fine, spirited, and re-warding adventure: "We shall not cease from exploration / And the end of our exploring / Will be to arrive where we started / And know the place for the first time."

Athens, Ohio
July 2002

Shakespeare at the Cineplex

The Long Decade

1989–2001

The twentieth century's long fascination with Shakespeare as material for film ended not with a whimper but a bang. The last decade of the century witnessed the greatest explosion of Anglo-American films based on Shakespeare's plays in the hundred-year history of the genre. Kenneth S. Rothwell has provided the comprehensive account of that history, and his work should be consulted by any serious student of Shakespeare on film.[1] In brief, that history can be condensed into five acts. Act 1 (1899–1929) was the silent era, featuring, according to Robert Hamilton Ball, more than four hundred one- and two-reel films based on Shakespearean material.[2] Act 2 (1930s) consisted of Hollywood's first attempt to merge Shakespeare with popular film. Act 3 followed World War II and was the great international phase in Shakespeare's absorption into film by directors as diverse as Laurence Olivier, Orson Welles, Akira Kurosawa, Grigori Kozintsev, and Franco Zeffirelli. Act 4, which stretches from Roman Polanski's *Macbeth* (1971) to Kenneth Branagh's *Henry V* (1989), was a barren wasteland in which Shakespeare almost completely disappeared from film. Act 5 (1989–2001) represents the revival of the Shakespeare film genre—what Rothwell has called "The Age of Branagh"—and is the subject of this study.[3]

This last decade consists of the most concentrated release of sound films based on Shakespeare's works in the century, similar to, but surpassing, the decade that followed the end of World War II. The long decade produced fifteen major Shakespeare films and an equal number of spin-offs ranging from Peter Greenaway's *Prospero's Books* (1991) to Al Pacino's *Looking for Richard* (1996) to John Madden's *Shakespeare in Love* (1998) to Gil Junger's *Ten Things I Hate About You* (1999) to Tim Blake Nelson's *O* (2001). Film's long romance with Shakespeare in the twentieth century ended with one cluster after another of new Shakespeare films appearing on screens around the globe. Some fine films—for example, Trevor Nunn's *Twelfth Night* (1996) and Julie Taymor's *Titus* (1999)—could not sustain their commercial glow; others—Branagh's *Much Ado About Nothing* (1993), for example, and Baz Luhrmann's *William Shakespeare's Romeo + Juliet* (1996)—competed brilliantly with more typical Hollywood fare at the box office.[4]

This study concentrates on the fifteen films directly committed to reproducing a Shakespearean text in the traditional language of the narrative film. These films confront a common set of problems and opportunities in attacking that challenge and form an interesting historical dialogue with previous English-language films by Olivier, Welles, Mankiewicz, Brook, Hall, and Zeffirelli. The spin-offs, even a film like *Prospero's Books*, which give us all of the text of *The Tempest* spoken gloriously by John Gielgud, present a different set of issues when working with Shakespeare on film and are best left to a separate study.[5]

It is a commonplace to note that the development of narrative film was a logical progression from the nineteenth-century theater's interest in spectacle. And once silent film developed beyond the nickelodeons, its logical home was in existing theatrical structures. When the first great movie palaces were built in the 1920s and 1930s, they resembled the elaborate and ornate Victorian music-hall theaters that had been film's first homes, just as the first permanent playhouse built in London exclusively for Elizabethan drama, James Burbage's Theatre (1576), resembled the polygon-shaped inns that had provided early modern drama's first commercial playing spaces.

The 1970s brought a radical shift in the design of screening space for the popular film. That shift led to the development of the American cineplex. The venue no longer was one large auditorium with a single screen but multiple small screening rooms, so that a single site could simultaneously project a dozen films or more. The suburban cineplex, in form and content, now more closely resembles a modern international airport than a nineteenth-century music hall or vaudeville theater. Rather than an ornate, multistoried urban building, the cineplex is a large, sprawling, suburban, one-story, cement-block structure, surrounded by acres of parking lot. I have visited some where the parking lots were so spacious that one looked, in vain I'm afraid, for the cinema shuttle. On entering the cineplex, one is not confronted with a typical theater lobby but with a giant electronic announcement board displaying arrivals and departures. After purchasing a ticket, one is directed down one of several long hallways radiating out from the popcorn-and-Pepsi kiosk and lined with screening rooms arranged like gates at an airport. Most of the flights are to exotic locations, film never-never lands, to which the spectators are transported with the guarantee that they will be returned, safely, in two hours or less, to their point of departure. The urban cinema art house, to be competitive, even on a much smaller scale, has had to subdivide, redesigning its former single screening space into a series of smaller projection rooms.

Multiple screens, like the proliferation of cable television channels, demand more product, which has paradoxically created a market for what has come to be termed the independent film—the category that encompasses most of the Shakespeare films released in the long decade. The gradual shift in screening space coincided with the collapse of the film monopoly enjoyed by the Hollywood studio system from the 1930s to the 1950s. By the early 1970s, Hollywood was no longer defined by the major studios, each with its own company of stars, directors, and writers making films on its own back lots and soundstages. The new Hollywood came to represent money and market, providing funding and distribution for films intended for a mass international audience and encompassing pictures as diverse as *Lawrence of Arabia* (1962), *Dr. Strangelove* (1963), *The Godfather* (1972), *Chinatown* (1974), and *Star Wars* (1977). Zeffirelli's *Romeo and Juliet* (1968) was the first Shakespeare film to represent the new Hollywood's combination of money and market, and it became the largest grossing Shakespeare film—in constant dollars—in history.[6]

By the 1990s, as the number of cineplex screens increased and the average cost of a major Hollywood film approached $60 million, the market expanded for smaller, less expensively produced independent films, made on budgets between $5 million and $15 million. One film company, Miramax, came to signify this market, originally purchasing the distribution rights for foreign or independently produced films and eventually financing and producing films itself. Miramax's triumph came in 1998 when *Shakespeare in Love* snatched the Oscar for best picture away from *Saving Private Ryan*, Steven Spielberg's blockbuster film about the Normandy invasion. Miramax spawned a series of competitors, often created as separate divisions of the major studios, such as Samuel Goldwyn,

Pathé, Fine Line, Fox Searchlight, and Castle Rock. As Russell Jackson points out, "The 'independent' distributors in Hollywood, such as Miramax, invest mainly in low-budget films, often made outside the United States. The movies are typified by their 'attention to theme, character relationships and social relevance, and targeted at a market somewhere between the art-house and the main-stream.'"[7] By the end of the decade, Miramax had become, in terms of box-office revenue, Hollywood's fifth largest studio and a major player in the world of commercial film.

The world of the independent film is the budget and market niche for most of the Shakespeare films released in the last decade, their directors hoping to attract a mainstream audience while working on an art-house-film budget. Some of these films, though, were originally marketed for a mainstream audience (Zeffirelli's *Hamlet* [1990], Luhrmann's *William Shakespeare's Romeo + Juliet* [1996], and Michael Hoffman's *A Midsummer Night's Dream* [1999]); in industry lingo, they opened "wide."[8] Others achieved wide distribution by their initial success on a few screens (Branagh's *Henry V* and *Much Ado About Nothing*), but most lived and died with the art-house audience. The most expensive of these films, Taymor's *Titus* (1999), was shot on a budget of $25 million. The size of the budget was rare for a Shakespeare film, especially one being made by a director making her first feature film, but it undoubtedly represented a gamble based on her amazing artistic and financial success with creating the stage version of *The Lion King*.

Though Taymor's film is the most visually stunning of the group, they all aspire to production values associated with mainstream Hollywood films. Only Branagh's *Henry V,* Christine Edzard's *As You Like It* (1992) and *The Children's Midsummer Night's Dream* (2001), Adrian Noble's *A Midsummer Night's Dream* (1996), and Michael Almereyda's *Hamlet* (2000) reveal, often like a badge of artistic honor, their budgetary limitations.[9] For many of these films, a major savings came in cast costs. For the opportunity to do Shakespeare, most of the actors were willing to work for scale.[10] Established Hollywood actors like Michael Keaton, Robin Williams, Michelle Pfeiffer, Ethan Hawke, Bill Murray, Alicia Silverstone, Glenn Close, Annette Bening, Denzel Washington, and Mel Gibson all waived the substantial fees they command for appearing in conventional Hollywood films.

In 1977, in his opening chapter of *Shakespeare on Film*, Jack Jorgens divided the major sound-era Shakespeare films into three categories: the theatrical, the realistic, and the filmic.[11] Though Jorgens was aware that these categories were fluid and that a single film might contain elements of each, it was clear from his descriptions that Olivier's Shakespeare films typified the theatrical, Zeffirelli's the realistic, and Welles's the filmic. Jorgens judiciously spelled out the strengths and weaknesses inherent in each, but he was prescient to see the staying power of the realistic mode: "This is the most popular kind of Shakespeare film, not merely because film makers are most familiar with it and mass audiences enjoy the spectacle of historical recreations, but because everyone senses that at bottom Shakespeare is a realist."[12] Though many would dispute this claim, Jorgens is describing a particularly modern response to the power, sweep, and multilayered density of Shakespeare's worlds inhabited by characters presented with a psychological acuity that seems more of our age than his. Harold Bloom, after all, has made the astounding claim that Shakespeare invented our modern notion of psychological self-consciousness.[13] As Jorgens comprehensively comments:

> If realism in film implies something more than a visual style or authentic costumes and settings, it seems to many that this playwright—who filled his Globe with duels, battles, shipwrecks, tortures, assassinations, storms, coronations, trials, suicides, feasts, and funerals, who juxtaposed the ugly with the sublime, the base with the noble, everyday with holiday, who ruthlessly explored both the need for and the dangers of centralized power, the conflicts of young and old, the rocking of order and tradition by frightening, invigorating forces of change—virtually demands screen realism.[14]

For Jorgens, the expansive nature of the realistic mode reaches out to include a wide variety of film styles: "It may be Zeffirelli's decorative, spectacular, orchestrally accompanied variety, which is a descendant of the elaborate productions of the nineteenth century, or the harsh documentary style of Brook's *Lear*, or a mixed style, as in Polanski's gory, twilight *Macbeth*, the fortress and tangled forest of Kurosawa's *Throne of Blood*, or the silences and wintery spaces of Welles's *Chimes at Midnight*."[15]

I quote Jorgens at length not just because he remains one of the most compelling analysts of Shakespeare on film but because the realistic mode has dominated the revival of the genre in the 1990s. Somewhat surprisingly, it is Zeffirelli, rather than Olivier or Welles, who has had the greatest stylistic impact on these recent Shakespeare films. While many of these films spring, like Olivier's, from theatrical productions, they are much quicker to bury or disguise their stage origins. All four of Branagh's Shakespeare films were made from plays he had performed in on stage, but only his *Henry V* revealed some of its theatrical roots in its visual style. Ian McKellen intentionally turned to Richard Loncraine, a film director with no previous experience of working with Shakespeare, to translate his noted stage performance of Richard III into film.[16] Nunn, along with Noble the most experienced Shakespearean among the directors of these films, had never directed *Twelfth Night* on the stage in his long reign as head of the Royal Shakespeare Company. Only Parker's *Othello* (1995), Noble's *A Midsummer Night's Dream*, and Taymor's *Titus* had their origins in productions of the plays they had directed on stage. And only Noble's *Dream* retained obvious elements of costume and design from his stage production of the play. None of these films, unlike films of an earlier generation such as Tony Richardson's *Hamlet* (1969) or Stuart Burge's *Othello* (1965), intentionally revealed their theatrical roots. In the 1990s, television, rather than film, became the preferred medium for capturing brilliant stage productions of Shakespeare like Trevor Nunn's *Othello* (1990) with Willard White and Imogen Stubbs, Richard Eyre's *King Lear* (1997) with Ian Holm and Michael Bryant, and Gregory Doran's *Macbeth* (2000) with Anthony Sher and Harriet Walters. Jorgens's theatrical mode has almost completely disappeared in the films of this period.

A similar fate has befallen what Jorgens terms the filmic or poetic mode. Only Branagh's *Henry V* and Almereyda's *Hamlet* acknowledge the influence of Welles in this group of films. Almereyda's film has a genuine Wellesian feel about it, landscape, camera work, and a self-conscious awareness of film's poetic potential becoming essential components of the narrative. Taymor's *Titus* is an even more daring exploration of film's ability to encompass different modes of representation and certainly strives to create a film poetry to rival Shakespeare's. In the history of Shakespeare on film, *Titus* contains the widest mixture of film and acting styles—perhaps rivaled only by the Reinhardt and Dieterle *A Midsummer Night's Dream* (1935). Though distinguished by a brilliant performance of Titus by Anthony Hopkins, some stunning shots and sequences that rival the best ever achieved in a Shakespeare film, and the director's eclectic visual imagination, the film failed to capture an audience initially lured to the cineplex by the knowledge of Taymor's success with *The Lion King* and her all-star cast.

The poetic mode appears to have met the same fate as the theatrical, leaving the field to the realistic or representational. This will come as no surprise to followers of contemporary film, for this is the mode that has triumphed in the broader film world as well. Hollywood, considered less as a specific place located in southern California than as a stylistic mode dominating commercial film and as a nexus for the confluence of money and market, has become the shorthand expression defining the international narrative film in the last one-third of the twentieth century. The realistic mode, imagined by Jorgens as a combination of historical period spectacle with the action film, has expanded its boundaries, pushed by directors as various as Francis Ford Coppola, George Lucas, Steven Spielberg, Ethan and Joel Coen, Jane Campion, Ridley Scott, and Ang Lee. The great international phase in the history of Shakespeare on film, lasting from the mid-1940s to the mid-1960s, also corresponded to the great period of European film dominated by Bergman, Fellini, Antonioni, Godard, and Truffaut. European cinema was more the model for Welles and Olivier than the commercial Hollywood film of its time.

Welles and Olivier may have learned their film grammar from John Ford and William Wyler, but their film rhetoric, particularly in Welles's *Macbeth* (1948) and Olivier's *Hamlet* (1948), shows the influence of German expressionism much more than that of the commercial Hollywood film, even film noire. Though both men craved a wide audience—they were after all both actor-managers who thrived on being in the spotlight—the Hollywood film had yet to achieve the critical approval or cultural status that would allow them, unlike Branagh and Luhrmann forty years later, to raid it for ideas and models for their own films. Welles's own *Citizen Kane* (1941), repeatedly recognized as the great American film, seems now to fit in style and structure more comfortably into a European than a Hollywood film tradition. Welles himself left Hollywood and America for Europe in the 1950s to help launch the great international phase in the history of film.

The Shakespeare films of the 1990s are distinguished by their willingness to incorporate Hollywood genres, tropes, technical innovations, and casting practices. Not all of these films participate in this process as fully as others, but if we can imagine a spectrum, within the realistic mode, of Hollywood's influence, it would be most pronounced in the work of Branagh, Zeffirelli, Parker, Loncraine, Luhrmann, and Hoffman and less so in that of Almereyda, Edzard, Nunn, and Taymor. One of the chief ways these new films differ from their predecessors is in casting. As Lynda Boose and Richard Burt note, "the sudden contemporary renaissance in filmed Shakespeare is British-led, but by 1995 even British casting practices had changed to reflect the exigencies of market capitalism."[17] While Welles's *Chimes at Midnight* (1966) was the first Shakespeare film to employ an international cast—it included Keith Baxter and John Gielgud (English), Jeanne Moreau and Marina Vlady (French), Norman Rodway (Irish), Walter Chiari (Italian), and Welles himself (American)—the practice became commonplace only in the films of Zeffirelli and Branagh. In each case, their prime contribution to expanding the popular parameters of the Shakespeare film was to merge and mingle established Hollywood stars (Elizabeth Taylor, Mel Gibson, Glenn Close, Denzel Washington, Robin Williams, Alicia Silverstone) with English stage and film actors (Richard Burton, Ian Holm, Alan Bates, Emma Thompson, Derek Jacobi, Julie Christie), with largely successful results.

While Olivier's Shakespeare films are now used as standards against which to compare (and often find wanting) the efforts of Branagh and Zeffirelli, they would have been immeasurably improved by a more expansive casting policy, even among his own countrymen. His own well-documented professional jealousies kept him, until *Richard III* (1955), from using his great contemporaries Ralph Richardson (who would have made a magnificent Polonius) and John Gielgud (who wanted to play Chorus in *Henry V* [1944]) or younger actors like Alec Guinness and Richard Burton.

For Olivier and Welles, film was still something of an infant. Their challenge was to discover, in very differing artistic fashions, if Shakespeare could be translated successfully into the language of film. For Olivier, that language was an extension of his work with Shakespeare in the theater. As Jorgens points out, using Olivier as his model, the theatrical mode conceives the film performance "in terms of the theatre . . . [so] . . . Shakespeare's tremendous range of verbal and dramatic styles from stark naturalism to meta-theatrical playfulness need not be narrowed in the name of film convention and decorum."[18] He goes on to argue that it is the "blatant *theatricality* of Olivier's *Hamlet* which permits him to instruct the players from off-camera in the simultaneous roles of film director, Prince of Denmark, and surrogate for Shakespeare, and allows us to enjoy the irony that the performances in 'The Murder of Gonzago' prove they weren't listening."[19] For Welles, the problem was less translation than transformation. His frequently expressed analogy for the relationship between Shakespeare and film was that between Shakespeare and opera. Film for Welles was like opera—an independent art form with its own language, structure, and dynamics. We understand that when Boito and Verdi set out to make their *Otello*, they were creating a new work, not just a version of Shakespeare's play with arias substituting for soliloquies. Welles wanted the same liberties granted the filmmaker when dealing with Shakespearean material.[20] Jorgens notes that "like the realist, the film poet uses many non-theatrical techniques—a great variety of angles and distances, camera movements. He substitutes for the classical style of playing *on* the lines, the modern style of playing *between* the lines. But unlike the other modes, there is emphasis on the *artifice* of film, on the expressive possibilities of distorting the surfaces of reality."[21]

For Branagh and his generation of directors, Olivier and Welles had proved that Shakespeare and film were not fatally incompatible. Spurred by the commercial success of Zeffirelli's *Romeo and Juliet*, they sought ways to take Shakespeare even deeper into the model of the popular film. Branagh's career is emblematic. Between 1989 and 2001 he directed nine films (including four based on Shakespeare's plays and one based on related Shakespearean material), starred in nine others, played Hamlet and Coriolanus on stage, directed and acted in stage productions of *A Midsummer Night's Dream* and *King Lear*, and directed and acted in radio productions of *Hamlet, Romeo and Juliet, King Lear*, and *Richard III*. His film roles in *The Gingerbread Man* (1998), *Celebrity* (1998), and *Wild Wild West* (1999) allowed him to work with auteur directors Robert Altman and Woody Allen and the young Hollywood hotshot Barry Sonnenfeld.

When asked about the relationship between his work in mainstream commercial films and Shakespeare, Branagh replied:

> As a cinema-goer, I'm quite eclectic in my tastes and watch a wide range of films. Part of the challenge with the Shakespeare films, which remain a sort of backbone to what I do, seems to be necessarily and healthily influenced by exposure to, as a performer and as a director, story-telling in other kinds of genres (with the idea being that one is constantly trying to challenge the ways in which Shakespeare can be offered up on film). Therefore, to be familiar with the ways in which popular cinema tells its stories is very important . . . the way in which to approach [a new Shakespeare film] continues then to develop . . . You have to see if there's anything you can pick up from that to ask . . . "How can we make [Shakespeare] more available?" or "How can we open up the plays more?" So being away from [Shakespeare] for a while helps me enormously.[22]

None of his contemporaries has had such a rich decade of varied stage and film activity, but Branagh's continuing desire to find meaningful ways of linking popular modes of storytelling on film with Shakespeare defines this generation of Shakespearean directors.

Hoffman is only the most obvious example. He is an accomplished Hollywood director with several successful screen comedies to his credit, including *Soapdish* (1991), *Restoration* (1996), and *One Fine Day* (1996). His *A Midsummer Night's Dream* is the only one of these films to be made by a Hollywood insider, and it takes the broadest and most spectacular approach to its material. In many ways it is a remake of the Warner Brother's 1935 *Dream*, which featured a diverse range of studio actors from James Cagney to Dick Powell to Mickey Rooney to Olivia de Havilland. Hoffman employs a similar host of stars drawn from the worlds of movies and television: Michelle Pfeiffer, Kevin Kline, Rupert Everett, Calista Flockhart, Christian Bale, and Anna Friel. His film seeks to capture, in lush Technicolor, the lavish production qualities aspired to by Reinhardt and Dieterle. His film features the same eclectic approach to capturing Shakespeare's forest world. Where Reinhardt and Dieterle imagined the fairies as ballerinas streaming down from the heavens on moonbeams, Hoffman goes Disney with Tinkerbell-esque fireflies dancing in the night. Where Reinhardt and Dieterle filled their woods with an odd congregation of stags, rabbits, frogs, unicorns, and a little orchestra of gnomes, Hoffman peoples his with creatures ranging from totemic Etruscan statues to exiles from Jabba the Hut's bar in *The Return of the Jedi* and a reprise of the Warner Brothers gnomes, this time using them to spirit away from Theseus's palace a gramophone that ends up in Titania's bower. Hoffman, who begins and ends his film on location in Tuscany, even follows Reinhardt and Dieterle into the sound stage for the forest scenes—this time to Fellini's old studio at Rome's Cinecitta. Hoffman returns sound-era Shakespeare to the Hollywood that gave him birth, now with all the technological advances of modern film.

If Hoffman's film oozes Hollywood from every frame, Edzard's *As You Like It* occupies the other end of the spectrum. Edzard, best known for her four-hour film of Charles Dickens's *Little Dorrit* (1987), shot her first Shakespeare film on a budget of $1 million in the tiny Thames-side Sands Film Studio and on location in a neighboring abandoned Rotherhithe building site. Her largely unknown cast featured only one established film actor, James Fox, and one veteran of the stage, Cyril Cusack. Her film's charm rests in matching its low-budget resources with the spirit of

Shakespeare's Arden, where the imagination, rather than power, reigns. To succeed, Edzard's film, of all those in the Branagh era, demands the greatest leap of faith, or willing suspension of disbelief, from the viewer. We have to piece out its imperfections with our thoughts to transform her version of Arden as an abandoned slice of urban renewal into a playing space corresponding to Rosalind and Orlando's forest-wooing landscape. As Hoffman's film strains the limits of spectacular Shakespeare, so Edzard's flirts with the dangers of minimalism when applied to Shakespeare's most festive comedy. A pair of Beckett tramps, sharing a joint and joining the chorus of "It Was a Lover and His Lass," pushes the festive moment as far into modernism as it probably can go.

The other Shakespeare films in this long decade fall somewhere between these two poles, but most are to be found at the commercial end of the spectrum. What distinguishes many of these films from those of the 1940s and 1950s is their willingness not only to take the Hollywood film as a model, but to delight in quoting from Hollywood genres and specific films as well: Hoffman, as noted, mixes Disney with Dieterle in his *Dream;* Zeffirelli raids the American western in his *Hamlet;*[23] Almereyda's *Hamlet* is loaded with film noirish ideas; Loncraine's *Richard III* (1995), as Rothwell notes, quotes relentlessly from Hollywood movies as disparate as John Woo action films and 1930s gangster films;[24] Noble's *A Midsummer Night's Dream* attempts to capture ideas from his stage production of the play, using the frame of childhood fantasies ranging from *Alice in Wonderland* to *The Wizard of Oz* and *ET;* Parker's *Othello* yearns to be a romantic spectacle; and Luhrmann's *William Shakespeare's Romeo + Juliet* brazenly careens from one Hollywood style to another with the relentless cutting and heat of the latest MTV video. Even Taymor's brilliant, often surreal, *Titus* can't resist cracking Hollywood jokes worthy of Quentin Tarantino. One such moment is when Aaron attaches a plastic baggie containing Titus's freshly lopped-off hand to the rearview mirror of his sporty Fiat as he zooms off into the night with the radio blaring a jazzy tune.

The director principally responsible for initiating this profusion of Hollywood quotations within the Shakespeare film genre is Branagh. His four Shakespeare films not only dominate this revival of the genre, they also provide the richest source of examples. Critics as diverse as Rothwell, Kathy Howlett, and Sarah Hatchuel all have responded to this element in Branagh's work. His genius as a popularizer of Shakespeare lies in his willingness to find and self-consciously champion creative energy from the commercial Hollywood film. Branagh's career as a film director is marked by his open admiration for directors such as Alfred Hitchcock, David Lean, and Lawrence Kasdan. Branagh's unique contribution to the Shakespeare film genre is to have found in Hollywood movies a film language that allowed Shakespeare to break free from the elite art-house audience to find a broader public, especially among the young. His films, from *Henry V* to *Love's Labour's Lost* (2000), trace his progress in uncovering a congenial film style for Shakespeare. Each of his films appropriates an established Hollywood genre: the war film for *Henry V*; screwball comedy for *Much Ado About Nothing;* the intelligent epic for *Hamlet;* and the American movie musical for *Love's Labour's Lost.* Within these basic genres, he is then free to quote from such varied directors of the popular film as Howard Hawks, Stanley Donen, David Lean, and Stanley Kubrick.

Branagh's influence was crucial to this revival because of his energy, focus, organizational skills, and Shakespearean credentials. Although he spent only a single season with the Royal Shakespeare Company, I associate his Shakespearean background with Stratford—symbol of Shakespeare on stage in England. There he became noted for being, at the age of twenty-three, the youngest actor to play Henry V for the company. His youth was crucial because it launched him into his career as a director of Shakespeare films before he had achieved an Olivier-like status as a classical actor. Whereas Olivier, by the time he came to make his Shakespeare films, was both a creation of the long English stage history of the actor-manager and a senior representative of that legacy (he had had his flirtation with Hollywood in the 1930s, but it did not rival, in his creative imagination, the pull of the Old Vic and the idea that came to be the National Theatre), Branagh brought the requisite English stage Shakespearean credentials to his film experience without a cultural sentimentality about the stage's superiority to the younger art form.

A surprising source, Marlon Brando, confirms Branagh's appeal. He cites Branagh's film of *Henry V* as demonstrating an art of playing and speaking Shakespeare that exemplifies Hamlet's famous advice to the players: "The evolution of the English theater came to full flower in Kenneth Branagh's [film] production of *Henry V.* He did not injure the language; he showed reverence for it, and followed Shakespeare's instructions [to the actors in *Hamlet*] precisely. It was an extraordinary accomplishment of melding the realities of human behavior with the poetry of language. I can't imagine Shakespeare being performed with more refinement."[25] For Brando, in this context, "refinement" is not an ironic twist to the compliment, but high praise, as he goes on to elaborate: "In America we are unable to approach such refinements, and of course have no taste for it. If given the choice between Branagh's production of *Henry V* or Arnold Schwarzenegger's *The Terminator*, there's hardly a question of where most television dials would be turned. If the expenditure of money for entertainment in America is any indication of taste, clearly the majority of us are addicted to trash."[26] Brando here demonstrates an American attitude typical of artists and intellectuals of his generation: a disdain for American popular culture and an exaggerated reverence for the English tradition of classical acting.

Branagh, however, is very much of *his* generation, and he has tried to erase the fault lines separating popular and elite forms of entertainment. Branagh's passion for commercial films has allowed him to attempt to return Shakespeare to his origins in the popular theater of his own age. Surely one of the glories of Tom Stoppard's contribution to the screenplay of *Shakespeare in Love* was his witty linking of the commercial world of Shakespeare's theater with that of Hollywood. As Russell Jackson notes about this element in the film's subplot: "The tension between the artist and the marketplace has always been a good source of humor in drama and fiction and on film, and the story is usually told in terms of the crassness of the producers and the crushed idealism of the 'creative' department."[27] This tension, and Jackson's description of its dynamics, has driven such recent films as Robert Altman's *The Player* (1992), Barry Sonnenfeld's *Get Shorty* (1995), and David Mamet's *State and Main* (2001). Stoppard's script repositions Shakespeare not as the cultural symbol of high art but as the delicious object of low comedy: he is pursued by his creditors, nagged by his producers, anguished by his writer's block, baffled by his early modern shrink, and saved by a beautiful aristocratic androgynous muse. The film's final witty stroke is a visual one. It reveals, appropriately, that muse, Viola de Lesseps, wading ashore in Virginia. Shakespeare has become America's adopted native son. He is central to our greatest literature from Melville's *Moby Dick* to Twain's *Huckleberry Finn* to Faulkner's *The Sound and the Fury* to Smiley's *A Thousand Acres*. He moved west with the settlers and made himself at home in Hollywood where he has provided the text and the subtext for countless movies, as Robert F. Willson Jr. has recently demonstrated.[28]

Branagh has led this new generation of Shakespeare film directors deep into the popular film tradition. Some, Luhrmann, Loncraine, and Hoffman, have found the territory even more congenial than their leader.

What has come to mark Branagh's films, however, and to distinguish them from those of his contemporaries, is his respect for Shakespeare's language. Branagh's Shakespeare is not as visually daring as Luhrmann's, as parodic as Loncraine's, or as lush as Hoffman's, but his films create the most unique balance between the spoken word and the visual image in the history of the genre. Pauline Kael has called Branagh a "flamboyant realist," which is one way of saying that he manages to merge Zeffirelli's lush, extravagant visual style with a cool, intelligent, and precise manner of speaking Shakespeare's rich verse and muscular prose.[29] Even his *Love's Labour's Lost*, which repeatedly abandons Shakespeare to swing into Tin Pan Alley, pauses to allow Branagh time to give full flight to Berowne's hyperbolic celebration of the dazzling relationship between love and learning. Branagh's delivery of the speech, begun by literally tapping out its iambics, makes sense of every word and the rhythmic music of its linear placement. The moment is as inventive in its own way as his much heralded delivery of Henry V's Agincourt battle cry or Hamlet's "To be or not to be" soliloquy. Branagh also has been successful in coaching his large multinational casts, many of them inexperienced as classical actors, into finding themselves comfortable with Shakespeare's rhythms. The most obvious exceptions are Keanu Reeves, Jack Lemmon, and Alicia Silverstone—but who wouldn't trade those mostly minor disappointments for the glories of Denzel Washington's Don Pedro, Julie Christie's Gertrude, Robin Williams's Osric, Billy Crystal's Gravedigger, Natascha McElhone's Rosaline, Timothy Spall's Don Armado, and Nathan Lane's Costard?

In fact, according to Gary Taylor, Branagh's success (and Luhrmann's) may already be affecting the audiences for stage Shakespeare. In an essay on the Stratford Canada Shakespeare Festival, Taylor quotes Richard Monette, the festival's current director, as remarking that established film stars are reluctant, for fear of artistic failure and financial loss, to commit to a lengthy stage season of Shakespeare. Noble, the director of the Royal Shakespeare Company (RSC), acknowledges similar casting problems at the home office in Stratford, and his radical attempt to address them has led to his announced intention to resign as director in March 2003. Taylor goes on to comment:

> The festival therefore cannot use the excitements of star power to overcome public resistance to Shakespeare. Indeed, it suffers from comparisons between its casts and those available to film direc-

tors. Reviewing the RSC's latest *Much Ado About Nothing* (1997), Neil Smith concludes: "My advice? See Kenneth Branagh's film version instead. It's bright, it's breezy, the cast is starrier . . . and it's a whole hour shorter." The disappointing box office of the 1997 Festival *Romeo and Juliet* may owe something to its inability to compete with the Hollywood version then only a few months old. And its *Midsummer Night's Dream*, which opened in June 1999, can hardly rival the Michael Hoffman film released in May, starring Kevin Kline, Michelle Pfeiffer, and a supporting cast any one of whose members the Festival would be thrilled to get—and special effects no theater in the world could match.[30]

This is a remark, it is safe to say, that would not have been made about an earlier generation of Shakespeare films having had the power to challenge the market for stage Shakespeare. If Taylor's gloomy prognosis should be confirmed, it would surely, for Branagh, be an unintended consequence of his efforts, which resolutely have been to use film to expand the audience for Shakespeare, not to contract it.

With Hoffman's *Dream* and Edzard's *As You Like It* positioned on either end of the realistic spectrum and with Branagh's films and Zeffirelli's *Hamlet* occupying the middle ground, what of the other seven films released in the long decade and their relationship to Jorgens's categories? As I indicated earlier, it is the theatrical mode that seems to have lost its power as a model. Noble's *Dream* is the film most attached to its theatrical roots. Entire elements from the stage production—including the costumes, props, many of the sets, and blocking of the action—were transferred intact from theater to film studio. For the film, however, Noble reimagines the *Dream* as emanating from the fantasy of a young boy (Osheen Jones) who serves as the film's frame and an Alice in Wonderland time traveler into another world. This allows Noble to superimpose images echoing Hollywood films from Disney to Spielberg, most obviously the twice repeated shot of Bottom and the boy riding a motorcycle up in the sky in silhouette against a full moon lifted from *ET*, on his stage conception of the play. In the film's opening shot, Noble's camera pans over the toy-laden contents of the boy's bedroom, lingering for a moment on a Victorian toy-theater model. That model will reappear as a frame for the Pyramus and Thisby scene, in which the film self-consciously evokes its stage roots and the play's metatheatricality. The film is a noble experiment, using Ingmar Bergman's wonderful film of *The*

Magic Flute as an example, as Michael Hattaway suggests, but ultimately ends up creating a never-never land somewhere between the theatrical and the filmic.[31]

Noble and Branagh collaborated, as director and star, on stage productions of *Henry V* (1984) and *Hamlet* (1992) for the Royal Shakespeare Company. Each production directly preceded Branagh's film versions of the two plays, and, as I have detailed elsewhere, his film of *Henry V* was deeply indebted, in conception and detail, to ideas that first emerged on stage.[32] Such was not the case with Branagh's film of *Hamlet*, which contains only the faintest traces of Noble's stage production. Noble's production, though also using a full text conflation of Q2 and F1 versions of the play, was relentlessly domestic, influenced by the bleak Scandinavian works of Ibsen, Strindberg, and Bergman. Branagh's *Hamlet* sought epic models, especially in the films of David Lean, and emphasized the political, rather than the domestic, reaches of the play. However, the film does feature the use of a toy-theater model similar to the one employed in Noble's *Dream* (though not, I should add, a prop used in Noble's stage productions of either *Dream* or *Hamlet*). Here the model is a significant part of Hamlet's book-lined study into which he periodically retreats through the set's several hidden doorways. The study is the setting for the "O what a rogue and peasant slave am I" soliloquy, which concludes with Hamlet's face peering out at the camera through the back of the theater model as he delivers: "[T]he play's the thing / Wherein I'll catch the conscience of the King" (3.1.604–5). Branagh's screenplay then anticipates the moment's final visual image and sound: "We move closer in on the tiny stage where the figure of the King stands over the trapdoor, which Hamlet releases with a violent *snap!* The model King is dispatched to 'the other place.'"[33]

Here Branagh has fully assimilated the toy theater into the realistic conventions of his film. It is used as a spur to Hamlet's imagination as it races to rescue him from the paralysis of self-abuse and refocus his mind on his task. It provides him with a stunning shot of Hamlet's face framed in the model's proscenium that conjures up the whirling theatrics of the character's sensibility. The "snap" prepares brilliantly for "The Mousetrap," which follows immediately—the most self-consciously theatrical moment in text and film—but does so within the narrative conventions of film, rather than the stage.

Parker's *Othello* (1995) and Nunn's *Twelfth Night* (1996) also are films made by stage directors, but imagined decidedly in the realistic mode.

Parker, even more than Branagh, is captured by the Zeffirelli aesthetic. He laces his film with romantic shots, washed over by soft, muted colors, and underscored by whispering violins and cellos. Nunn's *Twelfth Night*, directed by an experienced Shakespearean who made his major midcareer move into stage musicals rather than movies, is a more assured piece of filmmaking. He brings a sure ear to Shakespeare's most musical festive comedy and uses the resources of film imaginatively to expand the play's use of song to capture its melancholy awareness of the precariousness of the romantic moment. Nunn beautifully cross-cuts between Feste and the midnight revelers singing "O Mistress Mine" to spin the song's theme out to include Malvolio, in his bedroom having a nightcap in a nightcap, and Olivia, asleep in her bed with a smile playing on her lips suggesting that she dreams of Cesario, and Orsino and Cesario playing cards as the song's tune is being played on the piano. By cross-cutting between all of the play's lovers, often here at emotional cross-purposes, Nunn uses film imaginatively to enhance the Chekhovian wistfulness of his approach to Shakespeare's final festive comedy.

Taymor's *Titus* (1999) and Almereyda's *Hamlet* (2000) are the two films that most challenge Jorgens's realistic mode. Taymor's film is an intentional mix of clashing visual and acting styles, made immediately apparent in the jarring contrast between the film's first two sequences. The film opens in a conventional family kitchen, with a young boy (again, Osheen Jones) playing with his collection of toy soldiers that ranges from Roman gladiators to medieval knights to GI Joes. As he intensifies his imaginary warfare, spattering gobs of ketchup on his warriors, the battle suddenly comes literally crashing into his play world and he is scooped up and whisked away, again as in Noble's *Dream* down a long tunnel, by an oddly dressed figure. The film then cuts to the entrance of Titus's mud-caked troops, in tightly choreographed mechanical movements—Taymor now playing on a grand scale with *her* warriors—into Rome's Colosseum (actually shot in a similar arena in Pula, Croatia). The scene is shot at night and the parade of military vehicles that follows the troops stretches from ancient horse-drawn carts to modern tanks. These two scenes announce immediately Taymor's intentions to merge and mingle the American present with the Roman past, mediated by Shakespeare's play occupying a space somewhere between the two empires. Her film uses a heightened realism to swerve toward the surreal much in the way Shakespeare's play uses exquisite verse to describe horrific events like Marcus's prolonged description of Lavinia's ravishment. Taymor clearly wants her film to reach toward the poetic, but the combination of *Titus Andronicus*'s unflinching cruelties and *Titus*'s restless switching of styles produced a film that was doomed to find neither the mass commercial audience it sought nor even the art-house audience its producers would have settled for.

Almereyda's *Hamlet*—its preview screenings having received disastrous ratings—was a surprise success with that very art-house audience for which it was targeted. Almereyda's film is the only one of the decade that quite consciously evokes the influence of Welles and demonstrates what Edzard's *As You Like It* failed to prove: that it is possible to make an imaginative and convincing Shakespeare film, in current film culture, on a minuscule budget. Almereyda and Edzard are the only two of these filmmakers to set their films in a contemporary urban landscape. Mrs. Thatcher's Docklands development rises, across the Thames, from Edzard's construction-site Arden and is captured in the deep background of several of her shots of Ganymede and Orlando at play in an urban wasteland. Almereyda makes a bolder use of his *Hamlet*'s Manhattan setting: his film makes the slick, glossy, glass-and-steel city a perfect landscape for Claudius's powerful manipulations. Hamlet is trapped in Claudius's world. On the street he is dwarfed by the towers of capitalism; in his apartment high up in the Hotel Elsinore he is isolated and impotent and a prey to Sam Shepard's intense Ghost. Ethan Hawke's Hamlet is only liberated when toying with his pixel-vision video camera and constructing his own "independent" movie/video on his clamshell editing machine.

Almereyda and Taymor, in very different fashions, aspire to be film poets. They participate in the Branagh era's use of star casting and the mix of actors drawn from the worlds of the stage and commercial films. Almereyda is open in declaring that Ethan Hawke's participation in his *Hamlet* was critical to its securing financial backing.[34] Anthony Hopkins and Jessica Lange played a similar role for Taymor. Almereyda's *Hamlet* mixes experienced film actors like Hawke, Murray, Shepard, and Kyle MacLachlan with those noted for their stage work like Diane Venora and Liev Schreiber. Taymor's film follows more closely the Branagh pattern of mixing American film stars (Jessica Lange) with British stage actors (Alan Cumming)—in this case with Anthony Hopkins occupying a crossover role, the British classical actor and international film star having moved to Los Angeles and become an American citizen. Each director, however, puts his or her cast in a film context in stunning contrast to most of the mainstream Shakespeare films in this revival. Narrative drive is less intense, while mode of delivery is more self-conscious. The pleasures these films provide come as much from their radical treatment of their Shakespearean material as from the material itself. Taymor's film, because she is working with less familiar and tractable material and because she insists on confronting huge chunks of Shakespeare's early dramatic verse without apology or embarrassment, is ultimately the more interesting.

The four films that were released at the end of this prolific decade—Taymor's *Titus* (1999), Almereyda's *Hamlet* (2000), Branagh's *Love's Labour's Lost* (2000), and Edzard's *The Children's Midsummer Night's Dream* (2001)—all signal interesting new directions for the genre. Each of the four, in differing fashions, radically extends *(Love's Labour's Lost)*, stylistically complicates *(Titus* and *Hamlet)*, or humorously revises *(Children's Midsummer Night's Dream)* the realistic and naturalistic model forged by Zeffirelli and updated and revised by Branagh in his first three Shakespeare films. This trend reverses the usual pattern in genre revival, wherein the first films are often the freshest and most radical, while the subsequent efforts simply try to exploit the newly rediscovered commercial appeal of the genre in increasingly obvious and pedestrian imitations. Paradoxically, these last Shakespeare films have stretched the genre precisely at the moment it appears to have lost the commercial appeal that gave it life. The modest financing that flowed into the decade's Shakespeare films after the artistic and commercial success of Branagh's *Henry V* and *Much Ado About Nothing* appears to have been reduced to a trickle. There are rumors of Mel Gibson's plans to direct a film of *Hamlet* with Robert Downey Jr. and of Harold Pinter's working on a screenplay of *King Lear* to be directed by Tim Roth. Only Branagh remains confident that his plans for a film of *Macbeth* (rumored to be directed by Martin Scorsese) will come to fruition.[35] The sense in Hollywood is that the genre has become oversaturated and that it is time to give it a rest to allow audience interest to renew itself.

The flow of new Shakespeare films was quickly followed by a dramatic increase in the critical literature devoted to this revitalized area of Shakespeare studies. The field now has a journal *(Shakespeare Bulletin)*, a historian (Kenneth S. Rothwell), a bibliographer (José Ramón Díaz-Fernández), a pioneering critic (Jack Jorgens), and a host of contemporary theoreticians spanning the full range of formalist and postmodern approaches to Shakespeare on film. The first half of the long decade, roughly 1988–94, saw a flurry of books devoted to the genre, generally looking back to the films of Olivier, Welles, Kurosawa, and Kozintsev. These books, by critics and scholar/historians as diverse as Lorne Buchman, John Collick, H. R. Coursen, Anthony Davies, Peter S. Donaldson, Barbara Hodgdon, Bernice Kliman, Luke McKernan and Olwen Terris, Ace Pilkington, and the forementioned Rothwell, provided the essential critical and scholarly groundwork for the developing field.[36] In separate volumes, Rothwell and Annabelle Melzer and McKernan and Terris constructed comprehensive filmographies (including television and video productions) that gave us an exhaustive map of the territory up to 1994. Critics like Buchman, Coursen, Donaldson, and Hodgdon began to create the methodological boundaries or divisions of the enterprise, with approaches as varied as the psychoanalytic (autobiography as key to directorial decisions), the intertextual (dialogue between stage and film performances), the formal (reading films with the literary tools of the New Criticism), materialist (marketplace and means of production), cultural studies (resonances with the film's historical moment), and popular studies (Shakespeare and the mass media).

These initial studies were primarily concerned with looking backward at samples from the genre, but they clearly sprang from the energies released by the wave of new films that began to appear in the wake of Branagh's *Henry V.* Film papers, panels, and seminars at the annual meeting of the Shakespeare Association of America (SAA) went, between the mid-1970s and the mid-1990s, from the exotic and marginal to the mainstream and central. Shakespeare-on-film scholars, once put on display to be growled at by the literary lions, found themselves delivering their papers to tamed, purring throngs of colleagues. Branagh's crowd-pleasing *Much Ado About Nothing* pleased the Shakespeare crowd at the SAA meeting in Atlanta in 1993, and by the 2000 meeting in Montreal even Almereyda's risky *Hamlet* was greeted with respect if not rapture.

In the second half of the long decade (1994–2001), the flow increased. Now the attention turned to collections of essays, inaugurated by Anthony Davies and Stanley Wells's *Shakespeare and the Moving Image* (1994) and capped by Russell Jackson's *The Cambridge Companion to Shakespeare on Film* (2000).[37] In between came *Screen Shakespeare* (1994), *Shakespeare, The Movie* (1997), *Shakespeare on Film: New Casebooks Series* (1998), *Shakespeare, Film, and Fin de Siècle* (2000) and special issues of *Literature/Film Quarterly* (1992, 1994, 1997, 2000, and 2001), *Cineaste* (fall 1998), and *Post Script* (1997 and 1998) devoted exclusively to essays on Shakespeare films.[38] Increasingly, the essays in these volumes have focused on the films of the last decade, with Branagh's *Henry V* and *Hamlet*, Luhrmann's *William Shakespeare's Romeo + Juliet*, and Loncraine's *Richard III* receiving the most attention. Among the several collections either published too recently to be included in this study or still forthcoming are two edited by Lisa Starks and Courtney Lehmann and one edited by José Ramón Díaz-Fernández, a professor at the University of Malaga who organized and hosted an international conference celebrating the centenary of Shakespeare on screen in September 1999. Díaz-Fernández has published, in the two special issues of *Post Script* devoted to Shakespeare on film, the definitive bibliography of the critical literature in the field. His conference neatly coincided with the publication of Rothwell's *A History of Shakespeare on Screen* (Cambridge University Press, 1999),[39] which provides a comprehensive critical history of the first hundred years of the genre from a three-minute scene filmed from Sir Herbert Beerbohm-Tree's *King John* in 1899 to Branagh's four-hour *Hamlet* released at the end of 1996. Rothwell's account, from the silents to the spin-offs, is wry, witty, and exhaustive. As the genre's leading scholar and champion, Rothwell never forgets that both Shakespeare and film have common origins in popular entertainment. Though he writes persuasively about what he terms "Shakespeare in the cinema of transgression" as he investigates films like Jean Luc Godard's *King Lear* (1987) and Derek Jarman's *Tempest* (1980), it is clear that his own preference is for bigger, bolder films from directors like Zeffirelli, Luhrmann, and Branagh.

Other full-length studies devoted exclusively to Shakespeare films also appeared in this period: there were works by Howlett, Willson, Hatchuel, and Douglas Brode.[40] And H. R. Coursen continued his prolific exploration of the realms of stage, television, and film Shakespeare, producing six critical studies in the decade. Coursen, particularly in *Whose History? Shakespeare in Production* (1996), *Shakespeare: The Two Traditions* (1999), and *Shakespeare in Space* (2002), argued forcefully both for the director's right to situate a Shakespeare text within a specific historical context and for his subsequent responsibility to make the period or landscape work *with* rather than *against* the energies of the text. For Coursen, while Loncraine's 1930s setting for *Richard III* works against the text, Branagh's setting his *Love's Labour's Lost* in that same decade, using 1930s popular songs, enhances Shakespeare's comedy. Similarly, whereas Luhrmann's hip, dazzling, Latin, popular-culture-inspired *William*

Shakespeare's Romeo + Juliet fits the postmodern moment for Coursen, Edzard's contemporary, urban *As You Like It* does not.

Willson's *Shakespeare in Hollywood, 1929–1956* (2000) gave us a comprehensive account of Hollywood's first encounter with Shakespeare during the age of its domination by the big studios: MGM, Warner Brothers, United Artists, Paramount, Columbia, and Universal. Willson demonstrates that if Hollywood had initial difficulties in finding a film language appropriate for realizing Shakespeare's text, it had little problem using him as a subtext for films as varied as George Cukor's *A Double Life* (1947), John Ford's *My Darling Clementine* (1946), and Fred Wilcox's *Forbidden Planet* (1956). Howlett's work is the most saturated with theoretical ideas from the field of film studies. It thoroughly explores the way a variety of directors, from Welles to Kurosawa to Zeffirelli to Branagh, use the frame of the shot—what it contains, arranges, and marginalizes— to create their interpretive approaches to capturing the Shakespearean dynamic on film. Hatchuel provides the first study devoted exclusively to Branagh's Shakespeare films through his *Hamlet*. Hatchuel's book will now become the starting place for the future explorations of Branagh's work as he already, at age forty, has become the most prolific actor and director in the long history of Shakespeare on film. Finally, Brode's *Shakespeare in the Movies: From the Silent Era to Shakespeare in Love* (2000) is a hasty attempt to skim the surface of the territory explored in depth by Rothwell and Willson. The book's errors of fact, spelling, judgment, and style were so egregious as to lead one prominent reviewer to call for its recall from the shelves to save a distinguished press from further scholarly embarrassment.[41] *Shakespeare at the Cineplex* joins the continuing exploration of the territory by being the first to be devoted exclusively to the Shakespeare films produced in this extended decade of the fertile revival of the genre.[42]

What distinguishes this decade's Shakespeare films from their now-famous predecessors made by Welles, Olivier, Brook, Kurosawa, and Kozintsev is their embrace of popular film models and techniques. Only a handful of these films opened on the screens of the suburban cineplexes, but almost all of them aspired to find the mass audience that the cineplexes serve. Led by Branagh, this generation of Shakespeare filmmakers was unapologetic about wanting their films to entertain. Their embrace of Hollywood models released a new energy into the moribund genre and made it live again in new, exciting, and sometimes even profitable, ways.

Shakespeare the cultural icon did not frighten these directors; in fact, they championed the very elements in his work that had made him speak to his own Elizabethan audience in such a commercially, as well as artistically, successful manner. Welles had something of this spirit, but neither the resources nor ultimately the artistic temperament to achieve it. For Olivier, Shakespeare was bound up with an elite national legacy and a theatrical tradition that he could not imagine abandoning. He, proudly and understandably, was an emblem of a culture that equated Shakespeare with the nation and both with the long tradition of the actor-manager that Olivier embodied in his own time. To his credit, Olivier—after initial resistance—helped take Shakespeare into the movies, but always with an eye cocked toward the heavens rather than directed squarely at the groundlings. The new Shakespeare directors, especially Luhrmann, Loncraine, Hoffman, and Taymor, see themselves less as up-holders of a stage tradition than as experimenters with and revivers of a film genre. These directors all manage to revere Shakespeare without being reverential.

Branagh is, of course, the leading figure in this revival. His film of *Henry V* (1989) initiated it; the commercial success of his *Much Ado About Nothing* (1993) sustained it; his epic four-hour *Hamlet* (1996) created its centerpiece; and his musical version of *Love's Labour's Lost* (2000) pointed it in new directions. The chapters that follow provide detailed studies of the fifteen major Shakespeare films released in the decade. With a few exceptions, they follow the chronological release of the films except where critical profit can be made by juxtaposing several films in a single chapter, as I do with Branagh's *Henry V* and *Love's Labour's Lost*, Edzard's *As You Like It* and *The Children's Midsummer Night's Dream*, and Noble's and Hoffman's *Dream*s.

The 1990s offer a climactic and concentrated period for scholars of Shakespeare on film. The decade extends the history of the genre even as it revises it. Branagh and his fellow directors acknowledge the legacy of Olivier, Welles, and Zeffirelli even as they daringly push the Shakespeare film deeper into Hollywood codes and models. *Shakespeare at the Cineplex*, similarly, is in conception and intention both a successor and a departure from its predecessor *Shakespeare Observed*. That study originated from a closeup observer's perspective on rehearsals for a Royal Shakespeare Company production of *Romeo and Juliet* and moved to more long-range critical and speculative observations on the evolving dialogue among influential literary theorists of the period and directors of landmark productions of the plays on stage and film.

Now, a richly productive decade later, these dialogues have become still more distinct and various, and it is possible to track the initiatory impulses described in *Shakespeare Observed* to their current collective focus in the Hollywood of the 1990s. The Hollywood of the recent decade is the locus of manifold and complex rival energies: of Shakespearean celebrants and skeptics, of prodigal sons and filial guardians of Shakespearean film history and traditions, and of new alliances among all these voices. Like the physical and metaphysical artifact of the local cineplex, at once a vernacular hangout for audiences of every description, never-never land, and quasi terminal, Hollywood has become a connecting point if not a terminus for the most adventurous Shakespearean journeys of our day.

The Words of Mercury and the Songs of Apollo

Branagh's Journey from Henry V to Love's Labour's Lost

I
n 1977, in his ground-breaking *Shakespeare on Film*, Jack Jorgens concluded a stunning catalog of Shakespeare films released in the 1950s
and 1960s with a prediction: "It is an impressive list, and it will continue to grow."[1] Writing fifteen years later in 1992, not long after the release of Kenneth Branagh's *Henry V* and Franco Zeffirelli's *Hamlet*, I was
more cautious about prophesying the future, mindful that Jorgens's prediction had been followed by the most unproductive period in a century
of films based on Shakespearean material. I rather timidly ventured:

> Branagh's film, released in the autumn of 1989, ended the fallow
> period—stretching back to Roman Polanski's *Macbeth* (1971)—in
> large-scale English-language Shakespeare films. It was also the
> first Shakespearean film since Zeffirelli's *Romeo and Juliet* (1968)
> to reach and sustain a substantial audience and to more than re-
> coup its production costs. It was quickly followed by Zeffirelli's
> *Hamlet* (1990) with Mel Gibson and Glenn Close, raising expec-
> tations that we might be approaching another fertile period in the
> release of Shakespeare films, perhaps one to rival the glories of
> the 1950s and 1960s.[2]

I wish I had been bolder, for ten years later we can clearly see that
Branagh's *Henry V* did introduce the most prolific and dynamic decade in
the hundred-year history of Shakespeare on film, a period that Kenneth

Rothwell appropriately has dubbed "The Age of Kenneth Branagh." Rothwell comments: "By a shrewd merger of art and commerce, Kenneth Branagh magically resuscitated the Shakespeare movie just when everyone was announcing its death at the hands of television."[3]

The surprising critical and financial success of Branagh's *Henry V* has proved to be as influential in the history of Shakespeare on film as was the equally unanticipated success almost fifty years earlier of Laurence Olivier's film of the play released in 1944. Olivier's *Henry V* led, over the next two decades, to a steady stream of international Shakespeare films by such directors as Orson Welles, Akira Kurosawa, Gregori Kozintsev, Franco Zeffirelli, and Peter Brook.

Branagh's 1989 film has helped to create the most concentrated release of English-language Shakespeare films in the century. Branagh, surpassing Olivier, Welles, and Zeffirelli, has become the only director to have produced four Shakespeare films. An examination of Branagh's Shakespeare films will reveal that he has molded his own cinematic style from elements present in the work of his distinguished predecessors. Popular film culture, represented on one extreme by James Cagney and on the other by Orson Welles, lies deep in the soul of Branagh's creative sensibility. Branagh watchers have long recognized that he generates much of his artistic power—as an actor and director—from his unique stance as an outsider to mainstream English theatrical culture. His family roots are in Protestant Northern Ireland, but his artistic energy flows from the American films and their iconic heroes he absorbed as a boy in Belfast. Branagh's biography reveals that he draws potential rather than paralysis from finding himself placed between rival legacies, traditions, and cultures: Protestant and Catholic in Belfast; English and Irish in Reading (whence his family moved when he was ten); and Stratford and Hollywood in his Shakespearean career.

Courtney Lehmann is more theoretical and skeptical than I am about these tensions in Branagh's films. Working with Fredric Jameson's notions of postmodernism, she cleverly posits: "Thus, for Kenneth Branagh, the question becomes: how does the postmodern 'artist' escape becoming 'dead again'?"[4] Ultimately, using his film of *Henry V* as her test case, she sees Branagh as struggling to overcome the schizophrenic split between high art (Shakespeare) and popular culture (the Hollywood film) at the core of his aesthetic. I would argue that Branagh has fashioned an effective style for translating Shakespeare into the language of film and in the process has become as much of a film auteur as his great modernist predecessors Olivier and Welles.

Branagh's nerve and intelligence are his most original qualities. His genius as an artist is as a synthesizer: his imagination works like a magpie, stealing good ideas from others, but linking them in surprising and original ways. As Rothwell observes, "Branagh's gift is in knowing how to combine the theatrical with the filmic."⁵ His films, for instance, show obvious debts to Welles, Hitchcock, Kasdan, Coppola, Lean, Minnelli, and Donen. His play *Public Enemy* (the first work staged by his Renaissance Theatre Company [RTC]) reaches back to Cagney and the Hollywood gangster films of the 1930s—a prism through which to capture the fantasies of a young lad coming of age in Belfast in the 1960s. When it comes to film, Branagh has the courage of his conventions. He works toward a personal style by studying and appropriating masters (Hitchcock for *Dead Again*) and models (*The Big Chill* for *Peter's Friends*). As his synthesizing imagination might suggest, his four most successful films to date are his Shakespeare adaptations: *Henry V, Much Ado About Nothing, Hamlet,* and *Love's Labour's Lost.*

For the first three of those films, Branagh had strong stage productions as inspiration: Adrian Noble's Royal Shakespeare Company productions of *Henry V* (1984) and *Hamlet* (1992–93), with Branagh as king and prince, and Judi Dench's *Much Ado About Nothing* (1988) for RTC, with Branagh as Benedick. From each, Branagh took several dominant visual ideas: dark, somber, conspiratorial interiors for *Henry V,* distinguished by the use of backlighting to suggest the mystery surrounding the newly crowned king, and rain and mud for the exteriors (the Battle of Agincourt setting was heavily influenced by Welles's great battle scene in *Chimes at Midnight*); while *Much Ado* was all Italian summer sun and heat spilling over in festive energy (individual moments echoed Hollywood movies as diverse as *The Magnificent Seven* and *Singin' in the Rain*)—a bright, fleshy, romantic day in contrast to *Henry V's* dark night of the king's soul on a risky imperial quest for personal and national identity. For his *Hamlet,* Branagh extended and revised the family focus of Noble's RSC production, which looked back at Shakespeare's play through the Scandinavian eyes of Ibsen, Strindberg, and Ingmar Bergman. *Love's Labour's Lost* was his Shakespearean valentine to the great Hollywood musicals of the 1930s, 1940s, and 1950s. It completed his journey from Stratford to Hollywood.

In all four films, but particularly in *Much Ado*, Branagh was striving to reach the large popular American film audience dominated by teenagers. This was an audience that had been touched only once before by a Shakespeare film: Zeffirelli's *Romeo and Juliet* (since then, post–*Much Ado*, we have had Baz Luhrmann's *William Shakespeare's Romeo + Juliet*). As I mentioned earlier, Pauline Kael, in her review of *Henry V*, calls Branagh a "flamboyant realist," which is to see that he manages to merge Zeffirelli's lush, extravagant style with a cool, intelligent understanding of his Shakespearean material.[6]

Branagh is a product of the postmodern moment dominated by a sense of belatedness—a sense that originality is exhausted and that only parody and pastiche and intertextual echo remain. Rather than finding such a condition enervating, Branagh's work seizes on its possibilities. Branagh is a reconstructionist—an artist who creates out of the bits and shards of the postmodern moment. Peter Donaldson has brilliantly demonstrated how the gritty strenuousness of Branagh's *Henry V* was inspired not only by Noble's post–Falklands/Vietnam stage production but also by a powerful aesthetic struggle with Olivier's 1944 film, which had been prompted by Olivier's desire to bring Shakespeare—and the English cultural tradition he represented—to the service of the nation as the Allies launched the invasion to reclaim Europe from Hitler.[7] Branagh's *Henry V* insisted, in its historical moment, that coming home was as important as going over.

In his 1996 film of *Hamlet*, Branagh again offers us a bright, bold mirror in stunning contrast to Olivier's dark impressionist maze. Here he seeks to synthesize the Freudian operatic romance of Zeffirelli's *Hamlet* with the austere politics of Kozintsev's great Russian film of the play. Many reviewers have stressed the film's debts to David Lean, noting that Branagh's cinematographer, Alex Thomson, worked as a focus-puller on Lean's *Lawrence of Arabia*. Students of mine have found cinematic intertextual echoes in the film, ranging from Stanley Kubrick's *The Shining* to Franklin Schaffner's *Patton* and David Lean's *Dr. Zhivago*.

Branagh's route beyond Olivier as a British-trained Shakespearean who makes films lies in his infatuation with popular film culture, with what we have come to call "Hollywood." Branagh is, in fact, the first director of Shakespeare films to mix Olivier's attention to the spoken text with Welles's fascination with camera angle and movement and Zeffirelli's visual and musical romanticism. Branagh's Shakespeare speaks *and* moves, something of a rarity in the genre where word and image often jostle one another for dominance; his Shakespeare films are distinguished by their bold life and robust energy. He is a director willing to take chances, particularly by not treating his Shakespearean material, even in his full-text *Hamlet*, as sacred.

Branagh's bravura quality is apparent from the opening frames of *Henry V,* where he first introduces Derek Jacobi's Chorus striking a match ("Oh for a muse of *fire*") on a darkened sound stage, then throwing on the full lamps ("To ascend the *brightest* heavens of invention") as he manages to suggest that film requires the same imaginative participation by the audience as does the theater. Here Branagh also is subtly evoking and revising Olivier's famous opening of his *Henry V* in a replica of Shakespeare's Globe. In that film, Olivier gave himself a sly double entrance: first, backstage, he glided into the frame from the left, clearing his throat before making his move out on the Globe stage to be greeted (as Burbage) by the Elizabethan audience's enthusiastic applause.

Branagh was equally audacious by introducing his Henry, backlit and in longshot, framed in a huge door looming mysteriously like some medieval version of Darth Vader. Branagh, cleverly, then films Henry from the back as he moves down a row of his courtiers and finally turns to settle himself on the throne. Here we get the first close-up of the king—and it is a stunning contrast to the camera's initial elevation of his power and mystery: what we now see is the face and body of a tousle-headed boy— Luke Skywalker rather than Darth Vader—overwhelmed by the size of the throne on which he sits. Each of these actor-directors, then, gives himself a double entrance: Olivier invites the pleasure of our recognition of his status as both international star of stage and film and dynastic heir to a four-hundred-year-old tradition of Shakespearean acting; Branagh invokes the shock of the vernacular unknown—not the Shakespearean actor-king, but the cheeky pretender.

Branagh is not shy in his desire to entertain, to bring Shakespeare to a wider audience by "telling the story with the utmost clarity and simplicity."[8] Branagh wants "different accents, different looks" to produce Shakespeare films that "belong to the world."[9] His films seek, as the medium demands, a naturalistic style for speaking and acting Shakespeare. Branagh's Shakespeare films are unique in their attention to language, as Geoffrey O'Brien has pointed out in writing about Branagh's *Henry V:* "The job of the actor was to clarify, line by line and word by word, not just the general purport of what the character was feeling, but the exact function of every remark . . . the result was a more pointed, even jabbing style, a tendency to deflate sonority in favor of exact meaning, while at the same time giving the meter of the verse a musician's respect, and the rhetorical substructure of the lawyer's questioning eye."[10] Branagh's visual style is dynamic and direct, with signature moments in each film establishing its tone, atmosphere, camera style, and interpretive approach: murky interiors and muddy exteriors in *Henry V,* capped by the four-minute tracking shot of Henry V carrying Falstaff's dead page across the Agincourt battlefield; the highly charged festive opening in the sun-drenched Tuscan landscape of *Much Ado;* the epic, 70 mm scope of *Hamlet,* coupled with mirrored doors and trompe-l'oeil interiors reflecting one version of reality while hiding several layers of another; and the giddy segue in *Love's Labour's Lost* from Berowne's great speech on love, learning, and a lady's eye into Irving Berlin's "Dancing Cheek to Cheek" from *Top Hat.* And finally, lush original film scores from Patrick Doyle.

Doyle's scores are emblematic of Branagh's desire to employ an extravagant film vocabulary. In his *Henry V,* for instance, which features such gritty images as Bardolph's hanging (with his feet left to dangle in the top of the frame for the following scenes featuring first Mountjoy and then Chorus) and a grimy, decidedly unheroic mud-laden battle scene, Doyle's score, at the close of Agincourt, swells from a single voice singing a Non Nobis to a huge choir supported by a full orchestra. The score romanticizes the English victory in a way that the battle's images do not, opening the door for Branagh's detractors to accuse such moments in his films of being ideologically unstable and politically pernicious. Such critics are impatient with the contradictions in Branagh's style, contradictions that Branagh's eclectic imagination embraces and, in the case of *Henry V,* as Norman Rabkin has elegantly outlined, are built into the very fabric of Shakespeare's play.[11] Is Henry a tyrant or a Christian king? The answer is, both. Michael Manheim's analysis of the film understands the ways in which Branagh's performance of Henry captures that central ambiguity: "Not glamour but sincerity is the word for [Branagh's] Henry . . . [and] he is the Henry for our time basically because along with his ingenuousness, sincerity, and apparent decency—he is also a ruthless murderer. Branagh's characterization radically divides our sympathies."[12] This tension drives the film as it has driven the subsequent critical debate about Branagh's achievement.

Henry V, made on a shoestring budget of $6 million, in an age when the average Hollywood film costs almost ten times that amount, brought unexpected audiences and recognition, including Branagh's nominations for Academy Awards as best actor and best director in 1990. My first response to the film came in the context of *Shakespeare Observed*, which attempted to trace an intertextual dialogue between film and stage productions of Shakespeare in the post–World War II era. Then (1992), the film seemed a perfect climax to the book's thesis as it merged its own genesis in Noble's stage production of the play for the Royal Shakespeare Company in 1984 with Branagh's attempt, with a little help from Orson Welles, to offer a visual version of the play at radical odds with Olivier's heroic interpretation released in 1944.

Now, more than a decade later, Branagh's film seems more and more to reflect the chameleon-like nature of the play from which it springs. In 1989, it seemed to reflect the post-Falklands/Vietnam aesthetic as opposed to Olivier's more romantic and heroic version. Now, in the context of the end of the cold war and the collapse of the Soviet Union, it seems more an anticipation of the future than a reflection of the past. Branagh's film certainly launched the remarkable 1990s revival of the Shakespeare film genre. And as the Anglo-American culture, freed from the anxiety of opposition, looked back with something like triumph at some of its past literary glories, that revival joined a rash of interesting films based on the novels of Jane Austen, Henry James, and Edith Wharton. In most American universities, Austen, James, and Wharton were almost impossible to teach in the 1960s and 1970s, seeming, to the young headed to Vietnam or the streets, hopelessly irrelevant to their lives and contemporary politics. By the 1990s, the novels of these once-derided authors were being made into handsome Hollywood mass-market films by directors as radical and diverse as Ang Lee, Jane Campion, Martin Scorsese, Patricia Rozema, and Terence Davies, not just such traditional purveyors of the heritage film as Merchant and Ivory.[13]

As no less an authority than Al Pacino remarked, "Branagh opened it all up with *Henry V.* Now you say Shakespeare on Film in Hollywood and people listen."[14] Branagh's film opened up more than just the attention of investors, producers, and distributors. He reintroduced the triumphing-against-the-odds theme and sent film directors and writers—who also were spurred middecade by the fiftieth anniversary of the Normandy invasion—back to World War II as a subject for mass nostalgia. Books that followed included Tom Brokaw's *The Greatest Generation* and Stephen Ambrose's *Citizen Soldiers*, which climbed the American best-seller charts and stayed there. In film, there were Steven Spielberg's *Saving Private Ryan* and Terrence Malick's *Thin Red Line*. Spielberg's film, in fact, was just a thinly disguised American reworking of *Henry V,* with a Hanks replacing a Harry as the leader of a tiny band of brothers trying to define a nation's honor—in this instance, by saving a single soldier. The film repeatedly raids Shakespeare's play, opening with its equivalent of the siege of Harfleur ("Once more unto the breach") and then poaching from Henry's pre-Agincourt fireside chat with Williams, Court, and Bates about the nature of war, duty, leadership, and conscience as platoon leader Hanks and his men criss-cross the fields of France and camp out in a ruined cathedral debating their mission and the moral exigencies of war. If Shakespeare's king shows his humanity and reveals his common touch by moving among his men in disguise the better to engage with their anguish and fear on the eve of battle, Hanks plays his own game of hide-and-seek by keeping his men guessing about his background and occupation. He is eventually revealed as that democratic prince of the American past, the high-school English teacher quoting Emerson and Thoreau to comfort his charges.

In a wonderful irony, *Saving Private Ryan* soon faced its own battle—for the 1998 Academy Award for best picture, where it competed with John Madden's *Shakespeare in Love*. In the most lively and bitter best-picture campaign in decades, Miramax's Harvey Weinstein managed to outmaneuver Spielberg for the prize. Though Weinstein has become a Hollywood power, his Miramax company produces and distributes small independent films rather than giant studio blockbusters. In this instance, *Shakespeare in Love* had been produced by Branagh's oldest professional associate, David Parfitt, who helped him organize his Renaissance Theatre Company and produce, along with Stephan Evans, his first films. Little could Branagh have imagined in 1989 that a mere decade later his *Henry V* could have spawned an epic Hollywood battle between two movies representing two genres Shakespeare brought to perfection: the historical epic and the romantic comedy—genres that were represented as well in Branagh's first two Shakespeare films: *Henry V* and *Much Ado About Nothing*. The success of the latter is what finally provided the impetus for financial backing for *Shakespeare in Love*, an idea Marc Norman, the film's co-writer and producer, had been shopping in Hollywood for years. If Shakespeare bested Spielberg for the Academy Award, Spielberg quickly realized that he would make obvious the Shakespearean homage implied in *Saving Private Ryan*. He and Tom Hanks produced a ten-hour television series on the Normandy invasion and battle for Europe, *Band of Brothers*, which led to Spielberg's being named as an honorary knight commander of the British Empire (CBE) by Queen Elizabeth II in 2001.

That Branagh's *Henry V* and his performance as the soldier-king can now be read as much in the context of Churchill's ethos of "blood, sweat, toil, and tears" as in the antiwar spirit of the 1960s is perhaps one way of explaining the academic debate about the film. Critics such as Peter S. Donaldson, Michael Manheim, and Kenneth S. Rothwell found that the ambiguities in the ideologies of Branagh's film were either located in the text itself or were a source for its particular energy and dynamic. On the other hand, critics Curtis Breight, Donald K. Hedrick, and Kathy Howlett found the film fatally flawed by its attempts to present an ulti-mately heroic portrait of Henry against a decidedly antiheroic landscape. Breight, for example, while begrudgingly honoring Olivier's version for being straight-forward, condemns Branagh's film for masking its assumed politics:

> Olivier's agenda in *Henry V* is apparent and excusable. England embattled by a demonic regime, despite the historical casualties generated by the British Empire, was sufficient cause for a patri-otic version of Shakespeare's play. But Olivier's choice of *Henry V,* Shakespeare's most patriotic play in the view of traditional con-servative critics, also signals his subservience to the reigning pow-ers of British society. Hence *Sir* [Breight's italics] Laurence Olivier. Branagh's *Henry V* is more complex yet ultimately similar to Olivier's representation of political power. Branagh may actu-ally feel that he has made an anti-war film, but his personal ambi-tion has led him to construct a film ideologically conducive to Thatcherism.[15]

I cite Breight at length to demonstrate how both films, but particularly Branagh's, got caught up in the rhetoric surrounding war, class, and po-litical power in contemporary England. Here Olivier becomes a monar-chist, Branagh a market capitalist, and the old cold war ideological battles are framed and fought over through the two films' versions of the play's central characters and images. As Rothwell perceptively notes, Branagh's fiercest detractors are more likely to be British than American: "For many of his countrymen . . . Branagh had not only sold out to the Thatcherites and feel-good Shakespeareans, but also committed the unpardonable sin of being too successful too young. Branagh's movie was self-reflexively the equivalent of Hal's invasion of France. When this novice director's work then turned a handsome profit for its plucky backers, his success be-came unbearable."[16]

Rothwell is certainly correct to see that the critical controversy surrounding the film was inspired as much by its maker's biography as by its images. In the context of this study, Branagh's *Henry V* is significant because of its English origins. It sprang, as I noted above, from Noble's stage production for the Royal Shakespeare Company in 1984. Many of the film's ideological ambiguities were also embedded there. The majority of the film's backers were British, as were all of its actors. The film not only celebrated the return of Shakespeare to film but the return of a glorious age of English actors to filmed Shakespeare—from Paul Scofield and Robert Stephens to Judi Dench and Derek Jacobi. After fifteen years of the banal BBC television Shakespeare, the film came as a breath of fresh air and energy. As was true for Harry's archers at Agincourt, the film's power was in its surprise. As Donaldson pointed out, the film counterpointed fresh new faces, primarily Branagh's and Emma Thompson's, with weary old ones, primarily Dench's and Scofield's, as a younger generation of British-trained actors announced their appropriation of Shakespeare's performance legacy.[17]

The film moved, in contrast to the unimaginative handling of television's static three floor cameras in the BBC Shakespeare series. Branagh managed to achieve both intimacy and scope in his use of the camera from the opening tracking shot following Jacobi's Chorus in a studio sound stage moving past the props for a production of *Henry V*—chains, banners, armor, large standing candlelabras—and the film technology necessary for its reproduction: lamps, huge fans, and a Panaflex 35 camera, to the four-minute tracking shot of Henry V carrying the dead body of Falstaff's page (Christian Bale) back across the ravaged battlefield at Agincourt.[18] The film surprised, too, because it included, graphically, some elements from the ruthless side of the young king excised from Olivier's more heroic portrait: the unmasking of the traitors, Cambridge, Scroop, and Grey; the speech before the gates at Harfleur; and the hanging of Bardolph. The film's grit and realism were reflected in the speaking of the verse. Gone were the trills and flourishes of Olivier's soaring trumpet solos, to be replaced by Branagh's earthier, more conversational tones. Olivier gave us the English greyhound, fast and sleek, Branagh, the bulldog, solid and squat. The performance that perhaps best illustrated the move from the age of Olivier to Branagh's era in filmed Shakespeare was Ian Holm's Fluellen. Holm had been Peter Hall's Hal and Henry V at Stratford in the infancy of the Royal Shakespeare Company. He represented the shift in verse-speaking developed by Cicely Berry's voice work

with the company as it moved away from the sonorities of Olivier, Gielgud, Ashcroft, and Quayle to accents more regional and conversational—
for example, those of David Warner, Albert Finney, Glenda Jackson, and
Nicol Williamson. Holm's Fluellen did not have a trace of the comic
Welshman in his being, and the film moved as resolutely to his tear-
stained embrace with Branagh's king at the end of Agincourt as to the
more conventional union of king and Kate in the film's final frames.[19]

Branagh's *Henry V* was rooted in Stratford. It emerged from Noble's
1984 stage version of the play and featured several actors from that production (Richard Easton, Christopher Ravenscroft, and Brian Blessed)
and several of the leading actors from the thirty years preceding the film,
gathered from Peter Hall's RSC and Olivier's National Theatre (Paul
Scofield, Robert Stephens, Ian Holm, Geraldine McEwen, Jacobi, and
Dench). Its values responded to an English tradition of playing and
filming Shakespeare. As Donaldson has recognized, the film's anxiety of
influence was generated by Olivier's example in the English Shakespearean performance legacy in general and, specifically, in his film of
Henry V.[20]

Branagh's next Shakespeare film, *Much Ado About Nothing*, began to
reveal more clearly the new directions he was charting in his own career
and in his contribution to the revival of the Shakespeare film genre. As I
will develop more fully in my chapter devoted to the film, *Much Ado* begins to reveal more fully Branagh's Shakespearean film aesthetic and his
route to *Love's Labour's Lost*. Though, like *Henry V,* the film had its genesis in a stage production of the play—Judi Dench's, for Branagh's RTC—
it broke much more boldly with its stage origins than did his film of *Henry
V.* He retained a core group of RTC actors (Richard Briers, Brian Blessed,
Jimmy Yuill, Patrick Doyle, and Emma Thompson), but now, for the first
time, he reached out to a new generation of Hollywood actors (Denzel
Washington, Keanu Reeves, Robert Sean Leonard, and Michael Keaton)
and to young English actors with no experience of working in Shakespeare at either the RSC or National (Kate Beckinsale, Ben Elton, Alex
Lowe, Imelda Staunton). His desire was to create an Anglo-American al-
liance for filmed Shakespeare that would have an international appeal.

The film was shot on location at the Villa Vinemaggio in Tuscany in
July and August 1992. Except for the Agincourt sequences that had been
filmed in a field adjacent to Shepperton Studios, it was Branagh's first
experience of location shooting. The film's opening sequence, with the
women picnicking as the men come pounding home from war on

horseback, their right fists punched up high in the air as the film's title flashes in red across the screen, garnered both the film's first laugh and its first quotation: John Sturges's *The Magnificent Seven*. This giddy moment announced Branagh's first step away from Stratford and toward Hollywood in his Shakespeare films. As Sarah Hatchuel has detailed, Branagh's Shakespeare films become increasingly infused with Hollywood codes, conventions, and direct quotations.[21] Part of his film vocabulary comes directly from other films. All filmmakers learn from one another. Orson Welles watched a print of *Stagecoach* every night for a month to learn film's grammar and rhetoric before shooting his first film, *Citizen Kane*. But one would be hard pressed to discover any direct quotations from Ford's film in Welles's modernist masterpiece. Branagh, on the other hand, living in the postmodern moment, enjoys quoting from Hollywood films in his Shakespearean efforts. It is another way in which his Shakespeare films consciously set out to merge and mingle the canonical with the commercial. He is trying to reclaim Shakespeare for the popular culture that originally spawned and nourished his art.

His most daring use of such quotation comes in his four-hour, full-text film of *Hamlet*. Here Branagh takes on the play most associated with Shakespeare's elitist position as the world's most distinguished literary figure—England's Man of the Millennium. Branagh's film of *Hamlet* is audacious (and still baffling to most critics) because he breaks commercial film's most inviolable convention (length) even as his style continues to insist that he is making a popular film. Though *Hamlet* was shot at Shepperton (while Disney was remaking *101 Dalmatians* on an adjacent sound stage) and on location at Blenheim, it owes far more to the distant Hollywood than the neighboring Stratford. As I will detail later, unlike the case with Branagh's first film, in which Noble's *Henry V* had a powerful influence, Branagh's film of *Hamlet* bears little resemblance to Noble's 1992 stage production of the play starring Branagh.

Branagh's *Hamlet* revels in its exhaustive use of film language: montage, flashbacks, flash-forwards, and pictorial representation of material only mentioned in the text. His camera tracks, circles, zooms in and out, cranes high above. It is restless, like Olivier's in his *Hamlet*, but more attached to the horizontal than the vertical. Olivier's camera borders on the hysterical, poking into dark, forbidden corners or spinning out of control following Hamlet on his repeated dashes up those twisting stairs to be annihilated by either the Ghost or vertigo. Branagh's camera is, like his prince, on the prowl, but less confused and desperate. As I mentioned earlier, Branagh also delights in quoting from Hollywood films as varied as *Dr. Zhivago*, *The Shining*, and *Patton*. It's all part of his intoxicated fascination with popular film. Each of his four Shakespeare films takes one step further away from its origins in stage Shakespeare and one step closer to having the Hollywood film as its model and inspiration. In the realm of international casting, his *Hamlet* reaches far beyond *Much Ado* by including the most dizzy array of acting styles and traditions—from John Gielgud and Judi Dench to Jack Lemmon and Charlton Heston, from Julie Christie and Rosemary Harris to Gérard Depardieu, Jeffery Kissoon, Billy Crystal, and Robin Williams. These stars are mixed with Branagh regulars—Jacobi, Brian Blessed, and Richard Briers. The intention, again Hollywood-inspired, was to imitate the star-studded epic in which every minor role features a famous face. Many of his gambles (Christie, Heston, Crystal, Williams) pay off; others (Lemmon, Depardieu) do not.

Branagh's Hamlet is conceived as a soldier. When we first encounter him, he is dressed in a trim black military uniform, in stunning contrast to the white and gold glitter of Claudius and his court. In an age dominated by a series of possessed (Jonathan Pryce), neurotic (Alan Rickman), infantile (Mark Rylance), even pudgy (Simon Russell Beale) stage Hamlets, Branagh's is distinguished by having taken his cue from Fortinbras's final pronouncement that he should have a soldier's funeral, for had he been "put on" he would have proved "most royal." Branagh's Hamlet, like his military uniform, is neat, trim, precise. He has a racing mind and a keen wit. He is interested in the fencing lessons taking place at the court, and one can believe this Hamlet when he boasts to Horatio that "I shall win at the odds" in the match with Laertes. If he has a dark side, it is his military alter ego: Rufus Sewell's Fortinbras.

Branagh stresses Hamlet's military bearing because he is interested in Shakespeare's fascination with the soldier. Many of his major Shakespearean roles, on stage and film, have been soldiers: Henry V, Benedick, Iago, Coriolanus.[22] His next planned Shakespeare film role is yet another soldier, Macbeth. The two Shakespearean characters he has played on film who are not soldiers, Hamlet and Berowne, he transforms into military figures. Berowne spends his year of penance at the conclusion of Branagh's film of *Love's Labour's Lost* serving the wounded in World War II, thus literally learning to "move wild laughter / In the throat of death." Branagh's interest in the soldier may spring from the inevitable comparison and competition with Olivier, who served in the Air Guard for a period during World War II and was able to link Shakespeare to the war effort in his making of *Henry V.* Just as likely is the natural association of the actor-manager and film director with the "General"—the leader of the company. Branagh's prolific career is the mark of a man of action and organization. By the age of forty, he had already directed nine films, including four Shakespeares—the most by any film director—and appeared in other films by directors as diverse as Oliver Parker, Robert Altman, Woody Allen, and Barry Sonnenfeld. He is clearly interested in the genre of the war movie, as Sarah Hatchuel details, finding echoes in his *Henry V* and *Hamlet* of Stanley Kubrick's *Full Metal Jacket,* Sylvester Stallone's *Rambo* films, and Oliver Stone's *Platoon.* Branagh himself has commented:

> When making both *Much Ado* and *Henry V,* I've been influenced by a number of movies. I seem to know a lot of war movies, a lot of battle movies. I remember bits of Orson Welles' film, *Chimes at Midnight* and Kurosawa's *Ran* as also being very influential. Everything, from *The Great Escape* through *The Longest Day, The Magnificent Seven* . . . you name it. A whole pile of stuff that I can't coherently reference. Ideas stolen from everywhere.[23]

It is tempting to draw parallels between Branagh's interest in war movies and his embattled position with the English critics who have dismissed his last two Shakespeare films. But Hatchuel convincingly traces Branagh's experience with war and the movies to his first film role in *A Month in the Country,* where he played the part of a soldier traumatized by his experiences in World War I.[24]

Branagh's journey toward translating Shakespeare into the genre of the Hollywood movie reaches its culmination in his *Love's Labour's Lost.* The film is Branagh's obvious celebration of and homage to the great American movie musicals of the 1930s, 1940s, and 1950s. It is both his most joyous and most subversive screen treatment of Shakespeare, and its failure to recapture and expand the popular audience that his *Much Ado* found is something of a puzzle. The answer, I think, lies at the intersection of audience and treatment. *Love's Labour's Lost* is Shakespeare's great comedy of language. It overflows with rhetorical flights of poetry from his aristocratic lovers and tortured prose from a vast array of clowns. Though the remark is made about Don Armado, Holofernes, and Sir Nathaniel, Moth's pert comment, "They have been at a great feast of languages and stolen the scraps," could apply to the play's entire cast of characters. That language, in company high and low, is at the service of love and learning and their interconnections. The density and rhetorical exuberance of the play's language suggests that *Love's Labour's Lost* might be the least likely of all Shakespeare comedies to be successfully scripted for a popular-film audience.

Branagh had the wit and invention to see that Shakespeare's lovers break into sonnet as naturally as the romantic leads in movie musicals break into song and that dancing works as an implied metaphor for courtship throughout *Love's Labour's Lost*—from Berowne's opening query to Rosaline, "Did I not dance with you in Brabant once?" to the ultimate refusal of the women to "take hands and dance" to satisfy the men's wooing desires in the play's final scenes. The question, as Branagh has expressed it, begins with cinematically solving the problem of Shakespeare's language: "in the case of *Love's Labour's Lost* . . . a play so caught up with the idea of how language is used and abused, and so politically connected to its time, with that kind of language that [even in a] Shakespeare production we don't hear that often—how can we make that into a film?"[25] He found the answer in the American movie musical:

> The play responds very well to music. There are many references to music and dancing in it and the elegance, style, and wit of the play seemed to me to sit well in a context not unlike the Hollywood musicals of the thirties and forties. . . . Writers like Cole Porter or Irving Berlin or George Gershwin whose lyrics are arguably as witty, in their own way, as Shakespeare was in his time and just as full of conceits and verbal trickery. Shakespeare was trying to convey how silly and stupid and agonizing it is to be in love [and] the songs we have chosen convey all of the same vicissitudes of love.[26]

This witty and elegant idea borrows a technique from Dennis Potter's *Pennies from Heaven* and *The Singing Detective* and Woody Allen's *Everybody Says I Love You*, marrying it with the dancing of Fred Astaire and Ginger Rogers, Gene Kelly and Leslie Caron. The problem was that Fred, Ginger, Porter, and Berlin were as foreign to the fifteen- to twenty-five-year-olds who make up the vast majority of the popular-film audience as was Shakespeare's early comedy. H. R. Coursen is right to remark that "it is not too much to say that the songwriters of the 30s created more music that is still heard by the discerning listener than any decade ever," but the key word there is *discerning*.[27] The songs of the 1930s that I inherited from my parents—for example, those in the films of Astaire and Rogers—have not survived to swirl through the imaginations of the rock generation. So when Branagh's quartet of lovers first break from Shakespeare into song with Jerome Kern's "I Won't Dance," the song is as novel to this generation of teenagers as Shakespeare's play: not even Frank Sinatra's brilliant version with Nelson Riddle for Capitol on *A Swingin' Affair*, released in 1957, is alive in the minds of young moviegoers. They just didn't get the film's daft and deft musical jokes.

For the members of the audience whose memories do reach back to the Great Depression era of Branagh's film, his "actor-led" company—rather than "dancer-led" (Branagh's distinction)—too often fails to reach the sublime, and perhaps unreachable, heights of Astaire and Rogers dancing cheek to cheek or Kelly going solo on a rain-drenched street or windblown sound stage. For Wendy Wasserstein, as for many, "the great movie musicals defined romance and American exuberance," but she ultimately decides that Branagh's film fails to take flight because "the numbers in this musical *Love's Labour's Lost* are always performed with an arched eyebrow. And when the eyebrow becomes too arched, we can't help but suspend our suspension of disbelief and wonder why anyone's singing to begin with . . . dancing tongue-in-cheek is hardly as difficult or inspiring as cheek-to-cheek."[28]

I understand her response, though I think the tongue-in-cheekiness applies more to the treatment of the songs sung by the "fantastical" characters, especially Don Armado's (Timothy Spall's) version of Porter's "I Get a Kick Out of You" (where Porter's tongue *is* being very cheeky) than it does to those delivered by the lovers. The problem lies more, I think, in the very American nature of the movie musical. It is not a genre that travels well, unlike the Western, which has been successfully transplanted to cultures and landscapes as diverse as Italy and Japan. Like the stage musical from which it springs, it is a form that thrives on innocence and energy rather than irony and self-awareness, which is why Baz Luhrmann's *Moulin Rouge* was so disappointing. The movie musical, far more than Shakespeare, inherently resists the postmodern aesthetic; as a form —except in the hands of Bob Fosse—it refuses cynicism.

Love's Labour's Lost continues Branagh's Anglo-American casting mix of Branagh regulars, British stage actors, and young American film stars. For all of them, except Adrian Lester, this was their first venture into the world of musical comedy, which is another reason why Wasserstein, I think, mistakenly reads their efforts as parodic. Branagh genuinely is committed to his Hollywood song-and-dance material, and there are no arched eyebrows in the film's three best musical numbers: "I Won't Dance," "Dancing Cheek to Cheek," and "They Can't Take That Away From Me." In fact, in a remarkable feat of synthesis, Branagh's film manages to give us, in ninety-five minutes, most of the play's plot, about 25 percent of its text, and ten song-and-dance routines that echo movie musicals as diverse as Esther Williams's water ballets and Kelly's *An American in Paris*. As always with Branagh, there is often a sense of eager amateurism about these efforts, which some find more winning than others. This might be called the Andy Hardy strain in his production aesthetic ("Hey, gang, let's put on a play!") and his film of *Love's Labour's Lost* is his homage not only to Fred and Ginger but to Mickey and Judy as well.

The best of the dance routines, *Top Hat*'s "Dancing Cheek to Cheek," spins gracefully out from Shakespeare's verbal pirouettes on the relationship between love, learning, and a lady's eyes. Branagh's Berowne circumnavigates the library of Navarre's Oxbridge academy as he lectures his pals on the power of knowledge being derived not from leaden contemplation but from the "prompting eyes . . . of beauty's tutors." When he reaches "And when Love speaks, the voice of all the gods / Make heaven drowsy with the harmony" (4.3.341–42),[29] the film glides amusingly from Shakespeare to Irving Berlin as Branagh begins to croon, "Heaven . . . I'm in heaven" as he and his fellow lovers lift up and off, twirling into the library's great dome, carried aloft by their buoyant wooing spirits. C. L. Barber has written that Berowne's peroration on love "leaps up to ring . . . big bells lightly"[30]—a spirit captured nicely here by Stuart Hopps's choreography. When the men return to earth—now Fredied-up in white tie and tails—they spill out from the library into the courtyard to be met by their respective Gingers each dressed in a flowing pastel gown, and we are treated to a fantasy heavenly harmony among the four couples that we are denied in the text.

Branagh strings together his mixture of Shakespeare's song with Hollywood's dance by another long-usurped movie staple: the Movietone *News of the Week*, where his own voice (echoes of Olivier and Welles) serves as that of the rapid-fire narrator. The King (Alessandro Nivola) and his companions—Berowne (Branagh), Longaville (Matthew Lillard), and Dumaine (Adrian Lester)—have retreated into their little academe not only to deny themselves the pleasures of the world but also, one takes it, to avoid the growing winds of war, as the film is set in the long summer of 1939. The arrival of the French Princess (Alicia Silverstone) and her attending ladies—Rosaline (Natascha McElhone), Katherine (Emily Mortimer), and Marla (Carmen Ejogo)—calls the men back then, in Branagh's conception, not only to the pleasures (the songs of Apollo) but the pains (the words of Mercury) of the world.

A. O. Scott, like many of the film's reviewers, was sadly ignorant of Shakespeare's play, dismissing it "as Shakespeare's most forgettable early comedy,"[31] when, in fact, *Love's Labour's Lost* is the first of the Bard's great festive comedies. Scott appears to be as little familiar with the cultural and military history of the twentieth century (or the history of Great Depression–era movies) as he is with Shakespeare when he complains, "For no particular reason, Mr. Branagh sets the play in a dreamy technicolor Europe on the eve of World War II."[32] Mr. Scott might have thought about why those wonderful Porter, Gershwin, Berlin, and Kern songs were all created in the years of the Great Depression, along with screwball comedy—arguably the greatest contribution to the genre since the Restoration—the Astaire and Rogers films, and *The Wizard of Oz*. Coursen, the film's most perceptive reviewer, sees the connections between Shakespeare's text and its 1930s setting:

> Branagh's inter-war instant does not depend on historical parallels bound to break down under the most superficial analysis. The thirties were . . . a time of fantasy, of Hollywood films flying us down to Rio, or simply opening the doors in front of our dimes and quarters to art deco luxury in which William Powell and Myrna Loy traded witty comments or in which Fred and Ginger cavorted to captivating songs. . . . It is to this moment Branagh's comedy takes us. It is a zone that repels any history but its own, but it invites the kind of game-playing that goes on in Shakespeare's play and that was going on in the thirties, in spite of empty smokestacks and dust-filled midlands. As in Shakespeare's play, some of the "happy endings" were deferred, in 1939 because of another Great War. Some of the endings were not happy.[33]

As Coursen reveals, Branagh understands that the Hollywood comedies of the 1930s, musical and screwball, are structurally and thematically related to Shakespeare's elaborate wooing games. The elaborate verbal play and flights of wit that distinguish *Love's Labour's Lost*'s fascination with language are realized in the Hollywood musical in song and dance. Who remembers the dialogue (or plot) from *Top Hat*? Astaire and Rogers communicate in dance. Their wit is expressed in the way their bodies fly together, then separate, then tap, side by side, then dazzlingly swirl back together again. Branagh's film, even with amateur dancers, often catches this spirit, especially as the lovers spill out from library to courtyard in "Dancing Cheek to Cheek" and the Kelly-inspired "Let's Face the Music and Dance" number, which serves as the film's version of the Muscovite disguises the men assume in the play.

By beginning his film on September 1, 1939, as Hitler was rolling into Poland, Branagh provides both a motivation for and critique of the King of Navarre's decision to retreat into his academy. These gentlemen songsters off on a library spree are trying to avoid the unavoidable: entanglement with the wider world. In Shakespeare's play, that wider world is figured as female: learning can't trump love. Branagh's film complicates the issue by adding war to woman as part of the world's call, and thus it deepens the impact of Shakespeare's refusal to allow his play to end with the conventional happy ending. The arrival of Mercade, the messenger of death, at the play's climax suspends, on the women's insistence, the wooing games for a year. In the film, this moment is transformed to the arrival of the war and the call of the men from one set of arms to another. In a scene lifted from *Casablanca*, the men bid farewell to their respective Ilsa's at a foggy airport, and as the women's airplane disappears into the night, it skywrites, "You that way; we this way." This could have been the film's natural conclusion, leaving the romances and the men's fate unresolved, but Branagh gives us a miniversion, in black and white footage, of World War II, with the men (all except Boyet) emerging triumphant, to be reunited with the women as an orchestral reprise of "They Can't Take That Away from Me" swells on the sound track.

This World War II montage certainly sentimentalizes Shakespeare's less-conventional ending, where we learn that the "words of Mercury are harsh after the songs of Apollo." But the film's conclusion does pick up on an important strand in Shakespeare's development of the relationship between Berowne and Rosaline and adds another soldier to Branagh's Shakespearean creations. Natascha McElhone is the most accomplished of the young women, and in a few, deft moments she manages to suggest the essence of Rosaline's tart but generous wit. Branagh, wisely, retains almost all of her important exchange with Berowne when she sends him off to amuse the speechless sick so that he might learn that "a jest's prosperity lies in the ear / Of him that hears it, never in the tongue / Of him that makes it" (5.2.861–63). Branagh's Berowne, a bit of a 1930s sport with a lock of hair dangling down over his forehead, instinctively responds: "To move wild laughter in the throat of death / It cannot be, it is impossible: / Mirth cannot move a soul in agony" (5.2.855–57). The film then, in the black-and-white montage of war scenes, imagines Berowne as working in a field hospital, administering to wounded souls in agony. It is an appropriate touch and something of an act of recuperation for Branagh's Shakespeare roles from the unsure warrior-king Henry V, to the malignant NCO Iago with his eyes on the General, to a Hamlet condemned to fighting solitary battles against a smooth opponent and his own troubled conscience, to the clever wit Berowne sent into the world to test his tongue against rude experience. Coursen senses a connection between Branagh's Hamlet and Berowne: "What Branagh brings to Berowne is an amusement and a dawning sense of the insufficiency of merely the right background and the right schools. Berowne is a young man's part, and Branagh plays it with an aplomb he did not bring to that other young man's part, Hamlet, where he took his character and the entire project far too seriously."[34]

McElhone's ease with Shakespeare's language reflects her British training at the London Academy of Music and Dramatic Arts (LAMDA), but like the film's other young stars, her career has been in mainstream popular films—in her case, from Peter Weir's *The Truman Show* to John Frankenheimer's *Ronin*. Alicia Silverstone, amusing as a valley-girl version of Austen's Emma Woodhouse in *Clueless*, less adeptly negotiates Shakespeare's pentameters and never finds a vocal rhythm that allows her to inhabit the aristocratic Princess of France comfortably. Among the men, again a mix of young American and English actors most noted for their film roles, Adrian Lester rivets attention. He is most widely known for his film role in Mike Nichols's *Primary Colors*, but he was a brilliant Rosalind in Cheek by Jowl's all-male *As You Like It* in the early 1990s and the definitive Bobby in Sam Mendes's 1995 revival of Stephen Sondheim's *Company*. Subsequently, Lester was a vigorous Hamlet in Peter Brook's production that toured the world in 2001. The American actors Matthew Lillard and Alessandro Nivola, best known for their film roles in *Scream* and *Face/Off*, round out the quartet of male lovers. For the play's clowns—and *Love's Labour's Lost* has the richest assortment of any Shakespearean comedy—Branagh again turned to a mixture of English and American stage and film veterans, ranging from Timothy Spall to

Nathan Lane. Their roles suffer the greatest compression (and transformation, as the schoolmaster Holofernes becomes the lady Professor
Holofernia and Armado's pert page, Moth, is translated from a quick-wit-
ted boy to an old dullard). The film creates a flirtation between Richard
Brier's Sir Nathaniel and Geraldine McEwan's Holofernia and gives them
a sweetly daft dance version of Jerome Kern's "The Way You Look
Tonight" to mirror the love antics of the aristocrats. Nathan Lane as
Costard is perhaps the most successful of all the American comedians—
they range from Michael Keaton to Billy Crystal—whom Branagh has
preferred to cast in the clown roles, and Timothy Spall's Don Armado,
sporting a Dali-esque mustache, does a wonderful turn on Porter's "I Get
a Kick Out of You."

Branagh's film draws its inspiration from vaudeville and Broadway as
well as Hollywood. Lane's Costard is part Bert Lahr and part Zero Mos-
tel, and the Pageant of the Nine Worthies disappears into a Lane-led version of Irving Berlin's "There's No Business Like Show Business" *(Annie
Get Your Gun)*. Lurking, as influences, not far in the background are such
Broadway musicals adapted from Shakespeare as *The Boys from Syracuse*
and *Kiss Me Kate* and the more recent *Play On!*, which linked Duke
Ellington's music with a Harlem version of *Twelfth Night*. But it is over-
whelmingly the Hollywood movie musical that provides the film with its
animating force. The relationship between Hollywood and Shakespeare
that was echoed in certain visual moments in Branagh's films of *Much Ado
About Nothing* and *Hamlet* becomes more than a hint or an echo in *Love's
Labour's Lost:* it is the creative energy that drives the film, provides its
comic pleasures, and dictates its evasions and its elisions. As Branagh
notes, the idea to link *Love's Labour's Lost* with the movie musical was not
exactly a producer's dream: "Well here's one [a comedy] that Shakespeare
wrote [*Love's Labour's Lost*] that wasn't performed for 200 years after his
death and I'd like to do it in a genre that hasn't really worked for the last
forty years. You know, tough sell."[35]

It turned out to be a tough sell at the box office as well. For some, its
energy and high spirits could not compensate for a cast of actors who
were not trained singers and dancers. As Stanley Kauffmann noted: "Actors who are not singers and dancers are asked to do a great deal of
singing and dancing. Some of the singing may have been dubbed, but it is
still uncompelling. . . . The dancing is worse . . . what is the point in ask-
ing an audience to watch long dance numbers by people who are not, as
far as we can see, dancers?"[36] For those of us who are long-time Branagh

watchers, the pleasure comes as much from the chutzpa of his invention (and his continuing quest to be a Shakespearean version of James Cagney) as from its execution.

What the film ultimately runs up against is the particularly American nature of the movie musical. John Updike, in a fine essay on Gene Kelly, noting the European resistance to Hollywood musicals, speculates "that there [is] something specifically American about these films—a brassy optimism and a galvanizing work ethic. From the muscularity of the performers to the dizzily wheeling multitudes of choral dancers and swimmers, the atmosphere is cheerfully industrial. The style of the images may be insouciant—*Look, Ma, I'm tap-dancing!*—but their message is power, American power, the power released from every man by the emancipation of democracy."[37] It is that spirit that ties the American movie musical to its particular period, spanning the midcentury from the 1930s to the 1950s. America lost its innocence in the 1960s, and with it disappeared the movie-musical genre, swallowed by Elvis, rock'n'roll, and *Hair*. Dennis Potter, in his curious way, Woody Allen, and Branagh (and now Baz Luhrmann, with *Moulin Rouge*) have attempted to resurrect its loony spirit, but the genre and the times resist.

To his credit, Branagh's career reveals his continuing efforts to translate Shakespeare into established Hollywood genres: the war film (*Henry V*), screwball comedy (*Much Ado About Nothing*), the epic (*Hamlet*), and the movie musical (*Love's Labour's Lost*). If Branagh's *Henry V* is at least partially responsible for leading filmmakers backward from Vietnam to rediscover World War II, his ending of *Love's Labour's Lost* reminds Spielberg that the Normandy invasion was not just an American enterprise. In claiming the Hollywood musical for Shakespeare, Branagh continues his raid into film territory, appropriating forms that suit his Shakespearean purposes. In the process, he has created a new dimension to the genre of the Shakespeare film and successfully achieved what Reinhardt, Dieterle, and Cukor failed to do in the 1930s: to create a successful synthesis of Shakespearean material with Hollywood form and technique.

The Golden Girl and a Fistful of Dust

Zeffirelli's Hamlet

Franco Zeffirelli, whose *Romeo and Juliet* (1968) is the most commercially successful of all Shakespeare films, has received paradoxically less critical attention than any of the other major directors of Shakespeare films. Olivier, Welles, Kurosawa, Kozintsev, and Branagh all have found their work at the center of scrutiny in the growing body of critical literature devoted to Shakespeare on film. But not Zeffirelli. Of the six books that appeared between 1988 and 1992 and that constituted a small avalanche of critical interest in Shakespeare as a subject for film, only one, Peter Donaldson's *Shakespearean Films/Shakespearean Directors*, contained an extended analysis of a Zeffirelli film.[1] Zeffirelli was ignored by the others, as he had been by Charles Eckert's pioneering collection of essays on Shakespearean films that appeared in 1972, just four years after the release of Zeffirelli's *Romeo and Juliet*.[2] Only Jack Jorgens, in his ground-breaking *Shakespeare on Film* (1977), gave Zeffirelli his due, with chapters devoted to both *Taming of the Shrew* and *Romeo and Juliet*.[3] Recent collections, *Shakespeare and the Moving Image* (1994), *Shakespeare, The Movie* (1997), and *The Cambridge Companion to Shakespeare on Film* (2000), have tried to restore the balance somewhat by including omnibus essays on Zeffirelli's Shakespeare films, but even they are measured in their assessment of his achievement.[4] The attention paid to Kenneth Branagh's work may lead, as Robert Hapgood suggests, to renewed interest in Zeffirelli's, as Branagh's flamboyant realism is so obviously indebted to Zeffirelli's lush and energetic film style.[5]

Why has Zeffirelli's work been relatively ignored or discounted by Shakespeare-on-film scholars? His *Taming of the Shrew*, so obviously a vehicle for its famous stars Elizabeth Taylor and Richard Burton, did not transcend their limitations and appeared just at a moment when modern feminism was suggesting a host of alternative approaches to the play beyond treating it as broad, battle-of-the-sexes farce. Jorgens is right to see that the film's most innovative moments are its opening scenes with Lucentio and Tranio arriving in Padua just as the city breaks into festive swirl and abuse to celebrate the first day of the new university term.[6] Zeffirelli's frame clearly wishes to reimagine the play's farce as participating in the festive holiday atmosphere of Shakespeare's major romantic comedies. Branagh's boisterous opening of his *Much Ado About Nothing* was intended to create a similar festive atmosphere for his reworking of a later city comedy and was clearly indebted to Zeffirelli's example. But (Cassius to the contrary) the fault is sometimes in our stars, and Burton and Taylor fail to transcend the quasi-autobiographical impulses that led them to this Shakespearean project.

Romeo and Juliet perhaps suffered the opposite fate. Here was a film so bold and stunning that it immediately found and held a teenage audience: Critical analysis was largely superfluous. At least until Donaldson's suggestive essay, this film did not need interpreters: it spoke directly and powerfully to students, bypassing the Shakespeare establishment. Zeffirelli's film reflected the 1960s in romanticizing the passion, intensity, and beauty of the young destroyed by the quarrels and conflicts of their parents. The film became the first to reshape the teaching of Shakespeare in the American high-school English curriculum. For almost seventy-five years, *Julius Caesar* and *Macbeth* topped the list of the ten most-taught Shakespeare plays—a list on which *Romeo and Juliet* did not appear. By 1975, *Romeo and Juliet* had zoomed to the top of that list, where it has remained, sustained by countless replays of Zeffirelli's film, for more than twenty-five years. The film's immense popularity and its association, at least in the United States, with the high-school curriculum were perhaps two reasons for its critical neglect.

One might have expected that the huge financial success of Zeffirelli's *Romeo and Juliet* would have created the commercial atmosphere conducive to the making of more Shakespeare films, but the failure of Polanski's *Macbeth* (1971) to recapture and extend the young audience Zeffirelli's *Romeo and Juliet* had found doomed the genre for almost two decades until the advent of the Branagh era. Though the planning for Zeffirelli's film of

Hamlet (1990) long predated the release of Branagh's *Henry V* in 1989, the surprising success of Branagh's low-budget film certainly helped pave the way for Zeffirelli's return to screen-Shakespeare after an absence of almost twenty-five years.

Though some commentators feel that *Hamlet* presented the romantic Italian with a world less congenial than *Taming*'s Padua or *Romeo*'s Verona ("one cannot move from his Padua and Verona to his Elsinore without a feeling of sensory deprivation," Robert Hapgood perceptively remarks),[7] Zeffirelli's fascination and involvement with the play reaches back to his emergence as a major director for the stage. In fact, the first Shakespeare he directed after the remarkable success of his production of *Romeo and Juliet* for the Old Vic in 1960 was a prize-winning Italian version of *Hamlet*, with Giorgio Albertazzi, which went on tour to Paris, Vienna, Moscow, and London in summer 1964. That stage production was sandwiched between several operas he was directing, including Joan Sutherland in *I puritani* and Maria Callas in *Norma*. "This was the spring of both my divas," Zeffirelli comments in his autobiography, reminding us that his first *Hamlet* sprang to life in the midst of his work with two of the greatest divas of the age—one just emerging, the other beginning her decline.[8]

When, years later, Zeffirelli came to film his *Hamlet*, most attention was given to his casting of Mel Gibson, known primarily for his lead roles in the *Mad Max* and *Lethal Weapon* action films, and to Gibson's eventual performance as Hamlet. Because of Gibson, most responses to Zeffirelli's film sought to place it firmly in the film culture of its star. Kathy Howlett, for instance, argues that Zeffirelli "taps into aspects of Shakespeare's *Hamlet* that resonate within the context of American mythology and film. . . . Zeffirelli engages his audience in Hamlet's revenge tragedy through associations with the American gunslinger and myths of the American West."[9] Since I am always eager to see popular film conventions and genres at work in the films of the Branagh era, I find much of Howlett's analysis suggestive. However, I believe that the casting of Glenn Close and Zeffirelli's passion for the opera diva exerted an even stronger influence on many of his production decisions, with the result that, visually, Gertrude emerges at the center of the film. Zeffirelli's visual interpretation of the play makes an intriguing match with Janet Adelman's Gertrude-centered reading of the play in her *Suffocating Mothers: Fantasies of Maternal Origins in Shakespeare's Plays*, Hamlet *to* The Tempest, which appeared in 1992 just after the release of Zeffirelli's new film.

Adelman locates the reintroduction of the mother (in general) and

Gertrude (in specific) into the Shakespearean universe as initiating the tragic phase of his career. The successful negotiations with masculine legacy and female sexuality that Shakespeare dramatized in the Lancastrian tetralogy and the comedies—plays noted for their absence of mothers—collapse in Shakespeare's tragedies, where female sexuality intrudes upon and ruptures masculine identity. For Adelman, *Hamlet* initiates this tragic pattern, and Gertrude is at its core:

> Hamlet thus redefines the son's position between two fathers by relocating it in relation to an indiscriminately sexual maternal body that threatens to annihilate the distinction between the fathers and hence problematizes the son's paternal identification. At the same time, the play conflates the beloved with this betraying mother, undoing the strategies that had enabled marriage in the comedies. The intrusion of the adulterous mother thus disables the solutions of history and comedy as Shakespeare has imagined them; in that sense, her presence initiates tragedy.[10]

Julia Lupton and Kenneth Reinhard find a similar pattern at work in Zeffirelli's film, tracing it to Lacan's revision of Freud. For them, while Olivier's *Hamlet* provides a Freudian "reading that emphasizes Gertrude as the object of Hamlet's incestuous desire," Zeffirelli's film follows a Lacanian approach by presenting us with a Gertrude as the demanding mother, "at once over anxious and oversexed," whose "hungry kisses and caresses are resisted with barely concealed disgust by her son."[11] Because Lupton and Reinhard want to read Close's performance as Gertrude in intimate interconnection with her Alex Forest in Adrian Lyne's *Fatal Attraction*, their analysis of the film fails to account for the ways Zeffirelli's camera both adores and privileges Close's Gertrude and comes closer to giving us Adelman's reading of the play than Lacan's.

After establishing shots of castle and courtyard, Zeffirelli's *Hamlet* begins with a sob and a dumb show that silently and decisively answers the text's opening query: "Who's there?" The camera pokes its way down into the castle's crypt, where we discover ourselves at Old Hamlet's entombment. Our first close-up is of Close's Gertrude, whose pale, sobbing face is wreathed by thick, blonde braids. Gertrude approaches the coffin and removes a pewter rose from her hair and places it on the dead king's chest and then turns and collapses into Polonius's waiting arms. This misty moment is disturbed as a fist, clutching a handful of dust, enters the frame and slowly opens to allow the dirt to sprinkle down on the corpse. The camera follows up from hand to arm to capture the hooded face of Mel Gibson's Hamlet just as Claudius speaks the first lines of the film's dialogue: "Hamlet think of us / As of a father, for let the world take note / You are the most immediate to our throne."[12] As Gertrude's sobs mix with the film score's violins, Hamlet turns and exits. This tableau establishes Zeffirelli's decision to focus on *Hamlet* as a family romance, to place Gertrude firmly at its center, to compete extravagantly with Olivier's oedipal version of the play, and to offer a Hamlet defined more by that fistful of dust than by thinking too precisely on the event.

Gibson's presence as Hamlet has made comparisons with his work in the *Lethal Weapon* and *Mad Max* films inevitable, and Linda Charnes is right to see that the characters he played in those films share with Hamlet personalities made mad by marriages.[13] I am less convinced, however, by her desire to see Close's Gertrude as a combination of her good-girl/bad-girl roles in films like *The Big Chill* and *Fatal Attraction*. For Zeffirelli, Gibson comes out of film culture, but his context for Close is opera. Gertrude is conceived as the film's diva: she is the golden girl at the center of a drab masculine world. Zeffirelli's camera adores Close and repeatedly captures her glowing girlishness. Opera is, of course, as uncongenial a medium for *Hamlet* as are Howlett's westerns and Gibson's *Lethal Weapon* films, but in the visual tension between the two, played out in Zeffirelli's direction of Gibson's and Close's performances, the film generates an excitement in translating the play into a mixture of the artistic conventions that have governed Zeffirelli's professional life as a director and designer.

The poet Wayne Koestenbaum has written an extended rhapsody on homosexual fans of opera, *The Queen's Throat: Opera, Homosexuality, and the Mystery of Desire*—a work that explores gay fascination with opera in general and the diva in particular. While the communion between opera queen and diva is largely conducted by listening in the dark, with the diva's voice as the medium of ecstasy and thrill, Koestenbaum's text often and naturally links the diva with the female film star, from Gloria Swanson to Julie Andrews: "Callas sang in the era of *Sunset Boulevard:* in legend she became Norma Desmond."[14] He also understands that not all opera queens worship from afar and in the dark:

In a photograph, Visconti wraps his arms tightly around Callas and kisses her on the cheek—it looks to be a firm, authentic kiss—and she smiles, flattered and gratified to be kissed; Zeffirelli, doughy and devoted, kisses Callas, and she smiles radiantly, knowing the limits of the kiss; Bernstein holds Callas's hands and studies her, and they seem to be playing a seesaw game, figuring out whether their bodies are equivalent; gaunt and shirtless, Pasolini directs Callas as Medea, and she is attentive, obediently holding her hands to her face. These photographs attest to a specific historic configuration: the gay man venerating the theatrical woman and the woman responding gaily, the women imitating the gay man and the gay man imitating the woman, the gay man directing and then listening and admiring, the man and woman collaborating.[15]

A composite of those photographs showing Visconti, Zeffirelli, Bernstein, and Pasolini all giving rapt attention to Callas might serve as an analogue to the ways in which Zeffirelli surrounds Close's Gertrude with her quartet of male admirers: Paul Scofield's Ghost, Gibson's Hamlet, Alan Bates's Claudius, and Ian Holm's Polonius. The analogy breaks down, of course, because of the differences in the mystery of desire contained in the two tableaux. Close's Gertrude "smiles radiantly," is "flattered and gratified to be kissed," and wants to respond "gaily" to the men in her life. Zeffirelli's film keeps flirting with imagining Gertrude as the diva who, in the world of opera, releases her dazzle but keeps her distance with and through her voice. Shakespeare's queen is, however, as much body as voice, and her physical presence seems to demand intimacy rather than devotion. It is perhaps no surprise that the next role Close went on to create after her Gertrude was that of Norma Desmond in Andrew Lloyd Webber's opera-driven musical *Sunset Boulevard*, thus collapsing the roles of diva and film star into one. Zeffirelli's camera treats Close much as Visconti, Zeffirelli, Bernstein, and Pasolini treat Callas in Koestenbaum's reading of the photographs. The problem is that Shakespeare's males do not know the limits of their touch and kiss and keep trying to possess what Koestenbaum's opera queen simply wants to adore.

Zeffirelli's film, like Adelman's critical analysis, shapes the play with Gertrude, not the ghost or Claudius, at its center—or at the center of Hamlet's fractured consciousness. The film is much more about sons and mothers than fathers and uncles, and this is evident not only from the opening dumb show but in Zeffirelli's casting decisions as well. Close and Gibson are of an age; Scofield's Ghost is ancient and old enough to be Gertrude's grandfather; and while, by comparison, Bates's Claudius appears much younger than his brother, he is still almost old enough to be Close's father. Helena Bonham Carter's Ophelia (with eyebrows wonderfully sullen and defiant) is never a visual match for Gibson's Hamlet; she is out of his "star" not because of social standing but because she cannot compare or compete with his dazzling mother. She's a plain, puzzled child. Close is the film's radiant golden girl, and Gibson's Hamlet naturally (and unnaturally) finds it impossible to "step from this picture [Gertrude] to this [Ophelia]."

The predominant visual image of Zeffirelli's *Hamlet* is of the pale, blonde Close, dressed in virgin blue, shot in golden light, and surrounded by a host of swarthy, hairy males all dressed in drab colors. Even Ophelia's dress and coloring align her with the men rather than with the glamorous queen. The stunning poster for the film brilliantly reflects Zeffirelli's decision to make Hamlet's relationship with the female more powerful in the film than his struggle with the play's trio of father figures. The poster's foreground is dominated by the faces of Gibson's Hamlet and Close's Gertrude separated by the hilt of a sword whose blade Hamlet grasps with both hands. Close's face is positioned slightly above Gibson's. He stares intently straight ahead with beads of sweat glistening on his brow. Close's demeanor is serene; a white-and-gold headband pulls back her very blonde hair as she glances to her right. Tracking off in the distance behind Hamlet's head are portraits of Ophelia (hands to lips in puzzlement or fright), Claudius, Polonius, and the ghost. The order is significant. The poster properly anticipates the film in positioning Hamlet between Gertrude and Ophelia, rather than between Ghost and Claudius. Ghost is a distant, enervated presence in the film. Scofield's sweetly nuanced performance gives us the sad cuckold rather than the commanding king, while Close's Gertrude is a figure of appetite and vitality.[16]

Everyone in the film is fascinated by her. Anthony Dawson intelligently sees that "the gesture that seems to define Franco Zeffirelli's vision of the play is the glance. The camera moves, bodies move, but more than anything in his films, *eyes* move."[17] And, from the opening dumb show, those glances are directed as much at Gertrude as at Hamlet. She is the center of the male gaze and female gaze as well, as Bonham Carter's Ophelia repeatedly is found by the camera giving Close her puzzled scrutiny as if to say: What has she done to my man and how can I tap into that power?

Father is as absorbed as daughter. Holm's Polonius is clearly captivated by Gertrude. From his move to comfort the weeping queen in the opening scene to his report of Hamlet and Ophelia's romantic relationship and then to his preparation of Gertrude for Hamlet's arrival in the closet scene, Holm is more solicitous of Gertrude's opinion than of Claudius's. Holm's performance is subtle and meticulous. His Polonius is more the scholar (or pedant: note his cap) than the statesman, and his windy announcement of the Hamlet/Ophelia relationship is as much to Gertrude as to Claudius. Zeffirelli repeatedly places her at the center of attention. The play insists that it is Claudius who has usurped the center ("popp'd in between the election and my hopes") that rightfully belongs to Hamlet, but here Bates's Claudius seems just another male admirer of Gertrude's radiance. It is clear that his Claudius has murdered more for lust than power, but he appears shy and almost overwhelmed by his prize, rather than proudly possessive.

Zeffirelli's shift of the play's family-power dynamics is made most clear in his handling of the film's version of act 1, scene 2. As we have seen, he lifts a snippet of it as the first spoken dialogue in the film's opening scene. He cuts from the crypt to the court with elements of Claudius's opening address heard first as a general announcement (over an establishing shot of Elsinore's castle) and then from Claudius himself enthroned alongside his queen in the castle's great hall. Hamlet is absent from Claudius's slick congratulations to the court for their reception of funeral and wedding. He has to be sought out, and it is Gertrude who leads the search party. She nuzzles Claudius into accompanying her to Hamlet's room shrouded in darkness and filled with books and rudimentary scientific equipment. She swings open a giant curtain, exposing her son, certain that she is a light-and-life bringer. She laughs at Hamlet's crack about being "too much in the sun," having literalized his pun and missed its sting.

Close's Gertrude tries to soothe her son in the same manner she handles Claudius: with nuzzles and tender touches and kisses that become increasingly complicated and ambiguous. Here, when Hamlet sinks to the floor and capitulates ("I shall in all my best obey you, madam"), Gertrude goes to her knees to kiss his forehead, eyes, lips, and to press his defeated head into her abdomen. The sound of barking dogs and hunting horns recalls her to Claudius waiting on horseback in the courtyard below and she bolts out from her embrace of her son and down the stairs, where a great blue cape is swirled over her shoulders by her attendants. She dashes out into the courtyard, where she nearly pulls Claudius out of his saddle with an eager kiss before mounting and riding off, her blonde tresses billowing in the wind. Hamlet observes all of this from above as he spits out his bitterness at this "unweeded garden / That grows to seed. Things rank and gross in nature / Possess it merely" (1.2.135–37). Gibson slams shut the curtain to his window in an attempt to erase the scene below ("Frailty, thy name is woman"). In one of the film's most exquisite and apt transitions, as Michael Skovmand notes, the next shot—Hamlet's words lingering on the soundtrack—is of Laertes entering his sister's room, evoking the play's other key female: "Dear Ophelia, my necessaries are embarked."[18]

The sequence allows Close to give full rein to her winsome, vigorous Gertrude. The language of her power is physical: she exudes a sensuous vitality that, strikingly, is confusing to both of the men in her life. Hamlet, obviously, is both attracted to and repelled by her physical expressiveness, and Claudius, whom one would imagine to be completely caught up in her dazzle, is almost always filmed with a cup of wine, either in hand or at lip—a sign that he is anxious about their relationship even before Hamlet begins to work on exposing his guilt. The cup of wine, of course, will come back to haunt him in the film's final scene.

This scene also reveals the ways in which Zeffirelli uses the vertical and horizontal lines in his film to get at issues of enclosure and release embedded in the text. Denmark . . . prison; nutshell . . . infinite space; golden roof . . . congregation of vapors; paragon of animals . . . quintessence of dust; undiscovered country . . . no return; heaven . . . earth—all speak to Hamlet's sense of containment and desire for release. "What should such fellows as I do crawling between earth and heaven?" (3.1.126–28) he rhetorically asks Ophelia, staking out his boundaries and the central question of the human condition. Olivier visualized this cluster of images by his Hamlet's repeated flights up the stairs from Elsinore's bowels (Claudius's territory) to the high platform above (the ghost's). Donaldson suggestively has read these flights as speaking not only to Hamlet's story but to Olivier's autobiography as well.[19] Olivier's Hamlet is always trapped on the vertical; his Elsinore is an image of the mind's labyrinth from which there is no escape. There is only up and down for Olivier's Hamlet, never the possibility of in and out. He is horizontal only when leveled by the ghost's appearance on the ramparts and in Gertrude's bedroom and when, finally, making his flying leap to plunge his sword into Claudius.

Zeffirelli and Gibson present us with a Hamlet who wants to believe he has more options, avenues of awareness, and modes of attack. Zeffirelli does, like Olivier, exploit the perpendicular; he repeatedly positions Gibson's Hamlet above the action unfolding below: Hamlet is on a high catwalk above the courtyard seemingly overhearing as well as overseeing Polonius chastising Ophelia for being a "green girl" in accepting Hamlet's tenders of affection; he peers down from the ramparts through a grill to observe Claudius's (and the entire court's) reveling below as he awaits his rendezvous with the ghost; he is perched atop the shelves in Polonius's library in the fishmonger scene and pushes the library ladder away ("you yourself sir, should be as old as I am if, like a crab, you could go backwards") as Polonius attempts to climb up to reach him; he enters above Polonius and Claudius when they are plotting to "loose" Ophelia to him; and he hops up on the council table (wearing Polonius's skull cap) to play the fool with Claudius about the location of Polonius's body after the closet scene. In each of these instances, Gibson's possession of the high, vertical perspective is an expression of Hamlet's superiority to the carnal, duplicitous, and obtuse world below. Crucially, his one movement down and under comes as he retreats to the crypt after the nunnery scene to deliver the "To be or not to be" soliloquy, as if it were his attempt to share his anguish and impotence with his dead father. Zeffirelli is, of course, revising Olivier's spatial handling of the soliloquy here, though retaining Olivier's Q1 positioning of it after, rather than before, Hamlet's encounter with Ophelia.

But besides giving Hamlet a command of the vertical, Zeffirelli and Gibson also hold out the possibility that he might appropriate the horizontal as well. In Olivier's *Hamlet*, the only characters associated with the external, natural world are Ophelia and the gravedigger: the dead and the quick. Kozintsev, in his film's opening sequence, allows his Hamlet one breathtaking gallop home along the horizontal—then the castle swallows him up as the portcullis is cranked down after his horse clatters across the drawbridge. Gibson's restless Hamlet prowls Elsinore's upper and lower reaches and, in a stunning jump cut (immediately after he finishes the "To be or not to be" soliloquy) from dark to light, from inside to out: the film finds him outside Elsinore, sprawled out under a bold blue sky on a green hillside overlooking the sea, his horse grazing in the rear of the frame—a portrait of the hero who has lost the name of action.

The glimpses of the external world we get from Olivier and Kozintsev are gray, cold, melancholy landscapes mirroring each film's brooding Dane. Zeffirelli's romantic Italian blood cannot imagine a world where a vibrant sun isn't always shining and violent action is not always a possibility. Gibson's reverie is broken by the arrival on horseback of Rosencrantz (Michael Maloney) and Guildenstern (Sean Murray). The three men gallop off to a solitary log cabin, signaling the landscape of an American Western and reminding us of that fistful of dust that first introduced us to Gibson's Hamlet. Howlett argues that the Western is the film genre that Zeffirelli exploits in the framing and shaping of his *Hamlet*, and this scene of Hamlet exposing his two schoolfellows while sharing a cookout is central to her analysis.[20] But Zeffirelli is also creating his own scenic illustration here for Hamlet's "O what a piece of work is a man" speech, where the green earth we see is anything but a "sterile promontory" and the blue sky above seems much closer to a "most excellent canopy" than a "foul and pestilent congregation of vapors." In fact, the external world Zeffirelli gives us here bears a striking resemblance to the surface beauty of Close's Gertrude—soft and sparkling. The world, like his mother, puzzles Gibson's Hamlet precisely because for him it is not what it seems so obviously to be. Zeffirelli allows his Hamlet to move in a landscape beyond the confines of Claudius's poisoned court, but it finally offers neither solace nor escape, for its beauty seems only to echo the corruption of his mother's.

In a dazzling essay that nevertheless misreads Zeffirelli's *Hamlet*, Linda Charnes faults the film for failing to grasp the play's essential filmnoir quality.[21] But Zeffirelli's film style is as far removed from noir as slapstick is from screwball. Zeffirelli's sensibility is romantic and grandly operatic; his artistic blood beats in Technicolor, not black-and-white; his sensibility is passionate and sentimental, not cool and cynical. His solution to the oedipal conflict, complicated in his own case by his bastardy and homosexuality, is not to destroy the father but to glorify the mother.[22] This is the source of his lavish visual imagination and his attraction to the diva from Callas to Sutherland to Denyse Graves. That artistic attraction to the tragic female, the center of the operatic form, spills over into his Shakespeare films. Reading his autobiography reveals his much greater preoccupation with Elizabeth Taylor than with Richard Burton, for instance. The same pattern is at work in his *Hamlet*, where the landscape and atmosphere of the film seem more a reflection of Gertrude's radiance than Hamlet's intelligence.

This is reinforced by Zeffirelli's handling of the end of Hamlet's first encounter with Rosencrantz and Guildenstern. Hamlet's Western interlude, and its possibilities for flight and independence, is foreclosed by the arrival of the players, who literally transport him back into Elsinore and his reengagement with the family drama. Now, in the film's only reversal of the Hamlet-from-above perspective, it is Gertrude who peers down: from a high window, she sees her son in the courtyard below making merry with the actors. Hamlet acknowledges her presence with a glance before slipping into the shadows to formulate his plan for "The Mousetrap."

The actors have brought Hamlet back into the world of the female. Zeffirelli underlines the transition by transposing key lines between Hamlet and Ophelia from the nunnery scene, which creates a frame for the play-within. In fact, by doing so "The Mousetrap" becomes less about Hamlet's power struggle with Claudius than about the conclusion of his relationship with Ophelia and the preparation for his confrontation with Gertrude that follows.[23]

Zeffirelli shoots Hamlet's exchange with Ophelia about "country matters" in a tight two-shot; Hamlet's tone is more intimate than bitter or bad-boy bawdy, and Bonham Carter's Ophelia registers her puzzled understanding of his double-entendres with a raised eyebrow rather than a blush. Gibson's voice becomes more bold and bitter as he spits out "look you how cheerfully my mother looks, and my father died within two hours." Then, in an intriguing textual transposition, he replies to Ophelia's "Nay 'tis twice two months, my lord," with "So long? Then get thee to a nunnery. Why wouldst thou be a breeder of sinners?"—followed by a cut to the actors juggling with torches as a prologue to the evening's main event. Everyone is playing with fire here. Then the film cuts back to an anguished Hamlet almost pleading with Ophelia: "What should such fellows as I do crawling beneath earth and heaven?" After the film's brief (and largely mimed) version of "The Mousetrap" has caused Bates's Claudius to rise and stagger toward the platform with his hand pressed to his right ear before uttering a guttural laugh and exiting, the film returns to Hamlet and Ophelia for "Believe none of us. We are arrant knaves all." Long passionate kiss. "Farewell."

At this moment in Shakespeare's text, where Hamlet is most ecstatically fixated on Claudius and the way in which he has signaled his guilt, Zeffirelli's film insists on displacing Claudius in Hamlet's imagination with Ophelia and, by extension and cross-cutting, Gertrude. Certainly it is a bold idea to interweave the nunnery scene with "The Mousetrap," and there is a curiously apt logic to Zeffirelli's move to create a necessary link in Hamlet's mind between the confirmation of Claudius's guilt and his rejection of Ophelia (a replay of his visit to her room after his encounter with the ghost), but it is also simply further evidence of the way in which Zeffirelli's film repeatedly stresses that Hamlet's key relationships are with his mother and lover rather than with his uncle and father.

Zeffirelli's manipulation of text and performance here is an uncanny realization of Adelman's understanding of the ways in which Ophelia and Gertrude merge as the tainted female "other" in Hamlet's imagination. Zeffirelli's handling of Hamlet's relationship with mother and lover here is a visual gloss on Adelman's insistence that

> Ophelia fuses with Gertrude not only as potential cuckold-maker but also potential mother:
>
>> Get thee to a nunnery. Why, wouldst thou be a breeder of sinners? I am myself indifferent honest, but yet I could accuse me of such things that it were better my mother had not borne me. (3.1.121–24)
>
> The implicit logic is: why would you be a breeder of sinners like me? In the gap between "breeder of sinners" and "I," Gertrude and Ophelia momentarily collapse into one figure. It is no wonder there can be no more marriage: Ophelia becomes dangerous to Hamlet insofar as she becomes identified in his mind with the contaminating maternal body, the mother who has borne him.[24]

This pattern is again made evident in the film's dismissal of all but two lines of Claudius's attempt at confession and prayer, so that Hamlet can more quickly speed to the central confrontation with Gertrude that follows. The closet scene is the climax of Zeffirelli's film much as it is the climax of Adelman's analysis of the text.[25] This is the duet the entire film has been building to. Zeffirelli bathes Gertrude's bedroom in a golden glow that emanates as much from Close's face and hair (down and fully displayed for the first time in the film) as from the fire that blazes in her immense stone fireplace.[26] Besides her bed and the fire, two other props contribute to the setting: a huge wall hanging of a particularly ugly and ferocious Nordic wolf and a large white bear-skin rug. Olivier's and Kozintsev's bedrooms are cold and stark in comparison. Though Donaldson has cleverly described the draperies that hood Gertrude's bed in Olivier's film as suggesting the female genitalia, that bed remains the most sexually charged and exciting element in the room.[27]

Olivier's Hamlet is so overwhelmed by his oedipal confusion (and his age mismatch with Eileen Herlie's queen; he was forty, she twenty-seven, so obvious in close-up) that the scene fails to generate the sexual power and tension Olivier clearly and boldly intended. There's no oedipal subtext to Kozintsev's handling of the scene; his Gertrude is as cold and lifeless as her dressing dummies that are hidden behind the arras with Polonius. Oddly, Tony Richardson's *Hamlet*, so otherwise 1960s wild in its liberated sexual cynicism (Marianne Faithfull's Ophelia appears to have been intimate with both Laertes and Hamlet, for instance), does not seek to exploit the potential for incest between mother and son.

Gibson and Close give us the most intense and passionate encounter between Hamlet and Gertrude in the world of Hamlet on film. Anthony Dawson is right to quip that here "lethal weapon meets fatal attraction in what turns out to be a dangerous liaison."[28] Violence, lethal and sexual, infuses and comes to climax in the scene. Gibson's Hamlet threatens Gertrude with his sword, rams it home into Polonius through the wild animal embroidered on the arras, and later straddles his mother and thrusts away at her in a terrifying mock rape to the rhythm of the text's ugliest image: "Nay but to live / In the rank sweat of an enseamed bed / Stewed in corruption, honeying and making love / Over the nasty sty!" (3.4.92–94).

As Hamlet hammers away at Gertrude physically and Claudius verbally ("a king of shreds and patches"), Close finally pulls Gibson into a desperate, passionate kiss meant not only to silence his aggression but to express her own repressed longings. This moment is as primal as the murder of Polonius, and for Zeffirelli, as for Adelman, signals the ultimate release of Hamlet's wild discontent and opens the possibility for reconciliation with his mother. Scofield's sad, sweet Ghost (shot framed in a Romanesque archway to resemble a weary, worried saint in an altarpiece) seems oblivious to the action he has interrupted. The film's kiss is the climax here, not the text's conjuration of the ghostly authorial father. The murder of Polonius and the rape of Gertrude have made Hamlet an arrant knave and allowed him a perspective from which, finally, to understand and share his mother's flawed humanity. By finally enacting the ugly image that has both disgusted and transfixed him, Gibson's Hamlet has freed its powerful hold on his imagination. When Hamlet leaves, he gives

Gertrude his chain with the locket of old Hamlet on it, and she signals her acceptance of their compact by tucking the locket away when Claudius enters her room.

For Zeffirelli, this scene is as much about Gertrude as it is about Hamlet. Close's Gertrude is impetuous (she gives Gibson a vicious slap for his impudence) and passionate; she is a player here, and not a poor one. This scene confirms that for Zeffirelli she not only "earns a place in the story" but commands a central one. Again Adelman is extremely helpful in outlining the psychoanalytic pattern of interaction between mother and son that the film realizes visually in this scene. By reminding us that Hamlet's first and last words in the scene are "Mother," Adelman follows the progress by which Hamlet appears to rid himself of his ugly fantasies about the sexualized maternal body. For Adelman, "Hamlet cannot stop imagining, even commanding, the sexual act that he wants to undo."[29] Zeffirelli's film allows us to see that Gibson's Hamlet can rid his imagination of this contaminated vision only by reenacting it, allowing the expression of his own incestuous desire finally to obliterate Gertrude's, so that they can both be tarnished and thus capable of redeeming one another: "Once more, good night, / And when you are desirous to be blest, / I'll blessing beg of you" (3.4.172–74). Adelman comments about these lines, "As mother and son mirror each other, each blessing each, Shakespeare images the re-opening of the zone of trust that had been foreclosed by the annihilating mother."[30]

Hamlet's actions in Zeffirelli's treatment bring him down from his attempt to isolate himself in a superior position and perspective to his mother's flawed but all too human body. By finally admitting his own full participation in the complex mystery of the oedipal triangle, Hamlet can forgive Gertrude and restore her as the good mother. While Adelman remarks that in the text there "are no obvious signs of her separation from Claudius in her exchanges with him," Zeffirelli's film does provide, in the gesture where Close conceals the locket Hamlet has given her from her husband, such a sign, and it is a prelude to others that follow that indicate the reestablishment of the bond between mother and son.[31] Gibson's Hamlet becomes, after the closet scene, the performance embodiment of Adelman's reading of his reconciliation with Gertrude: "Trusting her he can begin to trust in himself and in his own capacity for action; and he can begin to rebuild the masculine identity spoiled by her contamination."[32]

This scene is obviously cathartic for Gibson's Hamlet, who suddenly is released into the action-hero mold that his performance, up to this moment, has strained against. While the text indulges the offensive vigor of Hamlet's wit in his exchange with Claudius concerning Polonius's whereabouts, Gibson's Hamlet is also physically energetic in this scene. He prances on Claudius's council table wearing Polonius's skullcap in an action that matches the topsy-turvey motion of his wit, turning the world, and its power and gender hierarchies, upside down. Gibson's Hamlet is never held captive in these exchanges, and he leads Rosencrantz and Guildenstern away on "Come, for England!" Then as Gertrude comes to bid Hamlet farewell, Zeffirelli gives us an extratextual moment. Before vaulting into the saddle and riding off, Hamlet pledges to her that he will trust his two schoolfellows "as I will adders fanged." This moment both mirrors and reverses Gertrude's abandonment of Hamlet as she rides off with Claudius at the end of the film's version of 1.2.

Gibson's Hamlet is again several steps ahead of Shakespeare's when, in Zeffirelli's visualization of the shipboard exchange of ambassadorial instructions, it is revealed that Hamlet has already prepared his revised version of the king's dispatch before he is fully aware of the contents of Claudius's. Zeffirelli returns Hamlet to Denmark on horseback, as befits the action-hero; and, as was the case, too, with the earlier change of emphasis, the climactic duel is less about Hamlet and Laertes and Claudius than about Hamlet and Gertrude. She is the golden seraphic mother dressed in virgin blue, her hair now in two long braids. He is the vigorous, clownish son mocking, for his mother's delight, the machismo of the duel. It is as if the two of them existed once again in a pre-Claudian state of innocence. There's no suspicious anxiety on either of their faces in the repeated cross-cuts that Zeffirelli makes between Hamlet's performance and Gertrude's spirited appreciation of her son's antics. Hamlet even signals one of his physical jokes with a wink, directed not at us, but at his mother. There's no physical or even eye contact between Claudius and Gertrude in this scene until she moves down from the dais to drink from the poisoned cup. Bates's and Close's reading of their exchange is wonderfully nuanced, capturing both his realization that he is the last person in this world to caution another about taking a drink, and her smiling girlishness in ignoring his warning. From this moment, the pace of Zeffirelli's cross-cutting between Gertrude and the duel intensifies, and she collapses at the moment Hamlet receives the fatal hit. Hamlet's eventual attack on Claudius is anticlimactic and is delivered with none of the energy and panache devoted to the strike by Olivier, Kozintsev, and, subsequently, Branagh. Claudius has never been the center of Zeffirelli's attention: Gertrude is at the core of his understanding of the play. And the film reminds us powerfully of the fates of the men who become infatuated with her golden-girl glow, from husbands and advisers to sons and lovers. The diva dies in an ugly parody of orgasm, having helped her quartet of male admirers to dusty death.

Zeffirelli's casting of the principal roles, his reshaping of the text, his use of cinematic space and landscape, the rhythm of his editing—all have established the family romance at the heart of his interest in the play. By doing so, his film gives visual substance and significance to Gertrude's central place in that romance—a place, as Adelman notes, that is much more opaque (but no less tantalizing) in Shakespeare's text. For Adelman, Gertrude remains "more a screen for Hamlet's fantasies about her than a fully developed character in her own right: whatever individuality she might have had is sacrificed to her status as a mother."[33] Zeffirelli and Close attempt to use the fantasies of another screen to shape a modern film version of Gertrude that has remarkable resonance with Adelman's powerful feminist and psychoanalytic reading of the play. For Zeffirelli, Close's Gertrude becomes the tragic diva—the golden girl of the West.

Shakespeare and Hollywood

Branagh's Much Ado About Nothing

F ranco Zeffirelli's *Hamlet* drove deep into Hollywood territory for its
    stars Mel Gibson and Glenn Close. The film, though respectfully
    received, did not generate the commercial buzz that followed the re-
lease of Zeffirelli's *Romeo and Juliet* almost twenty-five years before. The
film that, unexpectedly, did prompt a revival of that box-office excitement
was Kenneth Branagh's *Much Ado About Nothing*, released in May 1993.
Much Ado, raiding Hollywood for several of its stars and its romantic
screwball-comedy form, found the teenage summer-moviegoing audiences it so energetically courted.

Whether by accident or design, Branagh thrives on middle territo-
ries: his greatest achievement as an artist is as a synthesizer, between
Belfast and London in his personal life and between Stratford and Hollywood in his professional career. Such a situation, of course, leaves him
open to attack—from the Shakespearean purists for being a Hollywood
popularizer and from the cultural materialists for being a Thatcherite en-
trepreneur. What neither side seems prepared to admit is that Branagh is
almost single-handedly responsible for the 1990s revival of the seemingly
defunct genre of the Shakespeare film. In revitalizing the Shakespeare
film, largely invented in the post–World War II era by Laurence Olivier
and Orson Welles, Branagh absorbed the lessons of his masters but
reached boldly beyond them by incorporating into his films echoes of
Hollywood ranging from Errol Flynn and Tony Curtis to Wes Craven
and George Lucas.

As Robert Hapgood has pointed out, Branagh's Shakespeare films ultimately owe as much to the work of Zeffirelli, the Anglo-American outsider, as to Olivier and Welles.[1] Branagh works and creates in the postmodern moment, which, as Fredric Jameson and his followers argue, is dominated by a sense of belatedness—a sense that originality is exhausted and that only parody and pastiche and intertextual echo remain.[2] Rather than finding such a condition enervating, Branagh's work seizes on its possibilities. The Shakespeare film that most thoroughly and successfully embraces the postmodern aesthetic, Baz Luhrmann's *William Shakespeare's Romeo + Juliet*, would not have been possible, either conceptually or commercially, without the example of Branagh's *Much Ado*.

Hollywood elements infuse Branagh's Shakespeare films from their initial images to their endings. From his first double entrance as Henry V, inspired by *Star Wars*, to the final moments of *Hamlet* in which his prince performs a bravura Errol Flynn-esque rope swing down from the high balcony to pin Claudius against the throne, we can clearly see that Branagh reaches far beyond Zeffirelli in his willingness to marry Shakespeare and Hollywood. Courtney Lehmann has provided the most thorough and effective analysis of the ways in which Branagh's attempt to mix Shakespeare and film, Stratford and Hollywood, links up with the mingling of high and low culture in the cultural poetics of both the Renaissance and the postmodern eras. While her reading of Branagh's *Much Ado* through the perspective of a Gramscian cultural critique ultimately finds the film failing to deliver on its theoretical potential, her persuasive essay indicates the seriousness with which younger Shakespearean critics are beginning to regard Branagh's films.[3]

I am more concerned (and impressed) with the positive impact that Branagh's *Much Ado* has had on the revival of the genre. This includes its obvious influence on the making of Oliver Parker's *Othello* and Trevor Nunn's *Twelfth Night*. As Nunn argues: "It has become possible for many people to think in terms of filming Shakespeare almost entirely because of the achievement of Kenneth Branagh . . . the breakthrough success of his *Henry V*, followed by the even bigger box-office success of his *Much Ado About Nothing* has made the film world, and Hollywood in particular, become interested again when, for years, everything concerning the Bard was darkness."[4]

Branagh, Nunn, and Parker (like Olivier, Welles, and Zeffirelli before them), came to filmed Shakespeare via the stage. All four of Branagh's Shakespeare films grew from stage productions in which he starred but that he did not direct and from which he gleaned visual ideas that provided keys to the translation of his Shakespearean material into the language of film. From Adrian Noble's production of *Henry V* (Royal Shakespeare Company), we see rain and grit and the garroting of Bardolph; from Judi Dench's *Much Ado About Nothing* (for Branagh's own RTC) come hot Italian sun and festive energy; and from Noble's *Hamlet* (again for RSC), the nineteenth-century setting and use of a full-text collation of Q2 and F1. In each instance, Branagh's synthesizing sensibility reached out to link stage ideas with film images, traditions, and techniques. As Lynda Boose and Richard Burt point out, "even films which adapt the Shakespeare script as faithfully as does Branagh's *Much Ado About Nothing* speak within a metacinematic discourse of self-reference in which, through film quotation, they situate themselves in reference as much to other films as to a Shakespeare tradition."[5] I have already suggested a few examples of this phenomenon in the opening shots of his *Henry V* and the closing ones of his *Hamlet*. His *Much Ado About Nothing* brazenly lifts images and ideas from films as diverse as *The Magnificent Seven*, *Singin' in the Rain*, and *Some Like It Hot*, and Branagh's greatest achievement is to link ideas in Shakespeare's play with the witty Hollywood comedies of the 1930s that have come to be labeled screwball.[6]

As noted above, Branagh's film of *Much Ado* has its source in Dench's stage production. Branagh himself reveals that the specific images of the film's opening sequence—"heat haze and dust, and horseflesh, and a nod to *The Magnificent Seven*"—flashed through his mind one evening as his stage Benedick listened to Balthazar's song "Sigh no more, ladies."[7] Russell Jackson, text consultant for Branagh's Shakespeare films, places the film in the screwball tradition, and it is clear from the film's casting and its production values that Branagh wanted his film to merge Shakespeare and Hollywood.[8]

The most profound treatment of those wonderful films (they include *It Happened One Night*, *The Awful Truth*, *The Lady Eve*, *The Philadelphia Story*, and *Bringing Up Baby*) is by Stanley Cavell in his *Pursuits of Happiness: The Hollywood Comedy of Remarriage*. Cavell traces the structure of the screwball films back to Shakespeare's comic romances and their Old Comedy antecedents. Cavell argues that these depression-era films embraced the "creation of a new woman"—the symbolic daughter of the leaders of the first phase of the U.S. feminist movement that culminated in winning the right to vote in 1920. These Hollywood comedies "may be understood as parables of a phase of the development of consciousness in which the struggle is for the reciprocity or equality of consciousness between a woman and a man," with the recognition that this is "a struggle for mutual freedom, especially of the views each holds of the other."[9] Such films are romances; they "harbor a vision which cannot be fully domesticated, inhabited, in the world we know" for "they express the inner agenda of a nation that conceives Utopian longings and commitments for itself."[10]

Cavell sees that the intelligent play of wit that distinguishes the romantic commerce between the heroes and heroines of these films represents a movement toward a recognition of freedom and equality between the sexes in which each freely rechooses the other after the relationship has been ruptured, strained, or literally—in the case of Tracy Lord and Dexter Haven in *The Philadelphia Story*—divorced. Thus Cavell's decision to classify these films as comedies of remarriage. The witty bickering in these comedies leads "to acknowledgment; to the reconciliation of a genuine forgiveness; a reconciliation so profound as to require the metamorphosis of death and revival; the achievement of a new perspective on existence; a perspective that presents itself as a place, one removed from the city of confusion and divorce."[11] Shakespeareans, of course, can hear echoes of Northrop Frye and C. L. Barber in Cavell's language here as he rediscovers the structure and romantic energy of Shakespearean comedy buried in the heart of these remarkable films.[12]

While Cavell never mentions *Much Ado About Nothing* when he spins out from his close readings of individual films to seek and work a Shakespearean resonance, it strikes me that *Much Ado* is the Shakespearean comedy that most resembles Cavell's remarriage pattern. Though Beatrice and Benedick have not been previously married, the play does suggest a past romantic attachment between them that, as Beatrice reports, Benedick has broken off: "Indeed, my lord, he [Benedick] lent it [his heart] me awhile, and I gave him use for it, a double heart for his single one. Marry once before he won it of me with false dice; therefore your Grace may well say I have lost it" (2.1.275–79.) Beatrice and Benedick are surely the prototypes for the bantering pairs (most commonly played by Katharine Hepburn and Cary Grant) who distinguish the Hollywood comedies that Cavell writes about. The entire movement of the contrasting romantic plots in *Much Ado* is to bring each pair of lovers, in very different fashions, through the metamorphosis of separation and even feigned death into the revival of forgiveness and reconciliation. Beatrice and Benedick's progress through this pattern is self-created and unique, while Hero and Claudio's is socially generated and conventional.

Shakespeare's two plots are intimately linked in Cavellian terms because it takes Claudio's immature and cruel disruption of the socially sanctioned ritual of marriage to spur the creation of Beatrice and Benedick's privately conceived and imagined ceremony of reconciliation and reengagement. Claudio's slander of Hero spurs Benedick to exercise his independent intelligence in moving from the male camp to the female in response to Beatrice's wildly apt but unconventional rejoinder —"Kill Claudio"—to his hyperbolic, male wooing sentiment: "Come, bid me do anything for thee" (4.1.288). These two experienced and wounded lovers then create their own private pact as Benedick promises to enact Beatrice's consciousness of gender inequality (thus acknowledging her equality) when seeking revenge for slander ("Oh God, that I were a man! I would eat his heart in the market place!": 4.1.306–7) by allowing her anger to be expressed through his action: "Enough. I am engaged" (4.1.331).[13] This moment is the triumph of their unconventional courtship and represents their engagement as equals. Claudio and Don Pedro, and the conventional patriarchal social order that they represent and embody, can only be threatened and exposed by the united action of a woman and a man (Beatrice and Benedick) acting as a single consciousness and sensibility. Theirs is a singular social revolution, which is too often, in production and criticism, swallowed by an overemphasis on their "merry war of words."

I evoke Cavell here not because I believe Branagh was directly aware of his work but because I think Branagh had the screen comedies that Cavell champions in mind as one of several Hollywood ingredients he wished to bring to his treatment of Shakespeare's play as film. Rather than seeing his film as solely a vehicle for Beatrice and Benedick (as many stage productions do), Branagh is on record as desiring to give equal visual attention to Claudio and Hero by imagining them as younger versions of the older lovers: "Emma Thompson and I both wanted to suggest former lovers who had been genuinely hurt by their first encounter, which perhaps occurred at the tender age of Hero and Claudio in the play. For our own purposes we deliberately made the younger lovers around twenty . . . and Beatrice and Benedick a significant ten years older or so."[14]

Much Ado occupies a swing position in the development of Shakespeare's comedies. Its emphasis on the confusions of courtship and wooing places it with the earlier festive comedies, but its city setting, its concern with social mores and fashion, and its flirtation with rape and death all echo elements in the problem comedies that follow.[15] Branagh's film clearly seeks to highlight the play's festive elements made most apparent in his transfer of the play's locale from Messina, in Sicily, to the Villa Vignemaggio, in Tuscany—from city street to country estate. Anne Barton remarks that *Much Ado* is one of the most "resolutely urban of Shakespeare's comedies" and that in Branagh's film "Messina has disappeared" to be replaced by the "boldly rural and open air," which entails a "virtual obliteration of Shakespeare's carefully structured social hierarchy."[16] That hierarchy is probably well lost on film as its subtle distinctions are difficult to capture for a contemporary international movie audience, and, as I will argue later, Branagh wants his film to create a utopian green world vision based on the powers of imagination and intelligence rather than on social status.[17] Sarah Hatchuel regards Branagh's Tuscan setting as "an escape from reality . . . into a fairy-tale world,"[18] which, of course, is true of the pattern in the festive comedies, where the lovers are forced to flee the rigid rules of society to find the release of emotion and imagination in the green world.

Shakespeare's comedies have been notoriously difficult to translate successfully into film. Zeffirelli's *The Taming of the Shrew* (1966) is primarily a star vehicle for Richard Burton and Elizabeth Taylor, though the film's gaudy opening sequence, visually celebrating the carnival atmosphere surrounding the beginning of term at the University of Padua, provided a cinematic model for the visual impact of Branagh's lush opening to his *Much Ado*.[19] Peter Hall's *A Midsummer Night's Dream* (1968) certainly is the most textually faithful and probably comes closest of all the filmed comedies to making a synthesis between H. R. Coursen's desire for film productions of Shakespeare that merge "'conservative' criteria like clarity in the speaking of the lines" with a "radical [approach] to freshness and originality."[20] But much of what seemed filmically fresh and original in 1968—from the women's miniskirts to the use of a handheld camera and an editing style distinguished by the jump cut—has come to seem in a mere thirty years seriously dated in its impact. Christine Edzard's *As You Like It* (1992) found its inspiration in a series of parallels between the homeless in Mrs. Thatcher's London and the exiles in Shakespeare's Arden. Edzard's idea is provocative, but her film never fully releases the potential energy of its invention. The film lacks an animating visual energy to transport us willingly into its ideological conceit.

Derek Jarman's *Tempest* (1980) and Peter Greenaway's *Prospero's Books* (1991) are both the work of film auteurs who use Shakespeare, often stunningly, as one element in their own idiosyncratic aesthetic biographies. Jarman's film is, I think, the most interesting low-budget radical appropriation of Shakespeare on film, but it never sought (and certainly did not find) a popular film audience. The commercial success of Branagh's *Much Ado* created a climate that made possible the financing of Nunn's film of *Twelfth Night*, produced by Branagh's Renaissance Films Production Company. Nunn's version of Shakespeare's comedy makes an instructive contrast with Branagh's. If Branagh went for sun and flesh and festive energy, Nunn created a darker, more complex treatment of Shakespeare's farewell to festivity by emphasizing *Twelfth Night*'s affinities with Chekhov and our own culture's fascination with issues relating to gender, cross-dressing, and androgyny.

Hall, Edzard, Jarman, and Greenaway each used their Shakespearean comic material to make personal films intended for a very small slice of the potential international film audience. Branagh's plan for his *Much Ado*, encouraged by the surprising success of his *Henry V,* was more Zeffirelli-esque. Building on the popular approach to Shakespeare established by his RTC stage productions, Branagh wished "to tell the story with the utmost clarity and simplicity" for audiences "relatively unfamiliar with Shakespeare . . . we wanted audiences to react to the story as if it were here and now and important to them. We did not want them to feel they were in some cultural church."[21] Branagh's insistence on a realistic, plain style of performing Shakespeare turned him once again to America and to Hollywood: "The film presented a rare opportunity to utilize the skills of marvelous film actors who would embrace this naturalistic challenge. . . . In crude terms, the challenge was to find experienced Shakespearean actors who were unpracticed on screen and team them with experienced film actors who were much less familiar with Shakespeare. Different accents, different looks . . . [producing] a Shakespeare film which would belong to the world."[22]

There is an echo of Peter Quince (and Andy Hardy) here as Branagh assembles his cast and sets out to compete with Hollywood's one venture into big-budget, big-studio Shakespearean comedy on film: Warner Brothers' 1935 *A Midsummer Night's Dream*. That film, too, featured a wonderful assortment of Hollywood stars, including Branagh's own icon Jimmy Cagney and, of course, Andy Hardy himself—Mickey Rooney.[23] Now, some sixty years later, Branagh surrounds his Benedick and Emma

Thompson's Beatrice with young male Hollywood stars—Denzel Washington (Don Pedro), Keanu Reeves (Don John), and Robert Sean Leonard (Claudio)—which gives his film something of the flavor of Beatrice and the Brat Pack.

Branagh's visually romantic film, buoyed by the sophistication of his maturing cinematic imagination (several sequences, including the final swirling dance, are beautifully effective in their fluid use of a steadicam) and Patrick Doyle's lush score locate this version of *Much Ado* firmly within the festive tradition. Branagh shapes his translation of Shakespeare's text into the visual language of film through four sweeping cinematic moments in which the soundtrack abandons dialogue for swelling score or song. The film's opening sequence captures the men pounding home from war with a comic, fist-pumping brio lifted from *The Magnificent Seven*, while the women make a mad dash to prepare to welcome them. Then Branagh gives us two contrasting, wordless inner sequences in which Benedick and Beatrice celebrate the release of their romantic emotions in fountain and swing and Claudio and Don Pedro lead a winding, torch-lit vigil up to Hero's tomb. The film concludes with an evocation of Benedick's insistence on dancing before the wedding: the cast—intentionally absent Don Pedro—swirl out from the chapel, through the villa's courtyard, and into the garden. "Sigh no more, ladies" swells on the sound track and confetti dances in the air.[24]

Shakespeare is imagined here by Branagh as the first of a long line of English authors who send their characters to Italy to discover the joys of the flesh. Branagh can infuse his film with so much ripe romantic energy without destroying the more subtle and unconventional elements in Shakespeare's tale because of Thompson's remarkable performance as Beatrice. She is the film's radiant, sentient center. Intelligence and wit illuminate every moment of her performance. Thompson's Beatrice can register emotion, underline irony, change mood, raise alarm, deflect attention, suppress sorrow, and enhance wit by a mere tilt of her head, the cocking of an eyebrow, the flick of an eyelid, or a pursing of her lips. She can also capture just the right inflection for Shakespeare's muscular prose and deliver it in a rhythm properly suited to the camera. The economy with which she allows us to understand her previous romantic entanglement with Benedick and her embarrassment at unintentionally encouraging Don Pedro's marriage proposal is film acting worthy of association with Katharine Hepburn, Claudette Colbert, and Irene Dunne, the heroines of the great screwball comedies. Maria DiBattista, in *Fast-Talking*

Dames (her recent book on the heroines of Cavell's film comedies of re-marriage) describes those women in language that also speaks to Thompson's Beatrice:

> These women were sexy, but they were sassy, too. Most of all they were sharp and fast with words. They were quick on the uptake and hardly ever downbeat. . . . They weren't afraid of slang or shy of the truth. They called things as they saw them. . . . In their fast and breezy talk seemed to lie the secret of happiness, but also the key to reality.[25]

Beatrice's straight talk is what leads Benedick to an acknowledgment of the reality of Hero's slander.

The film cleverly leads us into its romantic landscape by allowing word and voice to precede image. The words of the first verse of the text's bittersweet song "Sigh no more, ladies" unfold on a blank screen, half-line by half-line, spoken by Thompson to the accompaniment of a guitar and cello. No bouncing ball appears above the words as in the sing-alongs that through the 1940s preceded films, but Thompson's carefully nuanced reading invites us to murmur the words with her and to register wry amusement at the way in which the song's description of male inconstancy and deception speaks not only to Shakespeare's comic concerns with the worlds of war and wooing but also to Branagh's delicate balancing of one foot on the verbal shore of the play and one in the visual sea of the film.

As we move into the song's second verse, the screen is suddenly filled with a painting (in progress) of a Tuscan landscape. As Doyle's score swells, the camera slides—in a single pan lasting more than a minute—from the canvas to reveal the painter (Leonato) and the landscape itself peopled with lolling picnickers, moving on from their tanned and laughing faces across the splendid vista to discover Beatrice perched in a tree reading Shakespeare's song to her fellow revelers. A bee buzzes about her face and birds chirp on the soundtrack. "A good song," as Don Pedro later observes—and one intelligently used here by Branagh to establish the mood of the women trying to distract themselves while the men are away at war, as well as to prepare us for the fickle behavior of those men once war gives way to wooing. This opening also allows him to move rapidly and cleverly from text to scenic representation (Leonato's painting) as we might find it in a stage production, and thence to his on-location Tuscan film landscape.[26]

In a flash, the messenger arrives. Down in the valley, the men are seen thundering home, and the women make a mad dash down the hill to prepare to greet them. The screen is filled with the rush of flesh and frenzy as men and women strip and plunge into baths and showers, perhaps, as Hatchuel suggests, a symbolic gesture of the film's desire to shake "the dust out of Shakespeare."[27] For an instant, Branagh's camera catches Beatrice and Hero framed in a high window—a shot he will repeat several times in the film—placing them with amused detachment above the splashing and shouting of the boys below and slightly separated from the shrieks and giggles of the girls wriggling out of their clothes and into the confusion of romantic excitement in the next room. Branagh concludes this sequence with an overhead shot of the women emerging from the house to welcome the newly spruced up men marching through the archway into the villa's courtyard. The two groups form a large X, underlining the film's prime interest in the battle of the sexes.

Branagh's visual insistence in these opening moments on landscape and the formation of the distinct groups of men and women serves his understanding of Shakespeare well.[28] *Much Ado*'s Messina setting and its concerns with social fashion has led some critics to place it, among the comedies, somewhere between Falstaff's Windsor and Vincentio's Vienna, where Shakespeare explores and tests comic themes in a recognizable social/urban context, rather than with the green-world, festive comedies where Branagh's setting chooses to align it. The festive comedies explore, like *Much Ado*, the gender confusions of love and loyalty prompted by wooing and tested by wedding. Here it is the men, specifically Claudio and Benedick, who are so prompted and so tested by the tension between male bonding, the confusions of wooing, and the commitments of wedding. By setting his film against the sunburned Tuscan landscape (only Don John, the anticomic villain, is repeatedly shot indoors, usually in the villa's cellarage), Branagh establishes the green world's liberating, socially leveling spirit. This carries over into costume design: all the women wear similar sheer cotton camisoles under mock corsets, and the men are either in identical uniforms or in white, linen vests worn over white shirts with open collars. Andrew Lane's response to these costumes was to remark that "*Much Ado* could become Ralph Lauren's favorite movie."[29] But Lane fails to see that Branagh's approach attempts to stress the democratic tendencies in Shakespeare's comic art, where we see the youthful egalitarian yearnings of emotion and romance. It is part of the stripping away, from fashion to bare flesh, that begins the film, and it provides one explanation for Claudio's eventual confusion of Hero and Margaret: both maiden and maid are dressed in almost identical white cotton dresses.

Branagh's film has its climax and its finest moment where wooing and wedding meet and clash: Claudio's shameful despoiling of his marriage to Hero and the genuine union of Beatrice and Benedick that rises from its ashes. It is also in these two antithetical moments that the film most closely approaches Cavell's comic paradigm. Leonard's Claudio is an insecure boy for whom confusion and embarrassment flush his face as quickly as does the blush of romance. By setting the wedding outside of the villa's small chapel, Branagh's camera gives ample space to Claudio's petulant tantrum. He savagely shoves his bride to the ground and makes a triumphant circuit of the scene, overturning benches and ripping away decorations before nestling in next to Denzel Washington's elegant Don Pedro to reestablish what he smugly believes to be the primacy of the male order. By contrast, Branagh's Benedick, going to his knees to join Beatrice at Hero's side, looks on in amazement as Leonato, with an ugly violence, makes the opposite move to join the male hierarchy by condemning his own child.

Now Beatrice and Benedick move into the chapel. There, first through her tears and anger and then through his commitment to her passion, they create a ceremony and construct a vow that issues not from social practice and tradition but from their own emotional and imaginative response to Hero's crisis. Branagh shoots a kneeling Beatrice in profile over Benedick's left shoulder so that we see and react to her through his perspective. They are not squared to the camera because they aren't yet square with each other. Beatrice's anger, and her frustration with her gender's limitations when it comes to taking appropriate action in the male world of "honor," leads her to kick over, in an exasperated parody of Claudio's earlier behavior, the communion bench she has been kneeling on. She cries out, "O that I were a man for his sake, or that I had any friend would be a man for my sake!" (4.1.317–18).

Branagh's Benedick is transformed by her passion. Earlier we had seen his nervous, cocky jester melt into the explosive comic romantic in the gulling scene. Now both of these excessive portraits are clipped, darkened, and matured as we watch his mind absorb and understand the issue that spurs Beatrice's fury. For the first time in the film, Branagh allows Benedick to look directly into the camera's eye as he determinedly confronts his emotional commitment to Beatrice.[30] Here he steadies and fixes his gaze: to engage the camera is to engage Beatrice. Branagh, as Benedick, plucks out the word *soul* to underscore in his quiet query, "Think you in your soul that Count Claudio hath wronged Hero?" (4.1.328–29): it is a word Claudio himself has flung about recklessly. Thompson, in her reply, chooses to emphasize *thought:* "Yea, as sure as I have a thought or a soul" (4.1.330), completing the marriage of mind and heart, thought and soul, between them. Their pact is then sealed by the vow that the entire scene has moved toward: "Enough. I am engaged; I will challenge him" (4.1.331–32). Benedick's commitment to action completes Beatrice's outrage and creates a surprise: a constant man. The words that lead man to woo and to wed will now be as consequential as those that lead him to war.

This scene is a perfectly realized Shakespearean antecedent to the "equality of consciousness between a man and a woman" that Cavell uncovers at the center of his Hollywood comedies. This intelligent moment, like Thompson's performance throughout, is what allows us to release our critical, skeptical selves freely to enjoy the film's exuberant excesses captured by Branagh's Gene Kelly–like splashing in the fountain, superimposed on Thompson's high-flying in a swing, that crowns the neatly segued scenes of the unmaskings of their true affections. Branagh's foregrounding of the absolutely serious gender issues at work in the play, which come into precise focus in his treatment of the chapel scene, makes possible the film's seemingly paradoxical indulgence of its giddy romanticism. Even as Shakespeare's comedies critique the follies and cruelties of love's social conventions, they provide evidence—however fleeting—for love's powers to cross class and gender divisions, as witness the relationships of Titania and Bottom, Ganymede and Orlando, Cesario and Orsino, Toby and Maria.

Branagh's film makes us laugh (a rarity in even the best films of Shakespeare's comedies)—from Thompson's wry reading of "Sigh no more" to the men pounding home, lifting in and out of their saddles in slow motion, and on from Branagh's struggle to position himself properly at the fountain to receive Beatrice's call to dinner (inspired, his screenplay tells us, by Tony Curtis's imitation of Cary Grant in *Some Like It Hot*), through Thompson's fiercely reluctant march down one of the garden's hedge-lined corridors to deliver that message, to the way each reads, admires, and seeks to improve the sonnets each has written to the other, demonstrating "our hands against our hearts."[31]

The Dogberry comedy is another matter. My first reaction was that it did not fit with the rest of the film's style. I found it cartoonish and fashioned after Michael Keaton's performance in *Beetlejuice* and the villains in the recent *Superman* and *Batman* films. But Dogberry is another reminder of the ways in which Shakespeare uses humor, along with imagination, as a device for crossing class lines in his comedies. Dogberry, working determinedly (and comically wrong-headedly) up from the bottom, does, like Beatrice and Benedick, finally *get it right*. It is another example of Shakespeare's utopian playfulness that, in comedy at least, the comics (high and low) should be the ones to expose and foil the villains.

Keaton and Branagh create a Dogberry who seems equal parts mixture of the Three Stooges, Monty Python, and some of the eccentrics who play off against the lovers in Cavell's comedies of remarriage (I am thinking here primarily of the major, the psychiatrist, and the town cop in Howard Hawks's *Bringing Up Baby*). Keaton, who chews the text into tatters, misses much of the way in which Dogberry creates unintended humor by proudly misappropriating the language of his social superiors. But, in compensation, he creates a similar visual comedy by a malapropism of gesture. Keaton's Dogberry and Ben Elton's Verges, for instance, imitate the thundering riders of the film's opening sequence as they mock gallop in and out of the frame, carried only by their own legs.[32]

The one corner of the play—and an important one—that is not well served by Branagh's lush emphasis on sunburned romance and comic mirth is his visual treatment of Claudio and Hero. His film fails to drive home the ways in which the play repeatedly favors the independent, unruly, intelligent wooing behavior of Beatrice and Benedick with the empty, socially conventional path followed by Claudio in his courtship of Hero. Claudio does not have to be played as a cad, as Barton suggests, but the text is at pains to underline his shallowness.[33] He seeks to confirm his love's beauty by soliciting the opinion of another male; he is quick to ascertain her fortune; and he is even quicker to seize upon the opportunity to allow a more powerful sponsor to conduct his wooing for him. Balthazar's song "Sigh no more, ladies" is also apt for Leonard's Claudio, who is constantly registering love's delight or anguish with an open mouth, a flushed cheek, and a watery eye.

Branagh's camera lingers on Leonard's face and finds no distinction there between the shy smiles he flashes at Hero in the opening sequences and the tormented grief he displays, first when he mistakenly believes Don Pedro has wooed Hero for himself and then later when he sees Borachio supposedly making love to Hero at her bedroom window. Branagh's decision to visualize for us this offstage moment and to make graphic Borachio's lusty coupling (rather than the text's more modest "talking") by capturing its effects on Claudio's face, shot in tight close-up, severely skews the audience's reaction.[34] This moment rarely fails to elicit an audible flow of sympathy—particularly from the teenagers who became the prime market for the film—for Leonard's grief. After all, this was the same actor who, as many in the audience know, had already suffered and died for Shakespeare in his previous film, *Dead Poets Society*.

Branagh and Leonard are, it seems to me, illustrating here a particularly American sentimentality about the precariousness of youthful innocence. American culture champions innocence over irony, and the literature of its high-school curriculum is dominated by the tales of the misunderstood and threatened young—from Romeo and Juliet to Oliver and Pip to Tom and Huck, and on to our century's contributions such as Salinger's Holden and Harper Lee's Jem, Scout, and Dill. Neal Perry (Leonard's role in *Dead Poets Society*) is a film equivalent of these characters, and Leonard's playing of Claudio in a similar manner imposes this American sentimental tradition on Shakespeare's more-tough-minded tale.

As I have already indicated, Branagh and Leonard do make Claudio's wedding tantrum properly ugly and savage, but the power of the moment's impact has been decidedly lessened. Rather than revealing Claudio's insecure and immature male malice (in contrast to Benedick's immediate move to support Hero's innocence), based on his superficial acceptance of the assumptions of the patriarchal order, Branagh's film asks us to understand the wounded lover's anger and to sympathize with Claudio rather than to judge him. This has the effect of making Claudio and Hero's reconciliation as romantically inviting and welcome as that of Beatrice and Benedick, allowing them a less problematical place in the concluding moments of Branagh's film than the one they occupy in Shakespeare's text.

Only in his handling of Claudio does Branagh's desire to be lushly cinematic conflict with his otherwise sure and intelligent translation of Shakespeare's comic energies into film rhythms and images. Branagh is not bashful about wanting his films to entertain; it's all wrapped up with his infatuation with the heyday of Hollywood from the 1930s to the

1950s. His cinematic imagination here incorporates a range of American impulses, from the egalitarian issues Cavell sees at work in *It Happened One Night* and *Adam's Rib* to the sentimentalizing of the young. Branagh's *Much Ado* is a marriage, resembling that of Beatrice and Benedick, between Shakespeare and Hollywood. With an intelligent, if necessarily inconstant, foot in both worlds, Branagh provides us with the most successful version we have of a Shakespearean comedy on film.

CHAPTER 5

Song, Sea, and Sexual Mystery

Nunn's Twelfth Night

Trevor Nunn's *Twelfth Night* (1996), clearly made possible by the commercial success of Branagh's *Much Ado About Nothing* (1993), takes a different approach to capturing Shakespeare's comic energies on film. Branagh's *Much Ado* translated the play into a bright, Tuscan romp darkened only by Claudio's immature tantrum. As I have argued, Branagh's model was the Hollywood screwball comedy of the 1930s. Although Nunn acknowledges his admiration for Billy Wilder's *Some Like It Hot*, his *Twelfth Night* finds its inspiration more in Chekhov and Mozart than in the world of film. His use of the play's songs to structure his bittersweet, autumnal approach to Shakespeare's farewell to the world of the festive comedies is subtle and exquisite. Music in Nunn's film of *Twelfth Night* fools with and feeds on love's tensions and excesses, fueling a melancholy, rather than midsummer, madness. Nunn conceives of Feste as the film's voice—its narrator, its troubadour. Before our eyes are engaged by images, our ears hear Ben Kingsley's voice lightly singing

> I'll tell thee a tale, now list to me,
> With heigh ho, the wind and the rain.
> But merry or sad, which shall it be,
> For the rain it raineth every day.

The words are a mixture of Nunn's and Shakespeare's, much in the manner of Nunn's fashioning the lyrics of "Memory" from bits and shards of

T. S. Eliot. That Nunn should find his way back to Shakespeare through song is appropriate since his film of *Twelfth Night* is the space through which he migrates from the world of contemporary musical comedy (*Cats, Les Misérables, Starlight Express,* and *Sunset Boulevard*) back to his roots in the classical repertory theater.[1]

Feste's soft voice at the film's opening, coupled with his omniscient, knowing perspective as the narrative unfolds, provides not only the frame but the filter through which Nunn chooses to explore his Shakespearean material. As Nunn admits, "I thought it was a good idea to provide an extra sense that Feste is an observer and to some extent a teller of tales, especially because of the content of his final song, so I liked the idea of Feste having some introductory material that gave us a context."[2] Kingsley is not a natural clown, but his Feste joins Imogen Stubbs's Viola at the film's center, and repeatedly he is associated not only with song but also with the sea. He is an ironic version of Viola's sensibility. As Ann Jennalie Cook remarks, Nunn presents "him as the quintessential outsider, welcomed and moving freely from one group to another but belonging to none."[3] We first glimpse him on a high bluff, watching Viola and her fellow shipwrecks wash ashore in Illyria, and he closes the film by emphasizing (through repetition) the "every day" in "And I'll strive to please you every day," as we catch him moving away from Olivia's estate, bag slung over his back, toward the now tranquil bay, off on another journey.

Nunn uses "The Wind and the Rain" in a manner somewhat similar to Branagh's use of "Sigh no more" to open his *Much Ado About Nothing.* There, the song's knowing acknowledgment of male inconstancy was associated with Beatrice's intelligent perspective on wooing and wedding, and its festive reprise at the film's end mirrored her move from the skeptical margins to the festive center of the world of romance. Nunn's film repeatedly insists on the everyday, which festive holiday both sweetens and threatens. As C. L. Barber has most prominently and perceptively revealed, Shakespeare's *Twelfth Night* tests the limits of holiday release: it both inscribes and incriminates festive abuse.[4] Nunn's film wants to find the right balance, the proper harmony in the play between everyday and holiday. The echoes of Chekhov in the film's period setting and autumnal landscape help to foreground the melancholy rather than the mad, both in the upstairs romance plot and its downstairs counterpoint in the conflict between Toby and Malvolio. The poles of holiday and everyday are captured in Feste's songs "O Mistress Mine" and "The Wind and the

Rain," and Nunn uses both songs in an imaginative fashion to frame the film's depiction of everyday travail and holiday romance.[5]

Nunn seizes upon song as the vehicle to open the film and explain action that, in the film, precedes Shakespeare's narrative. We find ourselves aboard a steamship, rolling on high seas, with passengers who are enjoying a Twelfth Night entertainment provided by twins wearing identical oriental costumes. One is playing the piano, the other a concertina, and both are singing "O Mistress Mine." Their mirth elicits laughter from their audience as they sing "your true love's coming / That can sing both high and low," with one voice clearly a soprano, the other a baritone. But which is which? The performers, disguised in identical yashmaks, then begin a comic process of self-exposure. As their veils are pulled down, we see that each sports a mustache. One twin reaches out and peels the mustache off the other; as the other makes a similar move, the storm intensifies, the tables and the piano begin to wander, and the entertainment comes to a crashing end as the passengers try to scurry to safety.[6] During all this, the camera has lingered on a solitary male figure in the audience who appears transfixed by the performance and whose eyes track the concertina player. As the storm batters the tiny ship, the twins are swept overboard into the sea, each reaching out, in the primal fluid, to try to save the other. The lonely observer from the audience clings to the ship as his eyes try to seek out the twins in the waves.

In a quick series of images, Nunn not only establishes a narrative line but folds in the play's lyrical nature, its gender confusions, its latent homoeroticism (the solitary onlooker is, of course, Antonio), its literal and metaphorical pattern of a rescue from drowning, and its association of the sea with various ideas expressed in the text about longing and appetite and the male ego. Nunn's opening fully creates that enigmatic figure, come from the sea, who can "sing both high and low" and who, in the disguised figure of Viola/Cesario, miraculously both destabilizes and harmonizes the Illyrian world into which she/he is reborn. As Eric C. Brown understands, Nunn's film skillfully plays with sexual identity so that "gender lines are hardly ever 'straight' but asymptotic, always nearing and becoming but never reaching or being."[7]

Such an understanding is reinforced by Nunn's wonderful treatment of "O Mistress Mine" when it reoccurs, in context, in the film's narrative. Here, through a brilliant series of cross-cuts, Nunn expands the song's audience from the text's revelers to include also Orsino and Cesario and

Malvolio and Olivia.[8] Nunn's film subtly interweaves elements of the text's act 2, scene 3 and act 2, scene 4 to create a wonderful composite portrait of the film's romantic yearners and holiday revelers all united by their varying responses to the song's lyric strain. The song begins with Feste sitting cross-legged on the kitchen table and accompanying himself on the concertina (an echo of the song's first appearance in the film). As he quietly begins to sing, the film cuts to Malvolio, dressed in a handsome dressing gown, sitting in his room with a glass of brandy, reading the naughty French magazine *L'Amour*, establishing his own bourgeois tastes and fantasies in a flash. As Feste reaches "That can sing both high and low," the film cuts to Olivia gently tossing in her sleep with a slight smile suggesting her own romantic dreams.

Then Nunn quickly cuts to Orsino's court and 2.4, where Orsino asks Cesario about "that old antique song we did hear last night" as we hear the tune of "O Mistress Mine" on the piano. The scene continues in this wistful atmosphere for several beats as the film interlaces the song's lyrics with the exchange between the card-playing Orsino and Cesario about the transitory nature of youth, beauty, and love. As Kenneth Rothwell perceptively notes, "Nunn's cross-cutting supports the cross-dressing that is so much a part of the play."[9] This melancholy strain deepens as Nunn cuts back to the kitchen crowd, where Maria has now joined Feste on "In delay there lies no plenty / Then come kiss me, sweet and twenty, / Youth's a stuff will not endure" (2.3.51–52). Imelda Staunton's haunting voice (she has begun a second career as a cabaret singer) captures the song's subtext of lost love and lost opportunity. This quartet (Feste, Toby, Sir Andrew, and Maria) are clearly no longer sweet and twenty but heading beyond sad and thirty-something. The wild outburst of loud singing and dancing that follows, as the rowdy crew bursts out of the kitchen and into Olivia's music room to bang away on the piano and kick up their heels, acknowledges their understanding that, Malvolio or not, their revels now are ending. His appearance, to silence their antics, is less a function of his puritanism than a temporal inevitability. Their desire to lash back at him and seek revenge is directed less, in Nunn's handling, at Nigel Hawthorne's Malvolio than at their own subliminal understanding that their best days are past: youth's a stuff will not endure.

Even H. R. Coursen, the film's most comprehensive critic, does not note how radically Nunn's screenplay revises Shakespeare's text as it repositions, and highlights, Feste's songs.[10] In the text, Feste's second song, "Come Away, Death," follows "O Mistress Mine" in the next scene, but Nunn divides 2.4 so that we get its opening exchange between Orsino and Cesario as part of the night revels I have just described, but then he delays the second half of the scene so that it follows the gulling of Malvolio (2.5), Cesario's second encounter with Olivia (3.1), and Sebastian's reunion with Antonio (3.3).

"Come Away, Death" is the radical, romantic extension of "O Mistress Mine." The latter urges the lovers to seize the day, while the former mourns the day that has been lost and romantically insists that the loss of love is also fatal. As a parallel with "O Mistress Mine," Nunn creates a nocturnal landscape for "Come Away, Death." Orsino and Cesario seek Feste out in the outbuilding that appears to be his quarters. Orsino wants "the song we had last night" because he wants to indulge his Frank Sinatra "in the wee small hours of the morning" mood as the rejected lover. Nunn uses the song to bring Orsino and Cesario into an awkward romantic encounter. Orsino's exaggerated melancholy causes him to move closer to Cesario to seek solace in another forlorn lover ("thine eye / Hath stayed upon some favor that it loves"), and in the process their eyes entangle and their faces move closer toward a kiss before they freeze, realizing that Feste has stopped singing. The spell has been momentarily broken, but Kingsley's face registers Feste's wry understanding of the emotions (and the physical realities beneath them) at work here. Nunn allows Toby Stephens's Orsino to experience some of the homoerotic desire expressed by the speaker of the sonnets, and here Cesario becomes the youth who is the master-mistress of his passions. This beautifully precarious moment also prepares for the crucial exchange that follows. Orsino, pursued by Cesario, bolts from the shed and heads for a bluff overlooking an angry sea; in the distance, the sky rumbles.

Nunn, appropriately, sets the crucial exchange of their relationship against the sea: Orsino repeatedly invokes the sea as a metaphor for his passion. Orsino indulges in his hyperbolic male-as-rejected-lover mode here, egotistically insisting on the primacy of his own superficial desires for Olivia, fueled by her rejection of his advances. Against his unattractive hyperbole and the melancholy fatalism of Feste's song, Shakespeare and Nunn set the example of Viola/Cesario. Denied, by disguise and circumstance, from speaking directly from her own voice, Cesario is forced to rely upon her imagination rather than her will to express her own quite genuine emotions. Her method is to fabulize: "My father had a daughter loved a man / As it might be perhaps, were I a woman, / I should your lordship" (2.4.107–9).

Nunn understands this moment well: he has Cesario challenge Orsino's outburst about his sea-hungry love—a challenge that has to be delivered over the roaring of the sea—with her hidden understanding of "the love women to men may owe." Orsino, suddenly intrigued, follows Cesario as she moves away from his roaring to find a quieter spot to respond to his query, "But what's her history?" Here Shakespeare provides, in Cesario's lyric expression of Viola's brave and generous melancholy, the response and the alternative to Orsino's egoism and the song's ("Come Away, Death") finality: "She pined in thought, / And with a green and yellow melancholy, / She sat like Patience on a monument, / Smiling at grief. Was not this love indeed?" (2.4.112–15). Stubbs's wistful delivery of these lines manages to quiet both Orsino and the sea.

Nunn's repositioning of "Come Away, Death" and the second portion of 2.4 allows his film to open and close with song and to use Feste's two internal songs to mark the two major turns in the narrative: the abuse of Malvolio and the education of Orsino. Nunn uses Feste's final song as an everyday counterpoint to the festive aristocratic weddings being celebrated (by a dance) within Olivia's great house. Again, Nunn uses the cross-cut between events within and without Olivia's house to establish the counterpoint between holiday and everyday that is at the heart of Feste's farewell song. Here the song's lyrics are specifically related to those members of the narrative who are excluded from the final celebration. While Shakespeare pointedly ends his festive comedies with a reminder that not all participants have been happily paired off or included in the festive conclusion, Nunn's film is at pains to detail the parade of characters exiled from this Illyria.

As Feste begins to sing his melancholy account of another possible (and more probable) version of life than the melancholy madness we have been watching—"When that I was and a little tiny boy"—we watch Richard E. Grant's Sir Andrew drive away in a trap piled with his luggage, shorn of the false expectations of the childish fantasy he had shared with Sir Toby. When Feste hits the next verse, "But when I came to man's estate," Nicholas Farrell's Antonio emerges and trudges off alone with his coat pulled up against the rough weather. The film cuts back to the lovers within embracing, and then as Feste moves to the next verse—"But when I came, alas, to wive"—the film returns to the exterior world as we watch Toby and Maria boarding a coach to carry them off to a less-than-festive honeymoon. Finally—on "with tosspots still had drunken heads"—Malvolio appears at the gatehouse and begins his own somber journey to revenge by the eventual triumph of everyday over holiday. The film cuts back to Olivia's crowded music room, where the wedding dance is in full swing. Against the lively tempo of that music, Nunn counterposes Feste's insistence on the "every day" in the song's final line: "And I'll strive to please you every day."[11]

Nunn's decision to focus on the excluded and the leave-takers at the film's end is in keeping with the autumnal atmosphere he has sought to capture throughout. Feste's sad final song casts a melancholy shadow back over the entire film. Nunn's house of love, which has been built on gender inclusiveness, seems oddly barren when it comes to imagining a similar generosity about class: fools, friends, uncles, maids—as well as stewards—are not entreated to a peace in a world where, evidently for most, the rain does rain every day.[12]

In his handling of Feste's songs and the play's lyric strain, Nunn reveals the formalist elements in his Cambridge education. When he dramatizes the gender issues at play in *Twelfth Night*, he marks his affinity with such postmodern approaches to the gender complications raised by the text associated with the work of Valerie Traub and Stephen Orgel or with such contemporary films as *The Birdcage*; *The Adventures of Priscilla, Queen of the Desert*; and *To Wong Foo, Thanks for Everything! Julie Newmar*.[13] Nunn, like Shakespeare, is creating for a mainstream audience, but he is interested in keeping touch with his cultural moment, in exploring more explicitly those corners of the text that enjoy the destabilizing of normative sexual and gender assumptions. Thus, as mentioned earlier, he foregrounds Antonio's unrequited longing (and the civil dangers his affections lead him into) by including him in the opening and closing sequences of the film and involving him—costumed as a priest—in an elaborate chase sequence to avoid apprehension by Orsino's officers.[14]

Coursen rightly sees that "Nunn makes the issue of depicting Viola/Cesario the major thrust of his film. The archetype to be developed is that of gender, its fusion and its confusion."[15] Nunn's film lingers on Viola's transformation from lass to lad (no eunuch, here)—her model being a picture of her brother in his military uniform. We watch her trim her hair, wrap a tight sash about her bodice to flatten her breasts against her body, stuff her crotch with a handkerchief, and finally refix the false mustache she wore in the film's opening sequence. This process is accompanied by tiny grunts and squeals indicating her struggle to be reborn in the image of her lost brother. This transformation continues as she shouts out above the sound of the sea in an effort to deepen her voice.

Stubbs has just the right attractive pluck to convince us of the desperate-ness of her undertaking, as well as its humor.

By transposing the text's first two scenes, Nunn is able to have Cesario already present in Orsino's world when we first meet him.[16] He is listening intently to a melody being played on a piano, and when Orsino signals for the melody to be repeated, the camera pans to reveal Cesario as the pianist. Here indeed is a curious creature come from the sea who can sing and speak "in many sorts of music" (1.2.58).

The film enjoys Cesario's initiation into Orsino's world—her trials with fencing, vigorous horseback riding, smoking cigars, and playing cards and billiards. These activities are culturally gendered as masculine, but Cesario demonstrates that they are open to mastering by anyone with will and imagination. Her comradeship is Orsino's rescue from self-indulgence. As is revealed in the "Come Away, Death" scene with Feste, the film suggests that Orsino's route to Viola and genuine romantic emotion must involve a swerving toward the homoerotic.[17] Nunn's film is here responding to latent energies in the text that have been the subject of intense interest by postmodern critics of Shakespeare. But what Traub ultimately concludes about the play ("Despite the attractions of homo-eroticism, the pleasure *Twelfth Night* takes in it is not sustained") is true of Nunn's film as well.[18]

Cesario is in a precarious romantic circumstance: she is simultane-ously, in her interactions with Orsino and Olivia, caught in both homo-erotic and heterosexual relationships. Nunn visually underlines her emotional depth and pain in a manner similar to his splitting of 2.4 to provide something of a before-and-after frame to the text's major roman-tic confusions involving Olivia, Malvolio, and Orsino. In this instance, he cuts Viola's soliloquy at the end of 2.2 into two segments, giving us the first nine lines (down to "I am the man") in context, and then returns to the rest of the soliloquy only after the screenplay's mingling of the ex-changes in 2.3 and 2.4. Here the film finds Viola alone in her attic room, staring at herself in a small table mirror as she takes off her uniform, un-binds her breasts, and removes her mustache. As she explores the confu-sions and complications caused by her masculine attire ("Disguise, I see thou art a wickedness"), she picks up the photograph of Sebastian. Her memory of him has been kept fresh, as though by the salt waves of the sea, and she shares her predicament with him: as a man she has sparked Olivia's passion and Orsino's interest; as a woman she has fallen in love with Orsino—a double bind. The film, by visually reuniting sister and brother, female and male, at this moment reminds us of the separation that is at the core of the narrative, a separation saturated with as much tragic potential as comic possibility.

Stubbs's wistful delivery of the soliloquy's concluding lines deepens our response to the remarkable gender complications of Viola's circumstances. Because she now entwines all of nature, she realizes that only nature's agent, time, can untie her entangled romantic situation. Brown, suggesting that the film recalls the past even as it projects the future, sees that Nunn employs a variety of cinematic techniques to create "a temporal description in the text that mirrors the temporal divisions unfolding in the film's thematics: that tension between an inward, stabilizing and seemingly constant present, and the outward, destabilizing, apparently mutable future. . . . The future of love, of mirth, is always in deferral, never now but passing away even as it matures to 'perfection.'"[19]

I have concentrated on the film's depiction of Viola/Cesario's relationship with Orsino, but Nunn is equally strong in his handling of her encounters with Olivia. Helena Bonham Carter's Olivia is a pre-Raphaelite beauty, with deep-set smoldering eyes, heaps of brown curls, and pouting ruby lips.[20] Stubbs's Cesario draws Olivia, much as she does Orsino, out of the shadows and into the light. Olivia's drawing room resembles its mourning mistress by being shrouded with dense, heavy drapes. The film presents Cesario as the bringer of life and light to a musty room and a misty recluse. She parts the drapes with her presence as she parts Olivia's veil with her impudence.

As Olivia becomes taken with this saucy ambassador, the film finds her pursuing Cesario out of the dark house into the sunlit garden. Her engagement with Cesario provokes Viola's fabulist imagination as she moves from reciting Orsino's limp text to responding in her own unique voice: "If I did love you in my master's flame." Here, as with Orsino, Viola can speak only as a hypothetical "other" rather than as a certain self. She is caught between two needy, powerful egotists and she must show them, and us, another way.

Play and film have flirted with gender transgression, but in the end, as Traub rightly notes, both return to normative assumptions about society's, if not nature's, heterosexual bias.[21] Nunn made two decisions that underline this. The first is to have Feste drop Viola's necklace, abandoned on the beach at the moment of her transformation from Viola to Cesario, over her head in the recognition scene—one step in her restoration to the feminine. The second is Nunn's decision, reaching beyond the text at the end as he does at the beginning, to show Viola in her "woman's weeds" dancing with Orsino in a foursome with Olivia and Sebastian that celebrates their joint weddings. The film's penultimate shot is of the four lovers enjoying a mutual embrace, with Viola and Sebastian clasping hands behind the backs of their lovers. When I first saw the film, I thought the clasped hands belonged to Viola and Olivia, and I smiled at what I thought was Nunn providing us with one last witty transgressive gesture, in gentle subversion of comic convention's triumph. But I was mistaken. The only challenge to this holiday remains Feste's song and its repeated echo of "every day . . . every day . . . every day."

Nunn gets so much of the upstairs romance so right that I was disappointed that the downstairs humor did not spark his filmic imagination in a similar fashion. Despite heroic efforts by Hawthorne, the Malvolio comedy fails to cohere. Hawthorne's Malvolio is too nice, and Mel Smith's Sir Toby too boorish and banal, to give the proper tension to their clash.

Nunn's film makes us care too much about Malvolio and not enough about his philosophical and cultural opposites Toby and Maria. Certainly Sir Toby can be conceived as a drunken sot, but that's the only aspect of his character Smith's performance projects. He does not provide a counterbalancing twinkle or spark to lend credence to his clearly apt charge about Malvolio's prim joylessness: "Dost thou think because thou art virtuous, there shall be no more cakes and ale?" (2.3.114–16). Maria can be played as an over-the-hill spinster grasping at her one last chance for marriage, but her desperate melancholy is all that Staunton, an admirable actress, finds worth exploring in her character. The clever, racy, witty woman who concocts the scheme to gull Malvolio and writes that brilliant letter of entrapment is nowhere to be found in Staunton's creation. The saddest and ugliest moment in the film is the drunken, sloppy kiss Sir Toby gives Maria before commanding her to "come by and by to my chamber." The helpless, empty expression on Staunton's face as Toby slouches off abandons the Chekhovian territory Nunn has been evoking and moves toward the darker marital intimacies we associate with Strindberg.[22]

Hawthorne's Malvolio is the most finely nuanced of the downstairs portraits, but the details of his performance all seek to create a "kinder, gentler" Malvolio. He reads naughty French romances before bed, wobbles after Cesario on a rickety bicycle, repositions a sundial (a bit of business lifted from Donald Sinden's great stage Malvolio for John Barton at the Royal Shakespeare Company) to conform with the time on *his* watch, clutches the cold torso of a garden statue as he imagines Olivia as his wife, and pathetically readjusts his toupee, dumped on his head by Feste, in front of the household staff as they listen to the story of his humiliation. There is never any sense that this Malvolio deserves at least some of what he gets. And some of the details cut against the grain of the character. *L'Amour* is the last thing Shakespeare's Malvolio would be reading; Machiavelli or Cotton Mather would be more likely.[23] Malvolio's fantasies are not about romance and sex; they're about class and power. He dreams of being "*Count* Malvolio," not Olivia's lover, which is why he can't unpack Maria's obscene anatomical anagram about "her very C's, her U's, and her T's." The toupee is another brilliant detail (which Coursen imaginatively links with Cesario's mustache) that does not quite fit.[24] Malvolio's vanity is in his self-estimation, not in his looks. He *is* a hypocrite, but not about fashion or style—they are foreign to his very being until Maria's letter provokes Olivia's supposed interest in his yellow stockings. The humor emerges from the outrageous contrast between Malvolio's customary black-suited sobriety and his cross-gartered giddiness. Hawthorne cannot paint that contrast because his Malvolio has never been severe—neither in manner nor fashion. The toupee is like *L'Amour* a glimpse into his human frailty long before we have any reason to suspect his vulnerability.

Nunn, Stubbs, Carter, Stephens, and Kingsley make the gender confusions of the romance plot crackle with suspense and humor, but the more obvious comic tension the play creates between Sir Toby and Malvolio fizzles.[25] In Nunn's reading, not just Antonio and Malvolio but all of the play's comic characters are excluded from the final harmony. The class battle between the soggy aristocrat and the crisp puritan is a take-no-prisoners affair: both end up as exiles from Illyria. Toby, in Nunn's interpretation, becomes the first of Shakespeare's many characters in the late comedies (Angelo, Lucio, and Bertram spring immediately to mind) to be sentenced to marriage, and Malvolio, dressed in a business suit and minus his toupee, is sent off to seek his revenge in trade.

As I mentioned earlier, Nunn generously credits Branagh and the success of his *Much Ado About Nothing* for creating the cultural and commercial climate that allowed him to raise the financing for his *Twelfth Night*.[26] As we have seen, Branagh's *Much Ado* owes much of its spirit to the great Hollywood comedies of the 1930s. The film can be seen as his effort to make a Shakespearean screwball comedy for teenagers—a bright, sun-drenched Tuscan romp interrupted by Claudio's caddish male immaturity and deepened by Beatrice's determined female outrage at the patriarchy's brutal treatment of Hero. Nunn's *Twelfth Night* is cast in more subtle hues, and its virtues are less obvious to the popular film audience. He seeks to underline the text's melancholy, its autumnal spirit, as opposed to its "midsummer madness."

In a revealing remark, Nunn allows that for him *Twelfth Night* "is one of those rare phenomenon, a perfect work of art, like Mozart's *Figaro* or Billy Wilder's *Some Like It Hot*."[27] Wilder's great film comedy about music and the mob, about sex and gender, about an escape to an Illyria called West Palm, was shot in black-and-white, and the high comedy was made more delicious by the peril of the film's cross-dressed heroes and the comic antagonism that sprang from their mutual attraction to Marilyn Monroe's Sugar Kane. One can see the influence of Mozart in Nunn's film, but little of Wilder, which may explain why it did not find the mass audience it sought. But it is one of the films in the Branagh era that most rewards repeated viewings. Nunn's use of song and sea to create a landscape for Shakespeare's tale of gender mystery, romantic longing, and holiday excess demonstrates the range of film's surprising ability to capture and transform Shakespeare's comic powers.

CHAPTER 6

Checkmate

Parker's Othello

Many elements of the Branagh style and aesthetic can be seen at
work in Oliver Parker's film of *Othello* (1995). Parker takes a bold,
romantic approach to his Shakespearean material, shoots on location in a ravishing Technicolor, employs a multinational cast headed by
an American (Laurence Fishburne), a Britisher (Kenneth Branagh), and a
French-speaking Swiss (Irène Jacob), and washes his film in a lush score
by Charlie Mole. Only Zeffirelli, in *Romeo and Juliet*, had employed, before Parker's film, such a ripe approach to a Shakespearean tragedy.

The great films of Shakespeare's tragedies in the international phase
of the genre were all—with the exception of Welles's *Othello* (1952)—
culturally specific in their casting, and much more influenced by the
European avant-garde than by the mass-audience commercial films produced by the Hollywood studios. Although there have been exceptions—
Kurosawa's *Throne of Blood* (1957) shows its debt to the Hollywood
western, and Olivier's deep-focus photography in *Hamlet* (1948) has its
source in Orson Welles's pioneering use of that technique in *Citizen Kane*
(1941)—the Shakespeare films of the 1940s and 1950s look to the Conti-
nent, not California, for their visual inspiration. Even Polanski's Technicolor *Macbeth* in 1971 derived its animating energy and style from an
Eastern European sense of history captured in Jan Kott's *Shakespeare Our
Contemporary*, rather than from Polanski's Hollywood experience in making *Rosemary's Baby*.

Parker's *Othello* wants to extend the Zeffirelli-Branagh aesthetic into the core of Shakespeare's most domestic tragedy, but the play's bitter intimacy keeps rubbing up against the film's romantic yearnings, and it never finds an effective visual language to resolve those ingrained tensions. The film also had the unhappy fate of being released in the United States during the media frenzy surrounding the O. J. Simpson murder trial,[1] which led many critics to read the film through an American, rather than British, cultural lens and to find the film culturally flawed in its representation of the relationship between society, race, and domestic violence.[2] This reading was further complicated by the casting of Laurence Fishburne as *Othello*. Fishburne's fame and reputation as a serious and powerful film actor had been expanded by his recent performance as Ike Turner (for which he was nominated for an Academy Award) in the film of Tina Turner's autobiography *What's Love Got to Do with It?* Ike Turner was notorious for his physical abuse of Tina Turner during their marriage, and Fishburne's performance of Turner did not blink when depicting his domestic viciousness. For American critics, the quartet of Turner, Simpson, Othello, and Fishburne made for an irresistible combination, even though the film was imagined and shot by a British director whose experience was not shaped by the American racial context.

The film foregrounds the Othello-Desdemona romance by opening not with Iago's racist invective but on the Grand Canal as two gondolas glide past each other in the night.[3] The camera closes in on one of the gondolas, and we spy two lovers huddled together, one black, the other white. The black male places a white carnival mask over his face as his gondola disappears in the night. The other gondola, we soon discover, is carrying Desdemona, and once across the canal she alights and scurries down a garbage-strewn, cat-infested lane to her rendezvous with Othello and their secret marriage. Parker's images here provoke our curiosity even as they irritate in their fuzzy ambiguity. Our initial surmise—that the passengers in the first gondola are Othello and Desdemona—proves to be mistaken. Is that interracial couple simply symbolic? or does Parker mean to suggest that the Othello-Desdemona relationship is not a unique one in Venice, the great mercantile city-state? Does the mask suggest it is, in fact, carnival in Venice, when holiday turns the world on its head, subverting the everyday social norms? Does the murky, shadowy opening, with Desdemona hurrying down that filthy calle, indicate that Parker wants to give us Iago's Venice: a nasty world filled with white trash and racist hypocrites, where the word *senator* is a pejorative and women "do let [God] see the pranks / They dare not show their husbands" (3.3.202–3)?

Parker's opening images provoke such provocative questions, but his film does little to extend or answer them. Like many other elements in his efforts to find ways of translating Shakespeare's images into those that will work in the language of film, Parker fails to find a coherent pattern for his bright visual ideas. After that initial image of the white mask covering the black face, Parker never returns to the idea of carnival as an appropriate landscape against which to shoot his Venetian scenes; nor does he return to the image symbolically in his treatment of Fishburne's Othello, where the Fanonesque idea (black skin, white mask) of colonial and cultural exploitation and appropriation provides a possible contemporary approach to the representation of Othello in image and performance. But nothing in Fishburne's proud, powerful Othello ever suggests that he has assumed the white mask, that he has deluded himself into thinking that he has become a Venetian insider. As Judith Buchanan notes, in a rich and suggestive essay on the film, Fishburne's "unapologetic otherness is undeniably part of his attraction. His Venetian garb does little to moderate the effect: his color, stature, bearing, earrings, unfamiliar gestures and half-mocking atmosphere make him less the supreme exemplum of Venice than an exotic misfit within it."[4]

Parker also never follows up on that fleeting opening image of a seedy Venice. In fact the film follows the text in making it clear that Iago's cynical attempt to dislocate Othello and his idealistic assumptions about the world cannot work in Venice. Iago's attempts to stir up trouble in Venice are blocked, first by Othello's supreme self-confidence and then by the senate itself in rejecting Brabantio's racially motivated paternal plea for authority over his daughter. As numerous critics have pointed out, the play's first act ends as a comedy, with the lovers triumphant over paternal and legal objections. Iago's poison can begin to work only when the action moves to the wilder outpost of Cyprus on the edge of the Venetian empire.

I realize that in insisting that Parker's images ultimately satisfy as well as provoke, I am holding him to high standards. *Othello* was his first film, and it reveals the work of an ambitious novice whose reach keeps exceeding his grasp. Those opening images promise more than they deliver, setting a pattern and tone for the entire film. I will cite another example. At the conclusion of the senate scene (act 1, scene 3), Parker's camera closes in on Branagh's Iago to capture his first soliloquy in intimate close-up. The crop-haired actor looks us right in the eye as he delivers, in a chilling, pathological whisper, "I hate the Moor," giving equal emphasis to each word in the phrase. In a master stroke, actor and director have taken us inside Iago's rancid imagination, but Parker is unwilling to stay in tight close-up as Iago begins his mental machinations. He pulls his camera back to reveal Iago toying with black and white figures on a chessboard (king, queen, knight) as he murmurs, "How? How? Let's see." Parker is not able to resist shooting the last lines of Iago's soliloquy with Branagh's face peering out at us through the pieces on the chessboard. Like the opening black and white figures in the gondola, this visual metaphor jumps out at us (my students never fail to cite the chess images in their papers on the film) and seems at first glance an effective device for capturing the busy plottings of Iago's mind: he is, after all, out to check a mate by turning him into his pawn. But this idea, too, is fatally flawed. Iago is not a chess player; he's a freelancer who picks up on what the immediate situation provides him and never thinks more than one move in advance. Chess is too rational and pure (a game more suited, perhaps, for that "great arithmetician," Cassio) for the nature of Iago's mind, which is motivated (particularly in Branagh's performance) by a welter of repressed emotions that the character never fully comprehends.

Parker returns to the chess image, with a flash cut, at the end of act 5, scene 1, on Iago's line "This is the night / That either makes me or fordoes me quite," as the tragedy hurtles toward its denouement. Here the chess pieces are swept off their board and down into a well, where the camera follows them to their watery grave. The image is meant to anticipate Othello's and Desdemona's shrouded bodies being given a burial at sea in the film's final frames. Here the chessboard is completely gratuitous, for as Iago's own lines indicate, he has lost control of the game. Iago is right when he says he is a creature of the night who works best in the murky world of doubt and suspicion. Branagh's Iago is a brilliant con man cozying up to camera and audience, never in jest but with the utter seriousness of one assured of and pleased with his superior intelligence. Branagh never makes Iago a joker as a means of winning our indulgence and approval. He wants us to admire him because he's so clever, which turns out to be the greatest con of all. Branagh repeatedly makes it clear that his Iago is a creature of twisted and tangled emotions—emotions he thinks he controls by the cool veneer of his rationality.[5] But by the time those chess pieces are swept down into that well, Iago has become the victim, not the master, of the events he has set in motion. His biggest con is to convince us—and not just us, himself, too—that he knows what he's doing.

Parker might have been wiser to pick up images from Shakespeare's text, most obviously those of nets and snares and musical discord, which Iago himself uses when plotting his fantasies. Undoubtedly, the strategies of Parker's predecessors—Welles's brilliant use of cage and prison imagery in his *Othello;* Sergei Yutkevich's use of fishing nets for similar purposes in his 1955 Russian film—closed off those possibilities for Parker. But chess, however initially inviting, proves to be a metaphor that works against not only the grain of the text but Branagh's canny performance as well.

The best thing about the film is the way Branagh's gritty, nasty Iago rubs up against, and complicates, the film's desire to be lushly romantic and erotic—much in the way Iago's cynicism in the text is always at work to sully Othello's idealism, about himself, his occupation, and his wife. Parker's film privileges Iago. Perhaps it is inevitable on film that Iago's cunning demeanor will work better than Othello's explosive passion. Olivier's Othello overwhelmed Frank Finlay's Iago on the stage, but in the film version of that production, Finlay restores the balance. Willard White's Othello, in Trevor Nunn's 1989 production for the Royal Shakespeare Company at The Other Place, was a huge commanding figure in that tiny playing space; but that same sense of his physical domination evaporates in the television version, leaving Ian McKellen's busy, mesmerizing Iago in complete control of the action and audience. Something similar happens in Parker's film, and not by accident: Iago's control is built deeply into Parker's design. As Buchanan perceptively notes, "Iago's desire to dictate the lens through which Othello is to perceive things identifies him as the film's internal cinematographer. It is Iago who explicitly instructs the spectator to 'look' . . . at Othello . . . [and] who determines how Othello should look both at others and at himself."[6]

Parker's camera develops two contrasting styles in presenting the fatal clash between the cynic (Iago) and the romantic (Othello). Parker allows Branagh's Iago to appropriate the camera, to make it his intimate, to ensure that it is always attentive to his text. The camera frames Iago's knowing soliloquies in tight close-up, often begun in profile so that Branagh can then draw us into Iago's gutter imagination with just a slight turn of the head to stare unblinkingly into the lens and confide in us directly. This device plays to Branagh's great strength as an actor—the ability to convey Shakespeare's language with absolute clarity and conviction. As with the examples of Olivier and Finlay and White and McKellen, some of the way the medium naturally embraces Iago is inevitable: Iago is made for the close-up; Othello needs the long shot; Iago's intimacies are whispered; Othello's rage must explode. Whereas film feeds on physical violence, the camera finds explosive personal passion disorienting. Olivier's Othello was bold and brilliant on the stage, when the audience was absorbing his masterful histrionics in long-shot; the same performance is embarrassing on film, where, in close-up, it repeatedly flirts with caricature.

Parker tries to avoid this trap by replacing Othello's text with his texture. Fishburne is a young, powerful, sexy Othello (no decline into the vale of years here) who radiates a natural authority and nobility.[7] There is no doubt that this man fetches his bearing and his being from men of royal siege. Fishburne's body fills the frame with his scowling presence, and Parker's camera lovingly caresses his shaved head—marked with tattoos and battle scars—giving us the warrior's menace, which can be quickly wiped away by the flash of Fishburne's dazzling, gap-toothed smile. From his left earring dangles a tiny pearl ("richer than all his tribe"), which Desdemona will clutch at in her attempts to pull away from his final, deadly, embrace.

Here is an Othello rich with potential, yet when Fishburne launches into what the filmscript has retained of Othello's big moments (from "Her father oft invited me," on), Parker's camera deserts the actor and moves into flashback (Othello moving among company in Brabantio's garden as Desdemona greedily inclines her ear to catch his tales), or later, when Iago's poison has begun its work, into projection (Othello imagining Desdemona and Cassio making the beast with two backs). For Parker, Othello's world is visual rather than verbal: Iago is word, Othello is image. One can understand Parker's filmic intentions here, and yet it deprives us of watching Fishburne work Shakespeare's poetry in a manner to complement Branagh's chillingly intelligent delivery of Iago's pestilence.

Though Parker is at pains, in the senate scene, to give us a multicultural version of cosmopolitan Venice, with a variety of British, European, and American accents swirling in the charged atmosphere, when we reach Cyprus only Jacob's Desdemona and Fishburne's Othello remain as linguistic outsiders.[8] Perhaps Jacob's French accent and Fishburne's American one sounded jarring to Parker's ears, which led him increasingly to conceive of their relationship in visual images, rather than verbal ones. I have already indicated how frequently Parker cuts away from Fishburne's Othello to give us visual illustrations of his longer speeches retained in the screenplay. He does something similar as a means of representing (and eroticizing) the relationship between Desdemona and Othello.

When Othello arrives in Parker's Cyprus, he comes mounted on a big black horse, rather than disembarking from a ship—to underline, as Lisa Stark's analysis reveals, that Fishburne's Othello is a young stud, rather than an aging general.[9] Several long, passionate kisses substitute for much of Othello's "It gives me wonder great as my content / To see you here before me" (2.1.183–84), and those kisses are registered by Parker's camera in a series of reaction shots from Emilia, Cassio, Montano, and Roderigo among the crowd gathered to welcome Othello. The nature of their relationship is further developed by Parker's depiction of the banquet that follows to celebrate the defeat of the Turks and the reunion of the newly-weds. As Barbara Hodgdon points out, the banquet and the lovemaking that follows are the film's most Zeffirelli-esque sequences.[10] What Shakespeare leaves to our imagination, Parker's camera and Mole's score romantically literalize. Jacob's Desdemona is achingly wide-eyed and innocent: her dancing, first for and then with Othello, at the banquet is erotic only in its honest physical expression of her affection for her husband. There is nothing coy or devious or even rebellious about Jacob's version of Desdemona.[11] Jacob's naturalness radiates a peasant earthiness, particularly in contrast to Anna Patrick's regal Emilia. Patrick's face, with its high cheekbones, long nose, and arched eyebrows, is the one that seems to step out of a Renaissance painting, not Jacob's. Visually as well as linguistically, Parker marks his Othello and Desdemona as outsiders; neither fits the culture that one is meant to represent, the other to defend and protect.

After the swirling public expression of their romance, Parker gives us the private version by following Othello and Desdemona to the consummation of their marriage. Here he extends the dance motif by having Fishburne twirl Jacob in his arms as they move to their gauze-curtained bed, which is strewn with rose petals.[12] Those petals suggest the blood that will flow from this encounter ("Thy bed, lust-stained shall with lust's blood be spotted") as well as those "spotted strawberries" interwoven in the famous handkerchief passed on down a long chain from an Egyptian charmer to a Venetian one. Parker's determination to displace language with image leads him astray. He thinks he is giving us a romantic, and liberally intoxicating, sexual encounter between a black man and white woman here, when in fact he is racially eroticizing two figures whom Shakespeare treats with more circumspection and less voyeurism.

Parker becomes a victim of his own romantic camera as he fails to understand how the drunken chaos that Iago releases in Cassio disturbs Othello's wedding idyll. The uproar Iago tried to provoke outside the Sagittary, which was immediately squelched by Othello's "Keep up your bright swords, for the dew will rust them," is now, on Cyprus, in the revels celebrating the defeat of the Turks and the general's marriage, allowed to ripen and explode. But in Parker's film, when Othello appears to restore order after Cassio's drunken spree, no chaos rages, no bell shatters the evening's peace, no riot violates the general's honeymoon. Parker's film gives us its own lush invention of the romantic commerce between Othello and Desdemona, but it refuses to capture the strident discord— "Silence that dreadful bell! It frights the isle / From her propriety" (2.3.175–76)—that Shakespeare's text is at pains to suggest interrupts the consummation of Othello and Desdemona's marriage and jolts Othello's imagination into establishing correspondences between love and war, sex and chaos, wife and enemy: "Are we turned Turks?" The absence of a raucous fight and the telling elimination of that tolling bell deprives Fishburne's Othello of the context in which to establish the psychological connection between the private riot of his passions peaked by his wife and the public riot of his troops provoked by his ensign.

Even though Fishburne arrives on the scene with his bedsheet draped about his shoulders, his Othello does not seem particularly annoyed at having been summoned from lovemaking to peacekeeping, though he does give Cassio a slap across the face on "I'll make thee an example," once Desdemona has arrived. This slap establishes a pattern for Fishburne's release of Othello's anger. His Othello is at pains to repress and restrain his obvious physical power, which makes it only more frightening when it suddenly erupts.

The movement of the text is to transfer Othello's insistence from "My life upon her faith" to "My wife upon his doubt." Iago seeks, of course, not just to displace Cassio, but Desdemona as well. He wants Othello's public approval and private affection. Iago's jealousy is motiveless only in the huge scope of its malignancy: race, class, and gender resentments all feed his particular pathology. Branagh does not shy away from letting us see the sexual jealousy at work in his Iago. Parker's screenplay underlines Iago's repressed homoeroticism by moving "I am not what I am" from its exchange with Roderigo in Shakespeare's text to Iago's first soliloquy at the end of 1.3, where it follows his suspicion that the Moor "twixt my sheets / Has done my office." Branagh delivers the line with just enough of a quiver to the lip to let us see Iago's sexual ambivalence. That quiver returns when Branagh's Iago relates to Othello his invented tale of Cassio throwing his leg over his thigh and plucking up dream kisses, intended for Desdemona, that grew upon Iago's lips. When Iago and Othello reach the climax of their partnership ("Now art thou my lieutenant" . . . "I am your own forever," which they seal in blood), the camera captures the tears in Branagh's eyes as he embraces Othello.

Parker's film is at its best visually and verbally as it moves to this embrace. He handles the long arc of act 3, scene 3 marvelously. Iago and Othello are first discovered exercising with long sticks, with Othello easily outmanning his opponent and sending him to the ground. Then they move into the entrance of the armory, where Iago helps Othello towel off as he casually begins to inquire about Cassio's relationship with Desdemona. As Iago's queries begin to sting, the camera follows them down several steps into the armory and captures Othello through standing racks of muskets, pikes, and swords, as we see him begin to succumb to suspicion. Here the film moves from the daylight world of military exercise, where Othello easily meets and parries Iago's thrusts, down into a murkier environment where physical blows are replaced by verbal ones and Iago quickly gets the upper hand. Parker visually captures the way Shakespeare's text allows Iago to turn Othello's attention from the military to the domestic, from issues of martial defense to ones of marital defensiveness, and locks Othello's consciousness onto the idea of Desdemona's infidelity and traps him in a world of doubt—the very world in which Othello is most defenseless. H. R. Coursen provides a detailed account of Parker's images here and their suggestiveness to Othello's vulnerable imagination: "The early phase of Iago's manipulation works well as he quickly translates Othello's mode from the conceptual to the experiential. We see Othello through a sword rack, in a kind of prison as he begins to hallucinate images of Desdemona and Cassio. A close-in shot of Othello's ear and Iago's whispering mouth captures the sensuous power of Iago's insinuations."[13] As Coursen observes, Iago is implanting images of the primal scene, and Fishburne's Othello quickly "takes the bait" and begins to transform "any innocent image of the past—a smile or glance" into an example of Desdemona's lasciviousness. Iago provokes Othello into remaking the history of his immediate past. As Coursen astutely comments, "Iago reshapes the past for Othello and makes it strange for him, alien. He becomes an alien not just to Venice but himself and what he knew, and a voyeur peeking through windows in his imagination at something that happens only there."[14] Iago, in short, transforms Othello into an image of himself—into an Iago.

Parker's screenplay cuts all of Othello's lines about his race and color, which indicate how thoroughly he has internalized Iago's racial and racist assumptions, but it does some radical rearranging of 3.3 and 4.1 to underline the emotional force of Othello's pact with Iago. "Now art thou my lieutenant" and "I am thine own forever" are transposed from 3.3 to follow Othello's epileptic fit, his overhearing of Iago's stage-managed exchange with Cassio, and his determination to kill Desdemona. Parker brings the two men up from the bowels of the fortress's prison, where Iago has put Othello behind bars and on the rack. This landscape is the visual extension of the armory scene; it finds Parker working with images not only from Shakespeare's text but in Orson Welles's great film of the play as well.

The film sets the pact between Othello and Iago on the fortress's ramparts (again echoing Welles), though here, rather than getting a version of Welles's famous tracking shot, we get a neat contrast between Othello's obsessive pacing and Iago's implacable stasis—eyes always fixed straight on the camera. Fishburne comes to rest only when he kneels on "Arise, black vengeance, from the hollow hell!" Iago joins him on "Witness, you ever burning lights above." Branagh now repeats the lip quiver on "heart" in "Iago doth give up / The execution of his wit, hands, heart / To wronged Othello's service" that he gave to his earlier evocations of his perplexed and repressed homoerotic relationship with Othello. Their perverse marriage is sealed by blood as each opens a cut in the palm of the hand, and then those hands are clasped together in a close-up to resonate with three previous close-ups of Othello's black hand uniting with Desdemona's white one at their wedding, in the senate scene, and in their marriage bed in Cyprus. It is here, in screenplay not text, that Iago urges Othello to "strangle her in her bed," which leads Othello to whisper, "Now art thou my lieutenant." The film is explicit at this moment in insisting that Branagh's Iago is as intent on displacing Desdemona in Othello's affections as he is in removing Cassio from his military post. Branagh's Iago squeezes his eyes shut as he allows his head to nestle down against Othello's neck and shoulders as the two men further seal their union with an embrace. Iago treats the camera not just as a conduit to an audience but also as the mirror that feeds his narcissism. As he infects Othello, he turns him toward the camera as well, for Fishburne increasingly confides his doubts about Desdemona directly to us.

Parker's screenplay and his camera seem often at a loss at how to best capture Othello. Fishburne is a powerful actor, but his Othello seems curiously contained; he smolders, but never erupts. Othello's music, his poetry, has to soar and command. He *is* hyperbolic ("My parts, my title, and my perfect soul / Shall manifest me rightly" . . . "I would not my unhoused free condition / Put into circumscription and confine / For the seas' worth"), but that self-esteem is central to his essence and proves fatal when it is dislodged by Iago's cynicism. Parker and Fishburne just cannot capture Othello's poetry: it is too big and dangerous for Parker's camera and too unfamiliar to Fishburne's training as an actor.[15] Fishburne has Othello's physical beauty and his power, and he is fine when fending off Iago's prosaic leading questions, but he is unable to carry us deep into Othello's tortured imagination through the images of Shakespeare's poetry. To compensate, as I have earlier argued, Parker replaces Othello's poetry with pictures—most significantly the enactment of Desdemona's coupling with Cassio that Iago projects onto the screen of Othello's imagination.

Parker increasingly deserts Othello in the second half of the film. Inexplicably, he cuts "Your napkin is too little" as Othello pushes Desdemona's handkerchief away from his forehead. This deprives Fishburne of the big gesture that would reveal why that napkin is "too little"—it cannot cover the cuckold's horns he imagines sprouting from his temples. This entire sequence, shot with Othello and Desdemona seated on their bed, is presented rather too casually by Parker. His camera is stationed behind the perplexed couple—perhaps so it can capture Emilia observing the exchange at the edge of the frame. Clearly Parker wants to treat the handkerchief as an afterthought, leaving it up to Iago to make something fatally momentous out of its private reality. But Shakespeare and Othello invest that handkerchief with magical, erotic powers, and Parker's film throws away any attempt to implant in this scene a suggestion of some of that symbolic significance.

Similarly, Parker perversely never allows Fishburne to "put out the light" or toy with the flame of the candle he carries into the murder scene, where his own heat is about to destroy his "moth of peace." Parker has Fishburne awkwardly carry the candle around the bed and use it as illumination as he performs a ritual cleansing of his hands and head before moving to the murder. The candle does not heighten the tension of the moment; in fact, its intrusiveness detracts from it.

Parker also alters our concentration on Othello in the film's final moments. He cuts all of Othello's agonizing recognition of his huge error—"O ill-starred wench! / Pale as thy smock! When we shall meet at compt, / This look of mine will hurl my soul from heaven, / And fiends will snatch at it" (5.2.272–75)—and he never has Othello cradle the dead Desdemona in his arms. Perhaps in keeping with the film's earlier depiction of their relationship, Fishburne's attention, and Parker's camera, focuses exclusively on Iago—so much so, that Parker even cuts away from Othello's silenced agony and the claustrophobic horror of the murder scene to follow Branagh's Iago when, after stabbing Emilia, he bolts from the bedchamber. In the chase that follows, Iago thinks he has eluded his pursuers by slipping through a door left slightly ajar. We quickly discover that he has entered the room into which the wounded Roderigo has been carried, and as Roderigo spies Iago, he spends his last ounce of energy to roll over and point an accusing finger at his victimizer. Here Parker gives us one of the film's two most unusual camera shots as Iago's full image is rotated in the frame to mirror Roderigo's perspective.[16] This cut away from Othello's agony breaks our concentration on his assimilation of his horrendous act. And once again, Iago's place in the story is privileged. In fact, Parker's camera allows Iago to "speak" even after Shakespeare's text has silenced him: "Demand me nothing. What you know, you know, / From this time forth I never will speak word." After Othello has died, Parker's camera does not focus on the lovers but rather on Iago as he inches his way up on the bed to curl into the fetal position and rest his head on Othello's knee.[17]

One final instance will serve to define the way in which the film curiously works to diminish Othello. The weapon with which Othello kills himself is slipped to him by Cassio. As Coursen recognizes, this dagger is the one we had seen Othello present to Cassio at the conclusion of his wedding to Desdemona.[18] This interesting detail seriously compromises Othello's suicide. Even if Othello remains powerfully divided and deluded in his final moments by turning against himself, by seeing himself as both the defender and the traducer (that malignant and turbaned Turk) of the Venetian state, at least Othello is his own victim and not someone who needs to be prompted (or even aided) into taking his own life by what might be interpreted as the action of a super-subtle Venetian. That the actor (Nathaniel Parker) playing Cassio and offering the dagger is the director's brother is the unkindest cut of all.

If Parker's camera is perplexed by Othello, it finds its true subject with Iago. Branagh gives us his fourth film version of a Shakespearean soldier.

His close-cropped, tight-lipped, false-faced Iago bears little resemblance to his worried, serious worker-king Henry V, his clownish Benedick, or his prim and precise Hamlet defined by his crisp, black uniform and his obvious interest in military exercises. Branagh's steely performance is cold and calculating, but he allows us, with one searing gesture, to shudder at the repressed heat that burns in Iago's festering emotional interior. In the aftermath of the drunken revel he provokes in Cassio, Branagh squats next to the remains of a campfire, pulls a still-smoking log from its midst, and grasps its burning end in his hand as he promises to turn Desdemona's "virtue into pitch, / And out of her own goodness make the net / That shall enmesh them all" (2.3.360–62). He smears the soot over his knuckles in a ferocious gesture of racial contempt and sexual envy. The masochistic white heat of this gesture acknowledges how deeply pathological Branagh's seemingly open and hearty Iago really is.

This ugly moment is coupled with a later one when Emilia brings the handkerchief to her husband. Iago is stretched out in bed on his stomach. Emilia approaches from the rear, and Anna Patrick delivers "I have a thing for you" as an inviting sexual tease. She moves to the bed to join Iago, and in one sweeping, cruel gesture Branagh rolls over, snatches the handkerchief, rolls Emilia over on her stomach, thrusts his hand up under her skirt with a disdainful power, and then pops up on his knees to toss the handkerchief in triumph in the air, where it spreads out and hangs suspended as he delivers "Trifles light as air / Are to the jealous confirmations strong / As proofs of Holy Writ" (3.3.322–24).[19] At moments like these, Parker's film is making inspired images. Branagh does not blink in revealing the nasty underside to his beady-eyed Iago. He resists the temptation to play cute with Parker's camera (unlike, in contrast, Ian McKellen's Richard III in Loncraine's *Richard III* film). His confidences are delivered with a knowing chill, rather than a clever wink. Branagh's line-readings manage to be both apt and intelligent: he delivers "I hate the Moor" in an ugly whisper, and in the space he allows between each word, Branagh makes us *see* Iago's gnawing jealousy. He makes words like "curse" and "snipe" and "pitch" hang in the air with the same vividness as his grasp of that smoldering log or his toss of Desdemona's handkerchief. Terrance Rafferty appropriately describes this aspect of Branagh's performance as expressing a "fierce glee," and he is right to see that Parker's film, his disclaimers aside, is relentlessly "Iagocentric."[20]

Branagh seizes the film because Parker is not able to summon a force to oppose him. He gives us soft-focused romance, pretty pictures, rather than the power of Othello's pride expressed through his soaring poetry or the roaring turbulence of that sea storm that dispatches the Turkish fleet and the clanging of that dreadful bell that calls Othello from his nuptial bed. When Desdemona sings her willow song, Parker cannot resist cutting to Othello, standing under the branches of a weeping willow, shot in silhouette against a moon-dappled tranquil sea. This is romantic, rather than ironic; sentimental, rather than tough-minded. Barbary's story and song are not about pretty pictures, they are about love and betrayal, madness and death.

Parker came to *Othello* as a relative novice in the worlds of film and Shakespearean stage production. His instincts were to follow the visual tradition begun by Zeffirelli and extended and transformed by Branagh by attacking his Shakespearean material with a sweeping, romantic visual style. His film is often handsome to look at, and it unfolds with a sure pace until its climax, where its tension, and the tale's tragedy, unravels. Some scenes, particularly those between Iago and Othello, are well conceived and executed. Branagh's performance rivets our attention, but ultimately it contributes to the film's decisive split in focus, allowing Iago, even in the film's final moments, to dominate the camera's attention, while the clash of Desdemona's blithe innocence with Othello's massive disintegration are allowed to fizzle, rather than reach a heart-rending climax. Parker never finds a visual means to get inside Othello's story in the same effective ways his camera and Branagh's performance manage to capture Iago's. Fishburne had the potential (and film experience) to be a brilliant Othello, but actor and director failed to allow the character to realize his full energy and power. Fishburne's performance is almost too sensitive and brooding, and Parker's camera and screenplay abandon his actor after Desdemona's murder, silencing the agony of his remorse and the fury of his retribution.

Changing Colors Like the Chameleon

Loncraine's Richard III

any of our greatest Shakespeare films have had their origins in stage productions: Laurence Olivier's trio, Franco Zeffirelli's *Romeo*, Peter Hall's *Dream*, Peter Brook's *Lear*, and Kenneth Branagh's *Henry V, Much Ado About Nothing*, and *Hamlet*, to name only the most obvious. Even Orson Welles, generally regarded as the most cinematic of Shakespearean film directors, had mounted productions of *Macbeth* and the Hal/Falstaff material before translating them onto film, and Welles later lamented that his theatrical production of *Othello* followed, rather than preceded, his magnificent film.[1]

In 1990, Richard Eyre staged a production of *Richard III* at the Royal National Theatre, starring Ian McKellen. This version drew attention for the audacity of its approach both to the play and to its dominating central character. Eyre set his production in the England of the 1930s, daringly evoking memories of an English aristocratic flirtation with fascism and Hitler that, through Edward VIII, reached into the heart of the royal family.

H. R. Coursen has deftly described the impact of the production's design:

> Eyre's setting was post–World War I Britain, home of Edward Duke of Windsor, Oswald Mosley, and photographs of Wallis Warfield shaking hands solemnly with Hitler. . . . [He] used the huge National [Theatre's] frame to create a panorama of a fascistic

rise to power. The staging itself reminded the audience of how fascists use such panoramas: Mussolini jutting his jaw from a balcony as thousands cheered in the square below, or Hitler at the Nazi Party Conference at Nuremberg in 1934 as re-evoked in the monumental *Triumph of the Will.* . . . Eyre created a modern world for his script to bustle in, which is always a dangerous approach when that world still lives in the memories of some of the spectators. The danger is that the world in which the script is set will fight the script itself and become the "play."[2]

McKellen's performance of Richard was the primary vehicle for defining the larger world that Eyre created for him to manipulate. McKellen conceived his Richard as the consummate aristocratic soldier whose military genius, surely primed at Sandhurst, was temporarily disabled by the Yorkist triumph ("this piping time of peace") he had helped to engineer. His first appearance set the tone. Following off-stage sounds of battle, the scream of a horse in agony, and then a silence, the words *Edward IV* appeared in Gothic script on a scrim that lifted to reveal a solitary figure emerging from a swirl of smoke, upstage-center. He was dressed in a military hat and greatcoat and moved slowly toward us with a slight limp that could as easily have been a swagger. McKellen's voice, like his posture, was tight and squeezed; he regarded us with the same disdain he did his brother's triumph. His delivery of the famed opening soliloquy was precise and clipped, swallowing vowels and striking consonants, producing on occasion an odd sound, deep in the throat like a death rattle.

Eyre has remarked, echoing Othello, that at the beginning of the play, "Richard's occupation's gone. He's a successful soldier . . . and [only] has purpose as a military man . . . [his] hunger to fill the vacuum left by battle is the driving force of the play."[3] McKellen's Richard resisted any impulse to play the clever clown winning us to schemes by the ingratiating nod and wink, which most actors find so irresistible when playing the part. This Richard was a repressed, tightly coiled cobra: a very different animal from Olivier's bird of prey, Anthony Sher's bottled spider, Simon Russell Beale's pop-eyed toad, or David Troughton's court jester. McKellen gave him a marvelous dexterity with his good right hand and arm, which were capable of the most remarkable feats: producing cigarette case and lighter in one fluid movement, or a tiny Bible to console Clarence on his way to the Tower, or a handkerchief to wipe away Anne's spit from his face. These moments were not only dazzling bits of the actor's legerdemain, but frightening examples of the character's single-minded power as well. Nowhere was this more evident or more mesmerizing than in McKellen's wooing of Lady Anne.

In the space of the thirty-five lines (twenty of them spoken by Richard) that elapse between Lady Anne's spitting and Richard's offer for her to kill him, McKellen managed to undress his upper body with one hand. Off came the greatcoat, then, from over his military tunic, the leather strap supporting the belt from which his sword hung; unbuttoning his tunic, he then dropped to his knees offering Anne his bright sword and his mocking heart in the same instant. Anne, like the audience, was completely disarmed by the slick force of will revealed by such a performance.[4] McKellen topped the audacity of this moment by using his teeth to remove the ring from his finger, offering it to Anne as a token of his contrition and affection. What woman could resist such wooing? What woman could resist such winning?

McKellen's performance was animated and defined by a thousand such imaginative details. One more extended example will suffice to provide the flavor of the actor's accomplishment. Eyre set the play's first great dynastic squabble, in act 1, scene 3, at, appropriately, the family dinner table. Richard, in white tie and tails, squared off across the length of the long table with his arch-nemesis Queen Margaret. The table held four candelabras, each holding three tall candles. When the quarrel ended and Richard was left alone to confide his plans to us, McKellen produced his cigarette case ("I do the wrong, and first begin to brawl") and lit his cigarette from the first candelabra, which he then puffed out as he verbally dispatched Clarence. He then toyed with the second set of candles, waving his hand above their flames, quenching them one at a time as he pondered how best to manipulate Derby, Hastings, and Buckingham. Using his napkin, he next flicked out the third trio of candles as he added Rivers, Dorset, and Grey to his list of future victims. On the lines "But then I sigh and with a piece of scripture / Tell them that God bids us do good for evil" (1.3.333–34), he produced yet another small Bible or Book of Common Prayer from his inner pocket and held it in his good right hand as he lifted the fourth candelabra in front of his face. His face visible through the flickering candlelight and cigarette smoke, he polished off his self-assessment: "And thus I clothe my naked villainy / With odd old ends stol'n forth of holy writ, / And seem a saint when most I play the devil" (1.3.335–37).

Shakespeare's Richard wins his audience by aligning himself with a

Bakhtinian conception of the grotesque body released by carnival freedom and laughter. Richard delights in (and delights us by) poking ironic
humor at his own physical deformity. McKellen turned this already subversive idea on its head. His Richard's agility at manipulating his rigid
rather than carnivalesque body became a metaphor for his skill in manipulating the body politic and bending gender relations to his own ends.
McKellen's display of his body on stage always radiated power, not laughter. Jack Jorgens has called Richard III "the gargoyle on the great cathedral of English history,"[5] and McKellen's physical genius transformed
Shakespeare's medieval gargoyle into a very recognizable twentieth-
century tyrant. One averted one's eyes from McKellen's Richard at peril.
When the production toured Eastern Europe, it struck an immediate
chord with audiences only recently released from the hold of despots. In
Bucharest, where the production played soon after the fall of Ceaucesceu,
the performance was stopped each night at the moment of Richard's
death with wild cheering and stamping. When it moved on to Cairo,
McKellen reports, "it all seemed like a new play about Saddam Hussein."[6]
What was a hypothetical metaphor for British audiences was lived reality
for their Romanian and Egyptian counterparts. As Eyre has remarked,
"The language of demagoguery in this century has a remarkable consis-
tency; Stalin, Mao Tse-Tung, Ceaucesceu and Bokassa share a predilec-
tion for large banners, demonstrations, and military choreography. . . .
Mass becomes the only consideration."[7]

    Here was a production and a performance that cried out to be reimag-
ined and translated into film: why, then, do I find Richard Loncraine's film
adaptation (with the screenplay by McKellen himself) so curiously at odds
with its theatrical inspiration? Why does the film, for all its interesting and
sometimes witty detail, fail to provide either the chilling impact of Eyre's
stage production or capture the essence of McKellen's brilliance as an
actor as expressed in his unique approach to Richard? Part of the problem
lies with representation. Bob Crowley's stage set established the 1930s
period by suggestion, rather than by any detailed recreation of a palace
interior. We were never in a realistic period set—one we might expect for
a play by Coward or Priestley, for example. When the Prince of Wales arrived in London in act 3, scene 1, he did so by train. Crowley and Eyre
playfully accomplished this by having a toy train hurry across the stage,
then stop to the squeal of steel braking on steel and a puff of smoke; a red
ceremonial carpet was then unrolled, down which the prince entered to
be greeted by Richard and Buckingham. That was all: it was left to the

imagination of the audience to fill in the rest. What was largely symbolic and suggestive on the stage becomes relentlessly realistic in Loncraine's film. Loncraine embeds Shakespeare's tale so thoroughly in the period settings of his film that it loses its power to represent more than what is shown or displayed on the screen. McKellen, who used the details of his stage performance to dominate his victims, here becomes the victim of Loncraine's visual details. The superabundance of those details—"Bentley limousines, Abdulla cigarettes, Sten guns, newspapers, railroad cars"— that so delighted James N. Loehlin, I found irritating and distracting. They, not McKellen's performance, became the film's focus. The frightening power of McKellen's "stiff and mannered" (Loehlin's description) stage performance was dissipated by decor.[8]

Loncraine is a journeyman film director who came to his craft from the world of television commercials. This is an artist who works and thrives in a materialist world. His camera work and editing are professional, but his film never reaches beyond its realistic premises. Welles, Ford, Bergman, Kurosawa, Truffaut, Buñuel, Hitchcock—to name only the most obvious directors—shaped film to reveal their own powerful aesthetic and psychological landscapes, thereby pushing the art of moviemaking in exciting new directions. Even the early Shakespeare films, from the Reinhardt-Dieterle *Dream* to Olivier's *Henry V* and Welles's *Macbeth,* found ways to mix and mingle established film conventions in ways that picked up on Shakespeare's similar creative experimentation with the conventions of the Elizabethan stage. Each of these films established a symbolic landscape (to use Kenneth Burke's still-relevant terminology) that created a vital resonance between the actor and the world created to surround him. Loncraine's problem is not his twentieth-century landscape, but how he uses it. By contrast, Christine Edzard's *As You Like It* uses a contemporary Rotherhithe setting to establish parallels between Shakespeare's exiles in Arden and the homeless in Mrs. Thatcher's London, doing so without having the landscape become the play. In Loncraine's film, his period details swallow Shakespeare's tale and swamp McKellen's performance to such an extent that we are deprived of the pleasure of watching a great actor create a character by vitally embodying a political landscape: the landscape in effect paralyzes the character. I realize that the problem here is as much mine as it is Loncraine's: even repeated viewings of the film, often experienced with classes of appreciative students, have failed to erase from my memory the thrill of the stage performance—an experience that I compare unfavorably with the tepid amusement provided by the film. I wish I had the imaginative and critical capacity to accept the film's virtues without also ruing its lost opportunities.

When McKellen showed an early version of his screenplay to Richard Eyre, he reports that "Eyre didn't approve of the modern props which had invaded the storytelling, particularly the telephones, motor cars, and battle machinery."[9] Eyre was alert to the danger that McKellen's approach would efface much of the energy and genius of the actor's performance by hemming it in with things. The problem was compounded when McKellen chose a film director relatively indifferent to Shakespeare—one whose visual imagination was not stimulated by Shakespeare's images and their possible contemporary parallels but by the period props, sets, and locations that McKellen had become so entranced with in developing his screenplay. In general, the best Shakespeare films have been made either by stage directors (Reinhardt, Hall, Kozintsev, and Brook) intimately familiar with their Shakespearean material or by actor-managers (Olivier, Welles, and Branagh) who had a driving ambition to translate a vision and a performance begun on stage into the world of film. McKellen found himself trapped between the two: Eyre's commitments at the National prevented him from accepting McKellen's invitation to direct the film, and McKellen lacked the ambition and creative confidence that drove Olivier, Welles, and Branagh to direct their own projects and performances.

Richard III is structured by two opposing tensions: Richard's pathological drive for power, always pushing, testing, manipulating the world in which he works, and the blocking forces—initially Queen Margaret and the duchess of York, later Richmond and the nobles—who attempt to impede and thwart Richard's progress, first by curses and then by arms. McKellen's screenplay fatally weakens both of these tensions—first by reducing the sheer theatrical power of Richard's drive, second by eliminating Queen Margaret and diminishing the choric power of those women who bear the brunt of the collective family suffering as it spirals murderously out of control in the last years of the War of the Roses.[10]

As Coursen argues, the distinction that Robert Weimann makes between *locus* (the thing represented, in this case the rise and fall of Richard III) and *platea* (the mode and means of that representation in a particular production) is helpful in illustrating the natural tensions and resonances that emerge in any performance, on stage or film, between the script and the production.[11] Weimann's terminology, adapted itself from the symbolic tensions between upstage and downstage space on the Elizabethan stage, expands upon Burke's notion of symbolic landscape and the Yeatsean and Jamesean metaphors (the dancer and the dance, the figure in the carpet) that were its inspiration. What happens in the McKellen-Loncraine film is that *platea* overwhelms and transplants *locus:* the figure disappears in the carpet, the dancer becomes indistinguishable from the dance. This might be an effective approach to Chekhov or a Shakespearean work like *Twelfth Night* or *The Winter's Tale*, but it doesn't work for *Richard III*, where the figure must dominate the pattern, where the dancer is the dance.

Paradoxically, the film that, McKellen insists, strives for a clarity of storytelling to make Shakespeare available for "everybody" has its best moments in clever little details that rip past so rapidly that their visual wit becomes available only to the Shakespearean insider. I will cite several examples just from the opening, precredits, sequence. We are in a manor house that has become a military headquarters. A ticker tape brings news that Richard and the Yorkist forces are closing in. Two officers, one older, one younger, exchange worried glances and murmur greetings: "Your majesty" . . . "Son." The elder retreats to prayer while the younger pitches a bone to his black Labrador and moves to his desk to eat. The camera focuses on the dog, who stops gnawing his bone, growls, and then breaks into a bark as his world begins to shake, soon shattered by a tank and its huge nozzle, followed by commandos in gas masks spraying machine-gun fire. The camera closes in on the masked face of one of them and we hear his heavy, rhythmic breathing. He shoots the kneeling, older officer and removes his mask as *Richard III* is spelled out in blood red on the screen. Here the movie audience is asked to absorb that the two officers are in fact King Henry VI and his son Prince Edward, that the tank's nozzle and Richard's gas mask are witty visual reminders of Richard-as-the-white boar—the rooting hog who wears many masks and can change colors like the chameleon—and that the curious focus on Edward's dog is, of course, conjured from Richard's own wry self-assessment: "dogs bark at me as I halt by them" (1.1.23). This jokey animal imagery is extended by having Richard first meet Tyrell (Adrian Dunbar) in the royal stables, where Tyrell is tossing apples into a stall containing a hog, and Dunbar is repeatedly shot in profile to accentuate the actor's own very prominent proboscis. Later Lady Anne's death will be visually noted by having a black spider scurry across her frozen face, evoking the "bottled spider," another of the menagerie of animals associated with Richard in the play.

Even though the visual wit of the opening sequence seems to me largely inaccessible to all but knowing Shakespeareans, it is promising; and that promise is extended in the long, establishing scene that follows the credits. Loncraine's camera introduces us to members of the royal family, one by one: Clarence (Nigel Hawthorne), the amateur photographer snapping pictures of the family with his Leica; Edward IV (John Wood), the old lecher being spoon-fed his medicine while he slips his hand up the nurse's skirt; Rivers (Robert Downey Jr.), Elizabeth's playboy-brother arriving on Pan Am with cowboy-and-Indian outfits for the young princes; the duchess of York (Maggie Smith), imperially presiding; and Queen Elizabeth toweling off her son. The family is preparing for the grand ball to celebrate the Yorkist ascension. As they move downstairs to join the party, the camera follows McKellen's Richard as he moves through the crowd, pausing to enjoy a whispered intimacy with Jim Broadbent's cigar-smoking Buckingham before moving on to a microphone on the bandstand, where the singer, Stacey Kent, has been warbling Marlowe's "Come Live with Me and Be My Love" as a lively foxtrot. It is in keeping with the film's camp cleverness that the first words we hear should belong to Marlowe, rather than Shakespeare.[12]

Richard's opening soliloquy is thus begun as a Yorkist victory speech, each line being interrupted by polite applause. As Richard moves from the family's triumph to his own feelings of dispossession by the end of military conflict and his brother's coronation ("But I, that am not shaped for sportive tricks"), the film cuts to the Men's Room, where he relieves his bile and bladder at once.[13] McKellen finishes his speech with a nice touch that establishes both his character's narcissism and his love of audience. The camera peers over Richard's shoulder as he admires his face in the washroom mirror, "Why I can smile; and murder while I smile; / And wet my cheeks with artificial tears / And frame my face to all occasions!"[14] Richard suddenly understands that he is not alone: we are there, via the camera, overhearing and overseeing; so he turns, with a wry smile, to take us into his confidence, speaking directly into the camera: "And, therefore, since I cannot prove a lover, / I am determined to prove a villain."[15] McKellen reports that he had some difficulty convincing Loncraine to allow Richard the ability to break realism's convention and address the camera directly. This is a convention long abandoned in Shakespeare films, from Olivier's *Richard III* (1955) to Oliver Parker's *Othello* (1995). But the film desperately needs more such moments. Richard's soliloquies are as important to establishing his character and his unique relationship with the audience as are Hamlet's. Loncraine's treatment of these opening sequences are his film's strongest moments, but he fails to build on them to discover visual metaphors and strategies that effectively translate either Shakespeare's stage devices or McKellen's strengths as an actor into the language of film.

McKellen's stage performance was built upon a wealth of gestures and details that established his approach to the character. With a few exceptions, those details have disappeared from the film. Rather than giving us the rigid autocrat who dominated by solitary self-reliance, the film traps the actor and paralyzes him by surrounding him with sycophants—primarily Ratcliffe and Tyrell. Richard's cigarettes are now instantly lit for him; he's given a manicure; he's handled and managed. The magnificent dining-room scene has been drained of its bitchy, crackling bite, and McKellen's soliloquy, accompanied by the snuffing out of the candelabras as he verbally dispatches his victims, is gone entirely. There is none of the mesmerizing flash of his undressing before Lady Anne, though the ring business is retained and given an added emphasis, courtesy of a close-up, as the camera allows us to see the ring momentarily disappear into McKellen's mouth before his good hand retrieves it and slips it on her finger. This gesture, as well as neatly paying Anne back for her spitting at him, appropriately reflects the vulgar daring of Richard's wooing and the oral fantasy of his devouring appetite for power: now it is *his* saliva that provides the lubricant for the ring.

By insistently setting McKellen within the film's realistic landscape, Loncraine drains both the character of its uniqueness and the actor of his power. A telling detail from McKellen's screenplay indicates how completely the actor became enamored of the film's reliance on period details and how far that carried him from the rigidly repressed soldier he created on stage. McKellen reports that he gave his Richard a pencil-thin mustache for his scene with Lady Anne because "Richard inspires himself by playing the fantasy role of a romantic lover. In the mirror he has razored a moustache of screen heroes like Clark Gable, Clifton Webb, David Niven, Douglas Fairbanks."[16] McKellen's stage Richard would have been oblivious to these Hollywood screen heroes, and the sexual fantasy he acted out on film with Lady Anne was a wicked parody of screen romance.

Reading the screenplay also reveals how much McKellen became interested in each of the film's locations. He describes them in detail. The attention to detail that distinguishes McKellen as an actor here gets sidetracked into his fascination with the film's landscape. Loncraine and his cinematographer Peter Biziou provide us with a decadent version of England in the 1930s, shot and lit to suggest a similar treatment of Mussolini's Italy in films by Visconti and Bertolucci. Bizou's camera becomes transfixed by the brutalist architecture of the South Bank and Battersea Power Stations (which do seem to echo Nazi monumentalism) and by the contrasting plush interiors of the prince's Pavilion at Brighton and Horace Walpole's Strawberry Hill House, which serve as several of the royal residences. Some of Bizou's shots are stunningly beautiful, but they never create an atmosphere to match the ominousness of Richard's quest for power. In fact, one wishes that Loncraine had poured less of his budget into filming the final conflict at Bosworth Field (here the Battersea Power Station) and more into creating a series of mass rallies and street activities to mark the growing spread of Richard's Blackshirts as his crude but powerful tyranny seeps into the culture. Loncraine does, on one occasion, make effective use of a film device by cutting from Richard's coronation to the royal party watching a movie of the event as they munch chocolates and sip champagne. More use of black-and-white newsreel footage would have been an effective film technique through which Loncraine might have captured more of the political flavor of the age he wishes to evoke.

The film does capture the general unattractiveness of the characters who surround Richard. Annette Bening's Queen Elizabeth is a feisty American parvenu whose brother Rivers is portrayed by Downey as a drunken lush stumbling down the steps of the Pan Am plane that has flown him in for the coronation ball. Later he will be dispatched by a giant stiletto that penetrates up through the bed on which he is making love to the stewardess he has picked up on his flight. Lady Anne pops pills and shoots dope; Nigel Hawthorne's Clarence sticks a camera in everyone's face and reads the *Times* in the tub in the Tower (Rivers, of course, reads the *Wall Street Journal*); Jim Carter's Hastings (reimagined here as the prime minister) nervously takes a nip from his flask during the council meeting to determine the succession; and Smith's regal duchess of York gets out of town (by plane) as soon as she can. The film might be retitled "Planes, Trains, Tanks, and Boats" for its insistence on incorporating almost every conceivable means of modern locomotion, creating more context than even the most ardent cultural materialist might imagine. Only Broadbent (who worked before with Loncraine in *The Wedding Gift*) finds a way to make his Buckingham—blinking with seeming innocence behind wire-rimmed spectacles—fit naturally into the film's environment.

The film introduces Princess Elizabeth, at her mother's side, in the opening ball sequence, where she is asked by Richmond to dance, another instance I think where only the Shakespearean insider can assimilate the storytelling. She then pops up in Richmond's traincar headquarters the night before Bosworth, where the archbishop marries them with lines plucked from Richmond's final speech. These two fresh roses then enjoy a night of sweet embrace, while Richard's sleep is punctuated by nightmare. It is typical of Loncraine's film that it cannot resist any cynical twist, even if to do so contradicts much of what has gone before. Richmond, from the outset, is presented attractively without a trace of irony. His morning's embrace with his bride is bathed in the lyric sentimentality of the lover, rather than with the carnal desire of the conqueror. But when Richmond finally traps Richard on a girder high above the battle and sends him plunging to his death, on the soundtrack Loncraine plays Al Jolson singing "I'm Sitting on Top of the World," and he cuts between the wicked smirk plastered on McKellen's face as his Richard wafts toward Hell's flames and a similar sly smile spreading on Richmond's face as he realizes that he is now top gun. The lovely irony of using the Jolson recording (Richard repeatedly listened to popular music in the film) is cheapened by having it cut two ways. This final image suddenly associates Richmond with Jan Kott's Grand Mechanism, while the film has consistently presented Richmond as a fresh-faced innocent, not as just another jackbooted thug out for self-aggrandizement. His self-satisfied smile, like so many other details in the film, is gratuitous rather than carefully placed, and in this instance it undercuts, rather than complements, our observing Richard's gnarled, contorted body floating free and heading home out of history and into myth.

Loehlin, in an admiring and intelligent essay that champions the film for many of the same reasons I find it wanting, provides a detailed list of the Hollywood-genre films Loncraine's *Richard III* raids and parodies. His exhaustive catalog includes a rich variety of popular genres, ranging from the slasher film to the Western to what he dubs "the modern heritage film," defined by the work of Merchant and Ivory.[17] The genre that Loncraine most relentlessly and effectively exploits is the 1930s American gangster film.[18] Loehlin convincingly argues that Shakespeare's play has uncanny and multilayered resonances, not only with the archetypal rise-and-fall structure of the gangster film but with its content as well:

> In the classic gangster movie . . . the anti-hero is an ambitious man who feels unfairly excluded from society. . . . The hero is often haunted by bitterness, shame or some unfulfilled psychological need, usually related to his family. . . . The hero's most important personal relationship is generally with his mother. His rise to power is often motivated by a need to impress her. . . . The hero has difficulties with other women; he often wins, and then neglects, a beautiful wife. . . . The hero's daring and ruthlessness earn him the admiration of the audience and a small group of followers. . . . The hero is almost always helped in his rise by a close associate or pal, whom he later rubs out for a perceived or actual betrayal. When the hero reaches the top he begins to forfeit audience sympathy; he becomes paranoid, violent and increasingly isolated as outside forces rise against him. He may be haunted by his past deeds; he begins to reveal his weakness. Cornered, he rises to a final heroic moment of defiance before being destroyed.[19]

Loehlin's models here are *Scarface*, *Public Enemy*, and *White Heat*, and he sees that while "Shakespeare's play bears some correspondence to this pattern . . . Loncraine's film follows it almost exactly."[20]

Loehlin's analysis, to my mind, is more interesting than Loncraine's film. In this instance, Loncraine's attempt to fuse a Richard III emerging out of the historically documented fascist leanings of some members of the British aristocracy in the 1930s with the Hollywood gangster film confuses, rather than clarifies, the parallels with either the historical reality or the Hollywood genre. Loncraine cannot resist piling one clever idea on top of another without regard to their impact on his film's narrative. Loncraine is a competent film director, but he has no feel for his Shakespearean material nor an imaginative grasp of the working assumptions of Eyre's stage production. This is a film whose period and politics certainly suggested that it be shot in black-and-white. Loncraine would have been wise to forego the expense of the mechanistic toys that litter the screen and to have invested instead in depicting the mass, mob activity that Eyre rightly associates with the tactics of the modern dictator. We are given no street scenes; no rising sense of multiplying Blackshirts suddenly alive in the land; no terror in the night; no mass rallies except for one poorly constructed shot of Richard's supporters hailing his acceptance of the crown. The film just doesn't create an urgent sense of Richard's inevitability. Even though McKellen was the creative inspiration and the driving force behind securing financing for the film, a reading of his screenplay indicates that he, too, bears responsibility for the film's imaginative failures.

Richard III reveals Shakespeare hitting his stride, particularly in the creation of Richard's mocking, ironic voice, in shaping the iambic pentameter line to his dramatic purposes. But McKellen's screenplay—with the exception of fragments of Richard's soliloquies that open the play and follow his conquest of Lady Anne—is decidedly prosaic. He does not trust the verse to work on film, even though Olivier and Branagh have convincingly demonstrated that the two are not mutually incompatible. He repeatedly tries to wrench the text into modern conversational rhythms for which it is particularly ill-suited. If the film cannot create visual images that convey Richard's terrifying rise to power, then it must let the actor have more of Shakespeare's words to allow us to see how he shapes the world he bustles in to his will. McKellen is a bravura stage actor whose brilliance largely dissolves on film; Olivier suffered much the same fate, never producing a film performance—with the exception of Archie Rice—to match his unrivaled power on stage. The film deprives McKellen of his vocal mastery of the play's great speeches, and because the medium privileges face over body and fragment over continuity, he is deprived of the sheer physical audacity of the way his body builds a character over time and in space on stage.

McKellen's performance lifted the stage production into the extraordinary, but he cannot carry the film. His Richard neither mesmerizes nor intimidates. For instance, on stage Richard was brought Hastings's head in a bucket; McKellen stuck his hand down in the bucket to close Hastings's eyes—a laconic touch not lost on his stage audience. By contrast, in the film Richard is brought a series of photographs of Hastings's hanging. He waits until he is alone, slips a popular tune on the victrola, nestles on a couch, and reviews each photo—flipping them casually in the air—as his foot keeps time with the music. The stage gesture had a terse and grim humor, and was done—like most of Richard's actions—for effect. The film's version of the moment is more Chaplinesque than chilling.

Stephen Holden suggests that the film's equation of the rise of fascism with upper-class ennui is made with "such a campy exaggeration that it finally seems tongue-in-cheek."[21] Holden's remark precisely captures what distinguishes the film from the stage production. Eyre and McKellen were serious about their Richard—deadly serious. Their Richard was not some bogeyman monster conjured first as an element in Sir Thomas More's Tudor propaganda and then translated by Shakespeare into the popular imagination as the mocking version of the Machiavellian stage villain. They provided Richard with a "local habitation and a name" and placed him squarely in the line of very recognizable twentieth-century tyrants. The film, ultimately, sends up this version of the character and the play.[22] Period details swamp, rather than suggest; poetry is compressed into prose; Richard's bold ruthlessness is translated into the petulance of the rejected child; and the cool, ironic soldier is transformed back into just another version—underlined by the film's final shot—of old Satan making his devilish mischief and getting caught.

Linda Charnes argues that Richard wants to replace stigma with charisma, which is one way to describe McKellen's stage creation of the character.[23] The film never finds a way to capture the charisma of the actor or the character, settling always for the send-up and put-down, rather than reaching for terror and menace. Welles once remarked, in a conversation about his *Chimes at Midnight*, that "the danger in cinema is that you see everything, because it's a camera. So what you have to do is to manage to evoke, to incant, to raise things up which aren't really there."[24] Loncraine's camera sees everything and thus suggests nothing; finally, his film doesn't just exchange Richard's kingdom for a Jeep, it exchanges his riveting power for a series of easy jokes.[25]

Shooting Stars

Luhrmann's William Shakespeare's Romeo + Juliet

B az Luhrmann's *William Shakespeare's Romeo + Juliet*, released in the fall of 1996, found and greatly expanded the international teenage audience that had made Branagh's *Much Ado About Nothing* such a surprise commercial success in the summer of 1993.[1] If Shakespeare's name had once been regarded by Hollywood as box-office poison, Branagh's two films had now made it possible for Luhrmann to propel that name directly into his film's title. The film's wild success has made that title both ironic and fitting, for both author and play have been effectively recanonized by this postmodern director. Luhrmann recasts Shakespeare as a secular saint, and *Romeo and Juliet* as revisionary film. Luhrmann's film opened simultaneously on more than thirteen hundred screens across the United States, and it led all the films released that weekend, in early November 1996, in box-office receipts—a first for a Shakespeare film.[2]

Even more than Branagh had for his *Much Ado*, Luhrmann carefully crafted his film for the teenage market. High-school students flocked to the film—pushed by their teachers (*Romeo and Juliet* is the standard Shakespeare play taught in high schools across the United States) and pulled by the androgynous appeal of Leonardo DiCaprio and Claire Danes. The film's young stars, coupled with its relentless, in-your-face MTV visual style and soundtrack, made its treatment of Shakespeare's tale immediately and excitingly available to its audience. In a wonderful twist of cultural irony, Franco Zeffirelli's film (also now a high-school staple), once attacked for its heady excess when released in 1968, now came to be regarded, in the face of Luhrmann's end-of-the-century dynamic assault, as the "classic" or "real" version of the play. A further irony results from Luhrmann's outsider status as an Australian. He not only has his way with an English classic, but his film was financed by his countryman Rupert Murdoch, the media mogul who became rich and famous while biting his thumb at the British establishment. The empire strikes back![3]

Luhrmann's first film, *Strictly Ballroom*, was a sweet, modern version of the Romeo and Juliet story set in Southern Australia. Nothing in its formal qualities prepared one for the pace and flash and dazzle of his *Romeo + Juliet*. Luhrmann takes his Shakespearean material more deeply into cinematic language than any other director in the Branagh era. Not even Julie Taymor's *Titus* nor Michael Almereyda's *Hamlet* are so loaded with the zooms, jumps, and slams that mark the opening of Luhrmann's film and become its cinematic signature. "This is like watching *Romeo and Juliet* under strobe lights," Kenneth Rothwell wryly observed.[4] The film is something of a paradox: it is at once the most radical and the most commercial of the Shakespeare films released in the last decade. It is the most radical because it was determined not just to find visual equivalents for Shakespeare's images but to overwhelm them with a virtual Pandora's box of cinematic devices, the most commercial because those devices provided a giddy rapture to the teenage audience, who found them exciting and amusing, rather than alienating. Luhrmann's film spoke their language. Janet Maslin, in her grudgingly positive review in the *New York Times*, rhetorically asked, "Where is the audience willing to watch a classic play thrown in the path of a subway train?"[5] The answer became evident in cineplexes across the country and the world: in the secondary schools.

The liberating energy of Luhrmann's camera work and editing and the film's remarkable ability simultaneously to transcend and deify its Shakespearean source has also made it attractive to leading figures in Shakespeare on film scholarship. To name only the most prominent, Kenneth Rothwell, H. R. Coursen, Barbara Hodgdon, Peter Donaldson, James Loehlin, and Courtney Lehmann have all produced essays championing the film, and a recent issue of the *Literature/Film Quarterly* devoted to Shakespeare on film commits three of its nine articles to *Romeo + Juliet*.[6] This attention should not surprise: the film is thick with images demanding to be read, saturated with enticing suggestions about the play's potential relationship with our media-dominated culture, and ripe with the postmodern collision and collusion of Shakespeare and popular culture. As Hodgdon humorously comments after a lengthy catalog of the way Luhrmann's film raids the cinematic canon from *Rebel without a Cause* to John Woo action films, "If this be postmodernism, give me excess of it."[7]

One of Luhrmann's achievements is to create a landscape for his multi-locale film that is recognizably urban and southern without specifically being Miami or Los Angeles or Mexico City. Like Ridley Scott's *Blade Runner* and Tim Burton's *Batman*, his *Romeo + Juliet* creates a celluloid city that fits the metacinematic qualities of the film. Within Luhrmann's generalized cityscape, as Coursen and Donaldson have pointed out, he fashions a series of spaces, from the Phoenix gas station, where the Montague-Capulet feud reignites in the film's opening frames, to the Sagrado Corazon de Maria church, where Juliet's bier has been placed, that become symbolic landscapes for his vision of Shakespeare's tale.

In between these flaming citadels (the gas station explodes, lit by a cigarette that Tybalt flicks to the ground as the shoot-out begins; the church is ablaze with the flames of a thousand candles surrounding Juliet's bier), the film stakes out three primary spaces: the Sycamore Grove Amusement Park, the streets and skyscrapers of the virtual city that comes to serve for Verona, and Capulet's palatial mansion, where the orchard ("whose walls are high and hard to climb") has been reconceived as a backyard swimming pool. The Sycamore Grove (a name cleverly lifted from Benvolio's report of having seen Romeo "underneath a grove of sycamore, / That westward rooteth from this city side") is a seedy, run-down, amusement park along the beach that is the hangout for the young Montagues. This space contains the Globe pool hall, a Ferris wheel, the abandoned shell of an old movie house, and the beach. This marginal space between the city (the land of the father) and the sea (the land of the unknown) is the territory of the young and restless. Donaldson perceptively understands that this crumbling boardwalk, though claimed by the young, is not the landscape that projects the future but is one that laments the past: "Luhrmann's film belongs to a pointedly *post-theatrical* approach to Shakespeare film adaptation. But 'the Globe' is acknowledged, and its passing lamented, for the playhouse puts in at least a cameo appearance. . . . The *lack* of a theatre is specifically called attention to in the film by the use of a large ruined proscenium arch, the ruins of a theatre or cinema palace, as a crucial location."[8] Luhrmann explores this submerged image of theatrical architecture even further in his subsequent film *Moulin Rouge*, where the stage is figured simultaneously as a place of romance and decadence.

Luhrmann, Donaldson argues, sees this space as a potential alternative to the modern, media-crammed cityscape dominated by the corporate towers of the Montagues and Capulets: "While this [media-saturated] culture is extremely attractive, the film offers tentative resistance to it, a resistance associated with the ruined theatre on the beach. . . . This location provides a hint of history at odds with the countermyth of autochthonous television . . . a free space for satire and poetry and drag performance."[9] But, as Donaldson acknowledges, it also becomes a space for death, for it is here that Tybalt fatally wounds Mercutio. Donaldson rightly sees that through Luhrmann's treatment of Mercutio's death, the film "suggests . . . that there is no liminal space from which the action can be commented upon in a world in which illusion and reality are so intermeshed."[10] Such is also the fate of that other space that might provide a critique of the film's dominant visual culture: the Capulet swimming pool. Here it serves as that dangerous territory, figured in the play as Capulet's orchard and Juliet's balcony, where Romeo and Juliet are momentarily free to discover and explore their quicksilver passion.

Most of the film's commentators are quick to read the visual metaphors Luhrmann employs to chart the rapid development of the romance between the two young lovers. The Capulet party is a raucous affair, more carnival than ball, dominated by Harold Perrineau's Ecstasy-inspired, drag Mercutio—a cross between Dennis Rodman and RuPaul—belting out "Young Hearts" to a pulsating Latin beat as he moves down Capulet's grand staircase in a silver corset. DiCaprio's Romeo, trying to break free from Mercutio's performance, bumps into a gross, red-faced Capulet (Paul Sorvino), caesared-up in a toga, who bellows at him over the din. To escape the blare of friend and foe and to try to clear his head from the Ecstasy buzz provided by Mercutio as a token of Queen Mab's inspiration, the film cuts to a shot of Romeo's head immersed in a basin of water. Submersion in water becomes the film's repeated signature image for the attempt by Romeo and Juliet to separate themselves from the crass, doomed world of their feuding parents: they seek another elemental existence. Luhrmann's next sequence of shots introduces DiCaprio's knight to Danes's angel as they peer at one another from opposite sides of a giant aquarium.

Crystal Downing provides an extensive account of the ways in which Luhrmann's images are inspired by Shakespeare's. She sees that the image of Romeo's submerged head parallels our similar introduction to a submerged Juliet, shot "as though the camera was looking up at her luminous face through the floor of a glass bathtub."[11] And Downing realizes that both of these images, linked to their eyes engaging through the aquarium, are responding to Shakespeare's repeated use of water imagery, from Romeo's "call me but love, and I'll be new baptized" (2.2.50) to Juliet's bold declaration that "My bounty is as boundless as the sea, / My love as deep" (2.2.133–34).[12] When Luhrmann's Romeo and Juliet are in their watery element, whether fish tank or swimming pool, the constant invasive rumble of the world recedes. Mercutio's wild version of "Young Hearts" slides from the soundtrack to be replaced by the ballad "Kissing You," which, the screenplay notes, releases its "first pure, achingly beautiful notes" just as DiCaprio spies Danes for the first time.[13] Here, and moments later in the balcony/swimming-pool scene, Luhrmann's camera steadies, holding the lovers' faces in close-up and two-shots; the pace of his editing slows; even Shakespeare's poetry is momentarily given leave to speak for itself, rather than having to compete with the music of the soundtrack. The film is given time, like the lovers, to catch its breath before racing away to the streets again.

Luhrmann's cityscape is dominated by two glass-and-steel, neon-signed skyscrapers, one marked Montague, the other Capulet. Between them is a giant statue of Christ, reminding Hodgdon of a similar Christ-figure dangling from a helicopter over Fellini's Rome in *La Dolce Vita*, swaying over a city where he is no longer embedded.[14] Luhrmann's, in contrast, has been digitally transplanted to stand between the Montague and Capulet corporate headquarters as a romantic reminder (like the Globe pool hall and the ruined theater) of a cultural past in which religion, duty, and family honor still mattered. The statue is at the center of a traffic circle, and the events of the film literally and figuratively swirl around its base. Luhrmann was attracted to Mexico City because he felt it provided a landscape where corporate values had not yet absorbed or destroyed the ties of traditional religious piety.[15] How well this tension between religion and family fits either Shakespeare's play or, ultimately,

Luhrmann's film, I'm not sure. Romeo and Juliet's passion derives its energy and beauty from being both iconoclastic and heretical:

> Romeo: What shall I swear by?
> Juliet: Do not swear at all
> Or if thou wilt, swear by thy gracious self,
> Which is the god of my idolatry.
>
> (2.2.112–14)

The church is represented by an equally freewheeling and meddling priest, who would be as problematic for today's Rome as for Shakespeare's Verona.

Something in Luhrmann's romantic sensibility gets swept away by the iconography of the Roman Catholic Church. Russell Jackson acutely observes that while "*Romeo + Juliet* has a stylized sense of actuality and modernity . . . [it] is no less romantic at heart and pictorial in values than Zeffirelli's film."[16] Nowhere is that sense of stylized reality and pictorial romanticism more evident than in Luhrmann's setting for Romeo and Juliet's deaths. In a scene that rivals and transcends the operatic Zeffirelli, Luhrmann places the drugged Juliet not in some dark and dank family vault, but on a raised platform in the heart of the Virgin Mary's church, surrounded by neon crosses, a blaze of candles, flowers, and rose petals. Loehlin, observing that this operatic finale is underlined and linked with the film's earlier evocation of aquarium and swimming pool, notes, "After the double suicide, the watery romantic isolation of the lovers returns for a poignant moment. The last phrases of Wagner's 'Liebestod' from *Tristan und Isolde* play during an overhead shot of the bodies surrounded by a sea of candles. . . . Juliet's violent suicide is washed over by the ecstatic love-death of Isolde, swooning in bliss over the body of her lover."[17]

Luhrmann's mingling of Romeo and Juliet's mutual idolatry with the gloriously illuminated church filled with the strains of Wagner's "Liebestod" is as daring in its own religious excess as is the couple's passion. To my mind and eye, Luhrmann's film provides no ironic or critical perspective on this moment, and by cutting Shakespeare's lines in which Montague and Capulet try to outbid each other in raising golden statues of their dead children, he perhaps recognizes that his film has already provided the equivalent visual apotheosis of the lovers. It takes no capitalist or Capuletist-come-from-the-grave to see that Luhrmann's film itself becomes absorbed by the very commercial world it set out to critique. Shakespeare's tale ends up being open to a reading tougher and more astringent than Luhrmann's film. Luhrmann's potential postmodern cynicism melts in the romantic blaze of his conception of Juliet's sin and the lovers' suicides.

The other significant element in Luhrmann's cityscape, beyond the world of church and corporation, is the street. After the opening shot of a television set buried in the center of Luhrmann's frame, presenting us with a newscaster's version of the play's prologue, the film cuts to the street, where the Montague lads roar down the highway in a bright-yellow truck. They gun past the Capulets, tossing their taunts to the wind. Street life in the film is defined by speeding cars, not gangs on foot. In the opening sequence centered around the Phoenix service station, no cut lasts longer than two seconds and point-of-view shots ricochet like bullets from the combatants' "Sword 9 mm Series" handguns. We are bombarded with lightning-fast cuts, slam zooms, supermicro slam zooms, extreme close-ups, and finally a crane shot up and over the mayhem, as the gas station ignites like a Gulf War refinery. Luhrmann creates the most explosive opening in the long history of Shakespeare on film.

Later, at the center of his film, Luhrmann will return to the streets for Romeo's murder of Tybalt. The famous confrontation begins at the Sycamore Grove. Prior to Tybalt's baiting, first of Mercutio and then of Romeo (the film's version of 3.1), this location has been treated as a place of play and plumage. This is where Benvolio first discovers Romeo, where the lads gather before heading to the Capulet ball, and where Mercutio tries out his mercurial gender posturings, perhaps inspired by his claim "That I am the very pink of courtesy" (2.4.61). Mercutio's final performance is as a stand-in for Romeo in the quarrel with Tybalt. The fight is staged amid the rubble of the ruined theater, and Mercutio is wounded with a shard of glass that perhaps has come from one of the old movie palace's gilded mirrors. Mercutio struggles up onto the stage, his mates as audience and the angry sea as backdrop, framed by the proscenium arch, to deliver his condemnation of the warring factions, "A plague on both your houses"—a shout that Luhrmann allows to echo on the soundtrack. As mentioned earlier, Donaldson argues that the stage, like the church in the final scene, fails to provide a space from which the action can be viewed with some distance or perspective.[18] Donaldson is right, for Luhrmann is not interested in providing such a control or ironic constraint on his material. He is more comfortable, as a director, on the street and on the move, and that is where his film zooms as Mercutio dies in Romeo's arms and the storm gathers. Tybalt speeds away, and Romeo, in his silver convertible, hurtles after him.

The ensuing careening car chase, more graphically presented in the filmscript than captured in the film itself, ends in a classic smash-up in the traffic circle at the base of the giant statue of Christ. Luhrmann here returns to the same frenetic camera work and editing that distinguished the opening street scene. As the cars are sucked toward Christ's outstretched arms, Luhrmann provides us with window-cam point-of-view and tumble shots, whip pans, and rapid cuts between Romeo and Tybalt, until their vehicles (Tybalt's sliding on its top) collide at the foot of the monument. The pace does not slacken until Romeo fires three bullets into Tybalt, and his body makes a slow-motion dive through the rain into a pool at the base of the monument. Luhrmann twice cuts to an overhead shot of this moment, with the camera peering down from the top of Christ's head. The water imagery previously associated with the innocence of Romeo's and Juliet's love has now been bloodied and compromised. As with the earlier street encounter, the violence of the quarrel gives way to the arrival of institutional force: the sky is suddenly filled with whirling police choppers and ambulance sirens as Prince, the chief of police, and the family heads arrive to witness the latest consequence of the feud.

The film makes its final return to the streets (and another visual linking of the Sycamore Grove with Christ and Mary) for Romeo's return from Mantua. Romeo is driven by Balthazar, in a dust-covered wreck out of *Mad Max*, first to the Globe pool hall, where Crusty, the owner, serves as the film's version of the apothecary. The police are in hot pursuit, and the film gives us one final chase as Balthazar and Romeo peel off toward the church as the cops (and Prince in his chopper) zero in on the young fugitive. This time it is the Blessed Virgin Mary's statue and sanctuary that become the lovers' and the film's destination, but neither the symbol of the spiritual world (the Christ statue) nor that of the profane (the Phoenix service station) can provide sanctuary or redemption. And here the film proposes a wild Marian merger of the grieving mother and her innocent, sacrificial children in the iconography of the film's setting of Romeo and Juliet's deaths.

Romeo and Juliet's suicides are imagined and envisioned not as a tragedy of fate, nor of bad timing or impetuous passion, but as a glorious apotheosis: a juvenile version of *Antony and Cleopatra*. They die in a blaze of religious and musical glory—not buried in the rotten jaws of the womb of death. DiCaprio's Romeo is pursued to the church by the police and is even shot at by a marksman in the chief's helicopter. Like Antony and Cleopatra, the film imagines them as being hunted, with death as the only possible consummation of their relationship, the only possibility for their union. The text's Romeo finds his entombed Juliet "a feasting presence full of light," but that illumination comes from the contrast between her beauty and its dismal surroundings. Luhrmann's film makes the church itself that "feasting presence." Donaldson reports that in "the making of the film so many Christian images were brought into the church by the production team that the authorities became suspicious and had to be assured that they were necessary to portray the culture of another place and time."[19] This lovely bit of cultural double-talk was obviously successful, but the only "other" place and time this scene belongs to is the universe of Luhrmann's imagination. We are asked to participate in an enshrinement of the lovers, all presided over by the welcoming arms of the Virgin Mary. Courtney Lehmann reads this moment as the natural culmination of the film's water-and-crucifix imagery. She persuasively sees that in the Capulet funeral monument, these two images "flow together in the spectacular image of the neon-blue sea of crosses. The force of this final image is so seductive that we can almost imagine Romeo and Juliet floating, swimming in the bliss of their first rendezvous in the Capulet swimming pool."[20]

As I have suggested, and the above examples illustrate, Luhrmann's film constructs a fascinating alternative universe for his retelling of Shakespeare's tale. The film's landscape is a mythic modern city (set on a north/south, rather than east/west, axis) of here and everywhere: Miami, Mexico City, Los Angeles. Within that built environment there are echoes and remnants of the past (the Globe, the ruined movie theater, the statue of Christ, the church) and signatures of the present (corporate sky-scrapers, police choppers, the ever-present media). As Coursen points out, the "film's fusion of specificity and the unknown gives it much of its power—this place we see emerges from some other place that cannot be known, though people know that it is there and know that ignoring it is as fatal as the results coming from it."[21] Coursen is referring both to the feud that is a perpetual open sore between the Montagues and the Ca-pulets—but that appears to have, in play and film, no known source—as well as to the mythic archetype of the Romeo and Juliet story itself. As Hodgdon, Rothwell, and Loehlin point out, "this place we see" does, at least partially, emerge from a place we know: other films.

Luhrmann shares with Branagh and Almereyda a powerful fascination with film culture and history. Loehlin quotes Luhrmann speaking on one of the film's many websites:

> In fact, what we've done is set the film in the world of the movies. You will notice that the film changes in style very dramatically, echoing very recognizable film genres, from Busby Berkeley to 70's naturalism to even European expressionism. The several changes of style refer to cinematic worlds or looks or ideas that audiences are familiar with on some level; using them to construct this "created world" will hopefully produce an environment that can accommodate a stylized language and make it easier for an audience to receive this heightened language.[22]

Luhrmann imagines "receiving" Shakespeare as a bit like taking communion; his film builds a temple to make the experience seem appropriate and natural.

Luhrmann's film is not as overtly metacinematic as Almereyda's (or even Loncraine's *Richard III*); nor does he quote other films as obviously as does Branagh. But this film is as resolutely postmodern as these other directors' work. As Donaldson has indicated, *Romeo + Juliet* is so media driven that it comes to "suggest the saturation of life by image."[23] This is certainly true of what happens to Shakespeare's language in the film; it becomes dominated by and absorbed into Luhrmann's cinematic language. We marvel at the ingenuity and intelligence of Luhrmann's images and their rapid-fire layering, but the success of the images drives Shakespeare's language into becoming the film's subtext rather than its text. Luhrmann's visual style consistently swamps Shakespeare's verbal one, as critics have complained. Geoffrey O'Brien insists:

> It's the skittish handling of the language, though, that reduces Luhrmann's film to little more than a stunt. While he gets a bit of mileage from the accidental intersections of Elizabethan with contemporary usage (as when his gang members call each other 'coz' and 'man'), any speech longer than a few lines just gets in the way, and the effect all too often is of sitting in on the tryouts of a high school drama club. The Shakespearean text begins to seem like an embarrassment that everybody is trying to avoid facing up to.[24]

A more generous slant would be to say that Luhrmann is so successful in creating a visual environment to match Shakespeare's language that his film ends up, perhaps unintentionally, overpowering it.

Another aspect of the film that has drawn attention is its resolute multi-culturalism—an American term created to stand for tolerance of a wide range of ethnic and gender diversity. On the surface, the film looks like dream Shakespeare for the agenda of the National Education Association: Afro-Americans, Latinos, gays, and cross-dressers are all given place of prominence in Luhrmann's version of Shakespeare's universe. The film's politics functions something like productions of Shakespeare did in Eastern Europe before the collapse of Communism and the Soviet Union: a means of smuggling in a critique of the regime under the noses of the authorities in the guise of presenting "Shakespeare"—a harmless, apolitical classic. But for all the film's inclusionary emphasis, it is still ul-timately focused on two very white young stars—DiCaprio and Danes.[25] Luhrmann, like Hollywood, can imagine a black, cross-dressing Mercu-tio, but not a black or Latino Romeo, nor a similarly ethnic Juliet. In fact, his film has to do some odd juggling with its ethnic impulses to produce the two pale creatures at its center. The Montagues, from Brian Den-nehy's Ted Montague and Dash Mihok's Benvolio to DiCaprio's Romeo, are all golden Angelinos, while the Capulets, from Paul Sorvino's Ful-gencio Capulet and John Leguizamo's Tybalt to Miriam Margolyes's Nurse, are all played as Hispanics.[26] In order for Capulet to produce a daughter as pale as Claire Danes, the film must make Diane Venora's Gloria Capulet blonde, white, and with an accent full of the deep Ameri-can South.[27]

Luhrmann's film, like Hollywood's America, wants it both ways: to celebrate ethnic diversity while not disturbing the conventional, com-mercial casting of the film's two young stars. It gestures toward a poten-tial subversiveness that it ultimately cannot sustain or deliver. In fact, it is precisely this paradox that makes the film, for all the outsider status of its Australian director and the radical energy of its style, such a hot Holly-wood commodity. The teenagers who flocked to the film on its huge opening weekend (and returned again and again, dragging along with them their reluctant friends) did so because they were urged to do so by their teachers and pulled in by DiCaprio. The film's MTV style came as a surprise and unexpected bonus. I saw the film on its opening night in our small university town. Oblivious to the promotional campaign and the DiCaprio phenomenon, I was surprised to discover the movie theater packed with high-school kids, rather than college students. I was quickly educated, however, by the squeals that erupted when the camera first discovers DiCaprio's Romeo trying to write his Rosaline poems on the shell of the ruined theater. These squeals, which sounded like weasels in heat, continued throughout the film, and at the moment when Romeo and Juliet first meet, a young girl behind me whispered: "Don't touch him, you bitch." While I admired DiCaprio's performance of the young Toby Woolf in *This Boy's Life*, I was unprepared for his transformation into a teen-cult idol.

Luhrmann capitalizes on his star's appeal by presenting him without irony or angst. The actor playing Romeo must provide him with an edge. Paris is the dreamboat: Romeo needs to be unconventionally attractive—or dangerous. Something in him has to speak to Juliet beyond being just another pretty boy or nice guy. This was the great failing of Leonard Whiting's Romeo in Zeffirelli's film. He was, finally, just another pretty face (and bottom); it was Olivia Hussey's Juliet that supplied all the power and breathless energy to their relationship. DiCaprio's Romeo suffers from a similar cinematic fate (and in this case, Danes's Juliet does not have Hussey's dark-eyed beauty or passion). Though Luhrmann's film provides the pair with an interesting symbolic landscape through their watery associations, they both end up being "wets," as well as all wet. Jim Bulman, writing to Hodgdon about her essay on the film, amusingly speaks for many in his response to DiCaprio's Romeo: "The most watery Romeo in film history? His acting is appalling, his affect minimal, and his intelligence—well, why go on? I can understand why teenage girls fall all over themselves for him. But you? Tell me it isn't so?"[28]

In fact, DiCaprio can act, as his performances in *This Boy's Life* and *Titanic* indicate, though he is not certain gold at the box office (his next film, *The Beach*, was an enormous flop). The fault is as much with director as with star. Luhrmann, for all the brilliance of his visual and technical imagination, is not yet an actor's director. When he wants to create a space and tempo for Shakespeare's poetry to live and breathe, as in the film's versions of the balcony scene and the lovers' one night together, his stars cannot provide the verbal dynamics to carry the scenes. They are conceived as an oddly passive pair; there's not a trace of passionate resolve or determined danger in their relationship: they're just cute—with one another and with the camera. The only performance in the film we are left to admire is Luhrmann's; there is a big space at the center of the film where Romeo and Juliet should be, but DiCaprio and Danes can neither fill nor hold it. To be fair, this is often the problem with stage productions

of the play as well, where Romeo's relationship with his mates is more exciting and fully realized than his relationship with Juliet, and the performance sags after the death of Mercutio.

Approaching this issue from another angle, Carol Chillington Rutter
writes that "Luhrmann's women do not repair, rather they register, postmodern fragmentation."[29] And, as I have argued, Rutter's observation extends to DiCaprio's Romeo. He is treated as an object, rather than as an
agent; even in his pursuit of Tybalt, he is as terrified of his violent passion
as he is overcome by it. The film repeatedly suggests that *Romeo and Juliet*
is more a tragedy of fate than of generational conflict or immature
passion. When Romeo reluctantly decides to attend Capulet's party, his
lines "But he that hath the steerage of my course / Direct my sail!"
(1.4.112–13) are followed by a flash-forward in which Romeo sees himself walking down an aisle flanked by blue-bordered neon crosses and
hundreds of candles. Neither he nor we yet know that this is the path to
Juliet's bier. But Luhrmann does. When Juliet bids farewell to Romeo the
morning after the consummation of their marriage, she imagines seeing
him disappear into a watery grave on "O God, I have an ill-divining soul! /
Methinks I see thee, now thou art so low, / As one dead at the bottom of
a tomb" (3.5.54–56). Interestingly, neither of these flash-forward sequences is included in Luhrmann's published filmscript. Fate, in the editing room, often directs the filmmaker's sail as well.

DiCaprio and Danes are at their most effective in their encounter
after the party. By plunging the scene into the Capulet's swimming pool,
Luhrmann puts his stars in a familiar element. His camera floats around
them, but frequently holds them in a sustained two-shot to allow some
flow to their exchanges. On "nor any other part belonging to a man"—
finding a touch of bawdy in the famous "what's in a name" speech—
Danes provides a teasing smile similar to the one she flashed earlier on
"You kiss by the book." As Downing indicates, the startled lovers fall into
the pool on Romeo's line "Call me but love, and I'll be new baptized"
(2.2.50), and the sea and journey metaphors (Juliet's concentrated and
deep; Romeo's wide and shallow) that Shakespeare employs to distinguish
his lovers are given an appropriate contemporary milieu here.[30] The best
favor Luhrmann does his actors in this scene is to shut down the perpetual soundtrack buzz. He resists scoring their exchanges until Romeo's
line "My life were better ended by their hate / Than death prorogued,
wanting of thy love" (2.2.77–78), and then only with a solo piano for several more beats before bringing in the full symphony to underline their
parting.

Some critics of the film have singled out the performances of the two British-trained actors—Peter Postlethwaite (Father Lawrence) and Miriam Margolyes (Nurse)—particularly their speaking of the verse, as superior to that of the cast's classical neophytes: Danes, DiCaprio, Perrineau, and Leguizamo. This is a common charge in Shakespeare films with international casts and has been levied against Branagh's and Parker's films as well. Postlethwaite and Margolyes do make much of the little text that is left for them in the screenplay, but both performances are immeasurably aided by the absence of the filmscore creeping (or pounding) in under their big moments. We are allowed to hear what they say without Shakespeare's rhythms being compromised or confused by competition from the soundtrack. Support for the film's use of a multiaccented cast comes from a surprising source: Alec Guinness. The sole member of the quartet of male English actors who dominated the classical stage in the first half of the century (the others were Gielgud, Richardson, and Olivier) also to have had an equally impressive career in films, Guinness comments: "The film has everything going for it except its greatest ingredient, the verse . . . but somehow Shakespeare survives. There are reasonably well-sustained passages; thoughts and feelings are always present; and what a relief it is to listen to American accents dealing with Shakespeare. They sound so much more authentic than our own overrefined suburban efforts."[31]

If the film too rarely slows its frenetic pace to allow Shakespeare his full voice, it is savvy to the myriad ways he has been absorbed into contemporary culture. In the opening shootout at the service station, we get snatches of the combatants' language lifted from other Shakespeare plays: "Double, double, toil and trouble"; "pretty piece of flesh"; "more fuel to the fire." Advertising billboards announce *The Merchant of Verona Beach*, *Such Stuff As Dreams Are Made On*, and *Shoot Forth Thunder*. Shakespeare is an implicit analogue to the film's religious imagery. That imagery, which many have cataloged, is ubiquitous: it ranges from micro to macro. Examples are the Christ painted on Tybalt's vest, the Madonna on the pearl handle of his pistol, the cross tattooed on Friar Lawrence's back, the shrine to the Blessed Mary in Juliet's bedroom, the crucifixes that dangle from the necks of just about everyone . . . and of course the Christ statue and the Church of the Sagrado Corazon. There is a sense that Shakespeare, like his two lovers, is being made sacred within a relentlessly demystified secular culture.

The film is boldly color-coded with blues, yellows, and reds. Romeo is blue, Juliet, white; the Capulet lads are black, the Montagues, yellow. Tybalt and crew wear stylish, tight-fitting black vests, trousers, and boots with steel tips and heels. Benvolio, Sampson, and Gregory sport loud Hawaiian shirts; Mercutio, appropriately, has no consistent sartorial style; and Romeo is the little gentleman in sports coat when we first meet him, and in a blue suit for his wedding. Blue and yellow—Mary's colors—come increasingly to be identified with Romeo and Juliet. The fish in the aquarium through which the lovers first spy each other are blue and yellow; the neon crosses that line the aisle leading to Juliet's shroud are outlined in blue and interspersed with the flickering yellow lights of the candles; the Mary shrine in Juliet's bedroom is a similar mixture of blue and yellow; and the color of the liquid in the vials provided by the friar and Crusty—who has hidden the poison in the false bottom of a Madonna lamp—completes the color pairing.

The film envisions the Romeo and Juliet story as a secularized version of the cult of the Virgin. The Blessed Virgin Mary, Shakespeare, and the lovers are all rolled up together in Luhrmann's cinematic imagination: for him, they all partake in an innocence and purity threatened by a commercial culture dominated by greed and violence. Even the Christ figure seems hedged in by the corporate towers of the Montagues and Capulets that flank his statue; his reach seems remote from the furious activity swirling about, far beneath his gaze. The film sees the image of Mary as more immediate and poignant, and it is to her outstretched arms that the lovers and the film relentlessly move. The mock altar on which Romeo and Juliet die is at the center of her church, and in its candle-powered brilliance it resembles the Virgin's shrine in Juliet's bedroom. Mary worship is a feature of the Mediterranean and of the Latin American Roman Catholic Church (it is also a strong presence in Australia) and provides a link between Luhrmann, Shakespeare's Italy, and the film's Hispanic flavor. Coursen provides an alert reading of the religious imagery at work here: "The film's major metaphor is religion and its irrelevance."[32] Institutional religion, in the figure of Friar Lawrence in both text and film, is not just irrelevant, but fatal. However kitsch the film's religious imagery may appear, the final sequences in the church are presented without irony. The lovers, cherubic of face and tiny of body throughout, become Mary's angels, secularized saints of star-cross'd love.

As the lovers lie blood-splattered on their bier, the strains of Wagner's

"Liebestod" soar on the soundtrack. After a high-angle crane shot of the bodies slumped together in death, Luhrmann provides us with a montage of the couple's happier moments. Then the screen goes white . . . and we realize that the camera is in close on their body bags as they are loaded into an ambulance. This shot is repeated as part of the television news broadcast that closes the film; another, we recall, framed its opening.

There is a lively critical debate about how ironically (or pessimistically) we are meant to read the media's enclosure of Shakespeare's tale.[33] I find the images within the Sagrado Corazon de Maria more powerful and lasting than those on the television screen. Luhrmann never allows, in the film's opening or close, the television screen to fill his own. His camera shoots the television set in long-shot, reminding us that it is contained within the larger, more dynamic frame of his film. The television screen is a snowy blank before the film's opening newscast begins, and it returns to that "dead time" after the concluding report. Shakespeare's story creates the news, and Luhrmann's film frames it. Shakespeare and film are being celebrated here. Luhrmann's frame reminds us once again that film, not television, is the modern medium that has found a way to capture and even transform Shakespeare. Zeffirelli and Branagh nudged the Shakespeare film from the art house to the cineplex; Baz Luhrmann's *Romeo + Juliet* made it feel as welcome there as his Romeo and Juliet are in the Virgin's shrine.

A Clean, Well-Spoken Place

Branagh's Hamlet

Kenneth Branagh's *Hamlet* (1996) is the most extravagant of his four Shakespeare films. If his models in *Henry V, Much Ado About Nothing,* and *Love's Labour's Lost* were, respectively, the war film, the screwball comedy, and the American musical, for his *Hamlet* he clearly had epic ambitions in mind.[1] He preceded it with a small, bittersweet, backstage comedy, *In the Bleak Midwinter* (1995), about a company of actors putting on a Christmas benefit performance of *Hamlet* to aid a rural village church. The two films are intimately interrelated, each representing one aspect or strain of British film history. *In the Bleak Midwinter* is Branagh's homage to the great Ealing Studio comedies of the 1930s–1950s, brought to their peak in Alec Guinness's performances in *Kind Hearts and Coronets* (1949) and *The Lavender Hill Mob* (1951). His *Hamlet* follows the model of David Lean's intelligent epics, from *Lawrence of Arabia* (1962) and *Dr. Zhivago* (1965) to *Passage to India* (1984), and it became the first British film to be shot in 70 mm since Lean's *Ryan's Daughter* (1970). Several excellent studies, most notably by Kathy Howlett and Emma Smith, have detailed the biographical, theatrical, and thematic resonances between the two films.[2] My focus here will be exclusively on Branagh's film of *Hamlet,* the way it enlarges and extends his film aesthetic and challenges and revises the major *Hamlet* films of the last half of the twentieth century, from Laurence Olivier's in 1948 to Franco Zeffirelli's in 1990.

Branagh's Shakespeare films are each distinguished by a signature shot or sequence that captures his way of translating Shakespeare into the language of film. These moments, each bold and dynamic in their own aesthetic composition and narrative context, also gather energy and resonance from the ways they echo earlier film images. The long, four-minute tracking shot of Henry V carrying the dead body of Falstaff's page back across the ravaged landscape of the Agincourt battlefield, as the Non Nobis swells on the soundtrack, places his gritty, post-Vietnam, post-Falklands perspective on *Henry V,* even as it recalls and reverses Olivier's equally long, but romantic, tracking shot that propelled the French charge at the beginning of his version of Agincourt. The opening sequence of *Much Ado About Nothing* deftly moves from text (the words of Balthazar's song popping up on the screen) to pictorial representation of landscape (the painting Leonato is making of his villa); we also see the Tuscan hillside itself, filled with female picnickers enjoying the sun, and the men, fists punched up in the air, riding home in the valley below. The sequence announces Branagh's giddy, festive approach to Shakespeare's comedy by appropriating images from films as diverse as *The Magnificent Seven* and *Gone with the Wind.*

In *Hamlet,* there are two such signature shots and sequences. The first is Branagh's visual treatment of the "To be or not to be" soliloquy and the confrontation with Ophelia that follows. The second is Branagh's handling of the "How all occasions do inform against me" soliloquy that closes the first half of the film. The first sequence is shot in Claudius's sparkling court, trimmed in white and gold and defined by a grand nineteenth-century salon lined by mirrored doors down its long walls. Branagh's film cleverly adapts this room so it serves not only as Claudius's court but also as Hamlet's playhouse, Ophelia's prison, and Fortinbras's prize. In a deceptively tricky shot, the camera peers over Hamlet's right shoulder, catching his full-length reflection in one of the mirrored doors. Hamlet is unaware that Claudius and Polonius have hidden themselves behind that door and are peering at him through a two-way mirror. As the soliloquy builds, the camera slowly closes in until Hamlet is present in the shot only in reflection, as if trying to discover there some clue to his recent discovery of the disparity between appearance and reality, loyalty and betrayal, deception and integrity. It is this disjunction that has disjointed his world and transformed his own identity within it from substance to shadow.

As Branagh's Hamlet finishes his rumination, delivered as a steely interrogation of the world he has suddenly inherited from his uncle and mother, he spies Ophelia (Kate Winslet), standing some distance away at the entrance to the great room, and he moves to her across an expanse of white-and-black checkered marble floor. Branagh delivers Hamlet's greeting to her in hushed and tender tones. Their exchange about beauty and honesty continues in this mood until Ophelia's guilty glance triggers Hamlet's query "Where's your father?" Winslet's embarrassed blush sets Hamlet off dragging Ophelia behind him in a furious move down the line of mirrored doors, opening and slamming them shut, searching for the spies. Flinging open the door into the room where Claudius and Polonius have been hiding, he knows he has struck home. Yet even when discovering Claudius's traces, Branagh's Hamlet can see only his own reflected image.

This sequence, one of the film's most stunning mergers of text and technique, was inspired not only by the way in which it radically revises Olivier's and Zeffirelli's filming of the linkage between the famous soliloquy and the "nunnery" scene but also by Orson Welles's magnificent funhouse mirror scene at the conclusion of *The Lady from Shanghai* (1946).[3] The mirrored doors pick up and extend the play's many literal and figurative mirrors, from Ophelia's "glass of fashion" to the "mirror [held] up to nature" that Hamlet affirms is at the heart of the actor's art and the "glass" into which he intends to transform himself in order to show Gertrude her "innermost part." Hamlet has been pushed from the center to the periphery; suddenly, he's on the outside looking in, and from that liminal position he develops a radical skepticism about what he sees. Hamlet is fragmented and fractured; his alert intelligence is troubled by the way in which he not only opposes but reflects Claudius. And while he repeatedly tries to hold the mirror up to Claudius's and Gertrude's natures, it keeps throwing back images more of his own turmoil than of their transgression.

Branagh literally positions the geography of the soliloquy midway between Olivier's ramparts and Zeffirelli's crypt landscapes, associated in both of the earlier films with the ghost of Hamlet's father. For Olivier, the soliloquy dramatizes the vertiginous allure of the deadly sea of troubles pounding both in Hamlet's mind and on the rocks below. His Hamlet, passively prone on the high platform, is literally caught sprawled between heaven and earth. For Zeffirelli, the move is not up and away but down and under, and Mel Gibson delivers the soliloquy in his father's burial crypt—a communication with death and the dead. Both films incorporate Q1's placement of the soliloquy; hence, for both Olivier and Gibson the soliloquy is sparked by Hamlet's escape from the charged emotional encounter with Ophelia in the nunnery scene. Olivier's camera, following his film's debt both to Freud and German expressionism, daringly bores into the back of Hamlet's head and equates the fuzzy images moving in and out of focus found there with the ever-changing pattern of the sea beating against the rocks below. Zeffirelli's crypt—where his film also begins—is presented in the same naturalistic style that dominates the film's atmosphere, very much in keeping with his conception of Paul Scofield's Ghost as startlingly human in its sad ennui, rather than supernaturally terrifying or imposing. Gibson's delivery of the soliloquy emerges as an imagined conversation with the absent father.

Branagh's version firmly embeds Hamlet in the perils of Claudius's world, not the Ghost's. His Hamlet is not trapped between above and below but between past and present, inner and outer, and the soliloquy becomes less a cry of hopelessness or despair than a determined thinking through of his own complicity in Claudius's corruption, his own bitter understanding of the way in which Claudius's narcissism releases and mirrors his own. Ophelia's appearance here, following Q2 and F1 ("Soft you now the fair Ophelia"), comes, initially, as a welcome respite from such intense self-preoccupation. Hamlet's rage, therefore, is heightened when he discovers her betrayal—a further confirmation of the puzzling and damning discrepancy he continues to discover everywhere between appearance and reality. Those mirrored doors become the vivid image for Hamlet of Claudius's court and world. For Branagh, they establish not only the nineteenth-century dynastic world he wishes to explore but the metaphoric reaches his film extrapolates from the text.

The second signature shot (the "How all occasions" soliloquy—done in one continuous take as the film's first-part climax) reverses the dynamics of the first. Whereas the "To be or not to be" soliloquy finds Hamlet embedded in the deceiving glamour and glitter of Claudius's world (he's boxed in, confined, trapped by a fierce, demanding father and a smooth, slippery uncle), the "How all occasions" speech finds impasse has given way to expanse. Now he is in Fortinbras's world, which is conceived as a snow-covered, rocky terrain something like that little patch of Poland the captain would not pay five ducats to farm but that Fortinbras and his army seek to claim.

Branagh begins the soliloquy with the camera in medium close-up and Hamlet in the right center of the frame. Patrick Doyle's score, unlike in the previous soliloquies, is present from the beginning. As the soliloquy builds, Hamlet remains frozen in the frame except to curl his right arm up into a fist, first on "I do not know / Why yet I live to say this thing's to do" and then again on "Rightly to be great." The camera slowly begins to pull back on "what is a man," and it does this so deliberately that

Hamlet's full-length figure is not revealed in the frame until "How stand I then." This reverses the "To be or not to be" soliloquy, where the camera closed in slowly over Hamlet's shoulder until only his reflection in the mirror was left of him in the shot. Branagh's extravagance now comes to dominate the treatment of "How all occasions" as his voice rises to a shout, the camera increasing its backward motion and suddenly craning up and away, reducing Hamlet to a tiny, black stick figure thrusting his arms out from his sides as he cries out, "O, from this time forth, / My thoughts be bloody, or be nothing worth!" (4.4.65–66).

The moment is a perfect emblem for one aspect of Branagh's film style: a willingness to risk all on a single flamboyant shot. Too often, I think, we respond to the flamboyance without considering the keen intelligence—what Mark Thornton Burnett calls Branagh's "cunning"—behind the hyperbolic excess.[4] Here Branagh gives himself and his Hamlet a huge screen moment, a moment that follows Olivier's film grammar for treating Shakespeare's soliloquies (start in close and pull the camera back as the speech builds, reversing film's normal pattern of moving from long-shot to close-up). But the extravagance of the shot is not self-indulgent: it is a searing critique of the character. Hamlet, in all this expanse of landscape, has been reduced to little more than a tiny black dot making grand but impotent gestures. Now that he has become, through the murder of Polonius, fully implicated in the world he has sought to expose and cleanse, he, too, has become one of those "black and grained spots" that Gertrude realizes "will not leave their tinct."

Branagh perceptively sees that Hamlet possesses the dual functions of actor and director; that in many instances he is "both in the moment and observing himself."[5] He translates that awareness to the impotence of the extravagance of the "My thoughts be bloody" moment: "Here's a man of grand passions where, in small rooms and with great intensity, his situation and his reaction to it can fill this vast screen and yet in a moment, which ought to strike us and him at the same time and with the same intensity, he can see himself as a very small part of a very large picture that is almost overwhelming."[6] Branagh has an instinctive awareness of Kenneth Burke's theoretical understanding of the relationship in Shakespeare between character and landscape. Director Branagh allows his Hamlet repeatedly to fill the screen—the "To be or not to be" mirror shot and Hamlet's head captured in close-up, framed in the model theater are compelling examples—and then to disappear almost entirely from it, in the "How all occasions" moment reducing him to a tiny, insignificant black speck against a northern landscape, with Fortinbras's army marching to Poland in the valley below. There is nothing quite like these two moments in the long history of *Hamlet* on film. The sheer ambition of Branagh's epic conception of the play allows him to create such stunning contrasts and allows him both to echo and to revise the work of the giants in filmed Shakespeare: Olivier, Welles, Kurosawa, Kozintsev, and Zeffirelli.

Considering Branagh's *Hamlet* in the context of the work of his distinguished predecessors raises the issue of his film style. He shares with the postmodern aesthetic a heightened sense of the past, in Branagh's case consisting both of Shakespearean stage and film history and an unabashed willingness to raid that past for ideas and images. But he also fits uncomfortably in the postmodern moment because his Shakespeare films are always striving to move beyond parody and pastiche to create big, bold, dazzling narrative images, to be populist and entertaining. As Peter Holland has pointed out, film has its roots in the nineteenth-century stage and its commitment to spectacle.[7] Spectacle Shakespeare does not work on stage, where it fights against Shakespeare's swift scenic and psychological transitions. But film can accomplish such movements in the flash of a jump cut or a close-up. Branagh is also associated with the nineteenth century because he emerges much more from its tradition of the actor-manager than from the contemporary British theater's dominance by university-educated directors. Branagh is unique in this tradition because, unlike Olivier, he has devoted his career to being the Shakespearean actor-filmmaker. Branagh has spent the decade of the 1990s making films, not moving back and forth between Shepperton and Stratford or the West End. Pauline Kael has called Branagh a "flamboyant realist," and that term points toward the cultural and historical synthesis Branagh makes in his films between a nineteenth-century aesthetic and a twentieth-century technology.[8] Perhaps his style can be best described as neoromantic.

Branagh's film style can be seen as a potent mix of two theories about the nature of the imagination summarized in M. H. Abrams's seminal work about romanticism, *The Mirror and the Lamp*. Branagh's films, most especially his *Hamlet*, regard the imagination as both mirror (presenting a selected and ordered reflection of reality) and lamp (creating and projecting a unique view of reality). One is struck by how these metaphors combine and become literal and mechanized in the art and technology of film, for film is a symbiosis of projection and reflection. Branagh's neoromantic imagination seizes on these metaphors to project his particular and unique mingling of text and tradition and technique in reimagining, on film, Shakespeare's powerfully fluid narratives.

Branagh's style derives from mind-as-mirror as, in *Hamlet*, for instance, it seeks to reflect the full text; to echo and revise earlier film treatments of the play; to provide something like a handsome illustrated version of the play by making visual much of the Fortinbras narrative, the love-making of Hamlet and Ophelia, Claudius's poisoning of old Hamlet, the First Player's evocation of Pyrrhus, Priam, and Hecuba, and the young Hamlet's enjoyment of Yorick. His style also seeks to provide an epic visual sweep to his Shakespearean material in keeping with his film's nineteenth-century setting and his homage to David Lean (acknowledged by his shooting in 70 mm and using Alex Thomson, a Lean veteran, as his cinematographer). In a fascinating essay on the film, Laurie E. Osborne argues that Branagh replaces textual editing with film editing as his primary method of shaping his Shakespearean material: "While producing the 'full text,' Branagh echoes and frequently exaggerates the cinematic strategies that reinforced the textual editing of earlier film productions."[9]

As Osborne understands, Branagh's style simultaneously projects rather than reflects an understanding of the popular film culture largely lost on other directors of Shakespeare films. While Holland is tempted to call Branagh a banal populist, we must remember that film culture is notoriously slippery and that often today's banal populist becomes tomorrow's auteur.[10] Branagh belongs to a relatively small group of film directors who have almost complete control over their projects, and his four-hour *Hamlet* is a stunning example of that independence. What Hollywood studio would have permitted such a commercial folly? Branagh's Shakespeare is romantic in its insistence on being visually bold and emotionally brash.[11] His very first film images, Derek Jacobi's Chorus striking a match into flame as he invokes "a muse of fire" and throwing a powerful stage light switch when he hits *invention* in "the brightest heaven of invention," demonstrate Branagh's affinity with the lamp of the romantic-school imagination. He is also not shy about allowing Doyle's lush film scores to pulse romantically beneath his films' images and Shakespeare's words.

Branagh's imagination is drawn to the bright and vivid. His *Hamlet* is film noir with all the lights on. The film's interiors are meant to echo a subtle merger of the dazzling Versailles Mirror Gallery and Inigo Jones's Banqueting Hall. Sarah Hatchuel quotes the film's designer, Tim Harvey, as remarking: "Ken wanted the sets to be . . . far removed from the rugged medieval gloom one usually associates with the play."[12] Branagh and Harvey clearly have Olivier's, Kozintsev's, and Zeffirelli's film versions of the play in mind here. Branagh's approach to the play and to character radically revises these major previous films of *Hamlet*. His Hamlet is less passive than Olivier's, less melancholy than Smoktunovski's, less manic than Gibson's. He is polite, precise, focused. His Hamlet is, even more than Gibson's, a man of action whose mission is frustrated more by lack of opportunity and a keen conscience than by inner resolve. His Hamlet is a military man without an army. His power and room for maneuver are limited by Jacobi's silky smooth Claudius and his relationships with Ophelia and Gertrude. When he is finally free from the super-subtle confines of Claudius's court, he finds himself trapped in Fortinbras's world—this time stymied by expanse rather than impasse.

The "How all occasions" soliloquy, discussed earlier, is a perfect example of how Branagh links his film's epic impulses with his interpretation of the play's central character. Terrence Rafferty understands well the purposes of this style at work in *Hamlet:*

> Branagh . . . rarely passes up the opportunity for a big visual effect: when the ghost of Hamlet's murdered father appears to him, the smoke and flames of Hell erupt from beneath the ground; after the murder of Polonius, a dizzying overhead shot shows us a great dark pool of blood; in the climactic scene, Hamlet's sword flies through the air, in close-up, and lodges in Claudius's back; when Fortinbras' soldiers invade Elsinore, they burst through doors of mirrored glass. Viewers who consider themselves sophisticated may be put off by . . . the director's obvious eagerness to please every segment of the audience; they may even mistake Branagh's intelligent showmanship for vulgarity. . . . Branagh attends [to playing Hamlet] with terrific ardor and an odd humility. He surrenders to the play's mysteries . . . and he persuades us, finally, that Shakespeare's intimate tragedy deserves nothing less than the grand-manner treatment it receives here—that the patient exploration of human behavior is itself an enterprise of great pitch and moment. The energy and animal vitality of Branagh's *Hamlet* actually make the play seem not less but more suggestive, because in this production action *is* meaning, and embodies mysteries deeper than any the hero's mind, or ours, can imagine.[13]

Branagh's film, in its epic sweep, nineteenth-century setting, and use of the full text, has the weight and scope of the great romantic Russian novel stretching from Tolstoi to Pasternak.

One of his earlier film projects, *Mary Shelley's Frankenstein* (1994), had taken him back to the nineteenth-century novel and introduced him to the film vocabulary of a big-budget epic. The *Frankenstein* film was not a critical success, but, contrary to common assumption, it more than re-covered its $40 million cost in worldwide distribution and video sales and rentals. As Branagh has observed, Victor Frankenstein is as obsessed with life as Hamlet is with death. Branagh invented a swirling, circling camera style, evoked first for a dance at the Frankenstein mansion before death intrudes on the family and then repeated more interestingly for Franken-stein's slippery, clumsy dance of life with the Monster when he first emerges from the mechanical womb that Frankenstein constructs to give birth to his creation. These circling camera shots return in his *Hamlet*, often centering on Claudius as the vortex of a centripetal force pulling the Danish court into the corruption of his crime. What is most remark-able about the epic visual ambitions of Branagh's *Hamlet* is that the film does not abandon the director's fascination with Shakespeare's language and his mad, Frankensteinian, determination to make the complete text come alive in a medium not known for its admiration for "words, words, words."

It is a commonplace in the criticism of filmed Shakespeare to place word in opposition to image. As Anthony Davies points out, that opposi-tion is most obviously revealed in the contrast between the Shakespeare films of Olivier and Welles.[14] Though Olivier's films radically cut Shake-speare's text (eliminating, for example, Henry V's ruthlessness, major portions of Hamlet's soliloquies, and Rosencrantz, Guildenstern, Fortin-bras, and Queen Margaret in *Richard III*), his films privilege word over image by consistently reminding us, through the mannerisms of camera and decor, of the script's stage origins. Welles's films, on the other hand, whether by necessity or invention, offer us a dazzling variety of camera angles, jump cuts, and vivid images, which carry the narrative far more powerfully than the substandard soundtrack that rumbles along, often awkwardly, with them. In Olivier's case, Shakespeare's words release a theatrical imagination; in the case of Welles, they release a cinematic one.

For Branagh, the words are not the means to an end: properly expressed and understood, they are the end itself. His films are not as theatrically evocative as Olivier's nor as visually complex and stunning as Welles's, but they provide a more satisfying synthesis between language and image than the work of his great predecessors. Branagh is determined to make Shakespeare's rich and dense language understood; he shines a light on the precise and concise speaking of Shakespeare's iambic pentameters and measured prose that brings to fruition the modern, naturalistic style of speaking blank verse that he has championed in his stage and film productions of Shakespeare. Geoffrey O'Brien got at the quality of Branagh's accomplishment with language when writing in the *New York Review of Books* about Branagh's film of *Henry V,* and his remarks are equally true for Branagh's *Hamlet:*

> The chief point of Branagh's direction was to keep language in front of the audience at all times, with Derek Jacobi's clipped . . . delivery leading the way. The job of the actor was to clarify, line by line and word by word, not just the general purport of what the character was feeling, but the exact function of every remark, as if some kind of match were being scored. Abrupt changes of vocal register, startling grimaces and seductive smiles, every actorly device served to maintain awareness that absolutely every moment had its singular thrust, and thereby to keep the audience from being lulled into an iambic doze. The result was a more pointed, even jabbing style, a tendency to deflate sonority in favor of exact meaning, while at the same time giving the meter of the verse a musician's respect, and the theatrical sub-structure a lawyer's questioning eye.[15]

This quality of intelligent attack on Shakespeare's language, which respects both its rhythms and powers to convey multiple layers of meaning, starts with Branagh himself and extends throughout his cast. It is immediately recognizable in those who have worked with him in previous Shakespeare films—Derek Jacobi, Richard Briers, and Brian Blessed; but it is also evident in the work of Shakespearean outsiders, on both sides of the Atlantic—Julie Christie, Kate Winslet, Robin Williams, and Billy Crystal. Language is essential in Branagh's romance with Shakespeare; it is not simply the launching pad or inspiration for filmic invention. Paradoxically, Shakespeareans once accused Olivier and Welles of being kings of shreds and patches in their treatment of the Shakespearean text, while now we fault Branagh for giving us too many words in his film of *Hamlet*.[16] Yet all those words are one of the most daring glories of the film. They are the verbal equivalent of its romantic, epic, visual style.

The challenge of filming a full-text version of *Hamlet* is what Branagh has in mind when he comments:

ILLUSTRATIONS

1. Henry V (Kenneth Branagh) and Exeter (Brian Blessed). Falstaff goes to war in Kenneth Branagh's *Henry V.* (British Film Institute)

2. Berowne (Kenneth Branagh), Longaville (Matthew Lillard), the King (Alessandro Nivola), and Dumain (Adrian Lester) about to be trumped by their women in Kenneth Branagh's *Love's Labour's Lost*. (Photofest)

4. Feste (Ben Kingsley) as narrator and troubadour in Trevor Nunn's *Twelfth Night*. (Photofest)

3.
Beatrice
(Emma
Thompson)
flying high in
Kenneth
Branagh's
giddy *Much
Ado About
Nothing.*
(Photofest)

5. Hamlet's (Mel Gibson) passionate assault on Gertrude (Glenn Close) in Franco Zeffirelli's *Hamlet*. (Photofest)

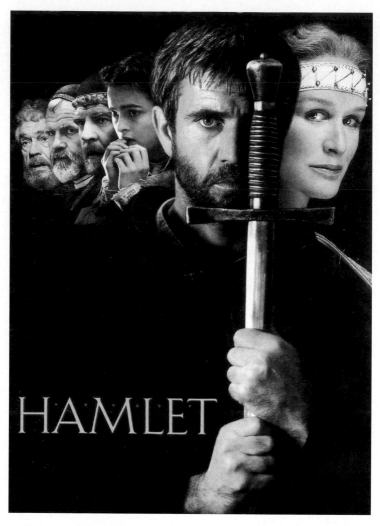

6. Hamlet trapped between Gertrude and Ophelia (Helena Bonham Carter) on the poster for Zeffirelli's *Hamlet*. (Photofest)

7. Othello (Laurence Fishburne) and Desdemona (Irène Jacob)—"a pearl richer than all his tribe"—in Oliver Parker's *Othello*. (Photofest)

8. Iago (Kenneth Branagh) catching Othello's and Desdemona's reflection in his knife blade in Parker's *Othello*. (Photofest)

9. Richard III (Ian McKellen) wiping away Lady Anne's (Kristin Scott Thomas) spit in Richard Loncraine's *Richard III*. (Photofest)

10. "A tank, a tank, my kingdom for a tank!" Richard III in the Battle of Bosworth Field, in Loncraine's *Richard III*. (Photofest)

11. Juliet (Claire Danes) peeking through her bedroom shrine to the Blessed Virgin Mary in Baz Luhrmann's *William Shakespeare's Romeo + Juliet*. (Photofest)

12. Juliet becomes herself a shrine in Luhrmann's *William Shakespeare's Romeo + Juliet*. (Photofest)

13. Hamlet (Kenneth Branagh), frozen between the newlyweds, Claudius (Derek Jacobi) and Gertrude (Julie Christie), in Branagh's *Hamlet*. (Photofest)

14. Ophelia (Kate Winslet), forced by Polonius (Richard Briers) to read Hamlet's letter aloud to Claudius and Gertrude in Branagh's *Hamlet*. (Photofest)

15. Hamlet (Kenneth Branagh) trapped in a film noir with all the lights on. The "To be or not to be" soliloquy in Branagh's *Hamlet*. (Photofest)

16. Emma Croft's tomboy Rosalind dressed in watch cap and jeans to mirror Orlando's attire in Christine Edzard's *As You Like It*. (British Film Institute)

17. Oberon (Dominic Haywood-Benge) in Christine Edzard's *The Children's Midsummer Night's Dream*. (Sands Film Studios)

18. Kevin Kline's Bottom discovered sitting at Monte Athena's Antico Caffé Greco just after a donkey has been led across the frame in Michael Hoffman's *A Midsummer Night's Dream*. (Photofest)

19. Hamlet (Ethan Hawke) and Ophelia (Julia Stiles) at the screening of *The Mousetrap* in Michael Almereyda's *Hamlet*. (Photofest)

20. Anthony Hopkins's mud-caked Titus Andronicus in Julie Taymor's *Titus*. (Photofest)

21. Aaron (Harry J. Lennix) and son in Taymor's *Titus*. (Photofest)

We needed to do those things which wouldn't pull the rug out from under our feet, but would keep us very alive to the inherent dangers and risks to the particular approach we took, and it seemed to me that that sharpened up all one's other instincts about this fundamental desire to communicate the play. And if you give yourself this extra challenge [using a full text] that can make you very canny and sharp and imaginative and inventive about how to communicate, how to make Shakespeare understandable, to make it to my mind naturalistic and entertaining.[17]

He might also have added *economical*, because on a budget of $15 million, Branagh's *Hamlet* is about twice the length of the conventional commercial film. During the filming, Branagh liked to joke about the size and shape of the project. When shooting the scene of Fortinbras's army smashing through the palace's windows, he quipped: "I'm making six films at once. This is *Die Hard*."[18] Length was always a pressure, and it meant that Branagh had almost no conventional film time (montage and action without dialogue) to exploit. He had to find a variety of ways to absorb the audience visually without ever having the liberty of interrupting the constant flow of the play's language. This is what has led some critics, most perceptively Bernice Kliman, to chastise Branagh for an overextended (and sometimes even confusing) use of flashbacks (Hamlet and Ophelia's love-making, the royal family enjoying a game of indoor curling or being entertained by Yorick, the murder of Hamlet's father) or parallel montage shots (the Priam and Hecuba scene or Fortinbras's army on the move and eventually storming the palace).[19] But these necessary sequences underlined the film's approach to certain key relationships (Hamlet and Ophelia) or characters (Fortinbras) in the play and varied the film's visual rhythm.

Branagh's lack of film time seriously compromised Hamlet's encounter with his father's ghost. As Branagh has indicated, the special effects meant to transport us (and Hamlet) into the ghost's purgatorial realm where he roasts in sulph'rous flames reveals the film's budgetary and creative limitations:

I wanted to scare people. I wanted to provide a very suspenseful treatment of it that I think works fitfully well. That's where I felt money and budget and quite frankly lack of imagination on my part didn't bring it off as well as I had originally hoped. I think that it was always going to be difficult . . . because it required time—time without dialogue. It required the sort of movie time we didn't have the luxury of creating when we knew there was another three and a half hours to come.[20]

Branagh's visual treatment of Hamlet's soliloquies stands in stunning contrast to these attempts at bigger movie moments. He films each soliloquy in one long, unbroken shot, requiring the utmost concentration on the part of both actor and cinematographer. Film acting is usually an endless series of snippets, tiny bits of dialogue repeated in numerous takes, reaction and point-of-view shots all being stitched together in the editing process with montage, action sequences, establishing shots, matte shots, and digitalized sequences. The economy of Branagh's Shakespeare films, and especially his *Hamlet*, rely on the actor's ability to sustain long stretches of Shakespeare's verse in a single take. This is particularly apparent in the work of Nicholas Farrell, Jacobi, Winslet, and, of course, Branagh himself.

Osborne was the first to note that, with one exception, Branagh films all of Hamlet's soliloquies in one continuous shot without any cuts, "foreshadowing Hamlet's consistent command over the camera's view whenever he offers . . . a soliloquy."[21] For Osborne, the circular movements of the camera in these moments signal "the authenticity and fullness of Hamlet's presence."[22] For instance, in the first soliloquy the camera begins its journey on the right, flows to the middle of the great hall as Hamlet steps down from the dais, and slowly pulls back, keeping Hamlet in medium-long shot as he releases his anger at his mother's remarriage. The camera follows Hamlet down the hall and pivots so that the soliloquy ends with Hamlet now framed by the huge doors at the end of the hall that is opposite from the throne. Remarkably here, at what would seem to be a natural moment, Branagh does not provide a cut, but continues the shot with the doors opening for the entrance of Horatio, Marcellus, and Barnardo. The unbroken shot then continues as the camera circles the quartet: Hamlet is pulled from his solitary (and very private) anger back into the world with the news of Horatio's revelation about the ghost.

The first cut since the beginning of "O that this too too solid flesh would melt" now comes when Horatio promises to reveal "this marvel to you" about the ghost's appearance, and it cues Hamlet to usher them into the privacy of his rooms just off the great hall. The sustained pace of this sequence allows first for the private explosion of Hamlet's repressed anger, then for the mercurial shift of his emotions into a lighter mood when he recognizes Horatio, and finally his amazed reaction to Horatio's report. The absence of cuts here, and the fluid, circular movement of the camera, creates a scene typical of Branagh's way of capturing Shakespeare on film: he risks letting the actors, rather than the director and editor, create the rhythm and intensity of the moment.

Branagh varies the pattern somewhat for the "O what a rogue and peasant slave am I" soliloquy. Rather than remaining in the great hall after the players have left (paralleling the departure of Claudius and Gertrude in act 1, scene 2), he takes his cue from "Now I am alone" to move into his private, book-lined study. His emotions are just as raw and lacerating here as earlier, but they are directed at himself, rather than his mother, and so they properly correspond to the landscape the film has marked as Hamlet's private space. Now the camera tracks him from left to right in medium-long shot before beginning to close in on "Bloody, bawdy villain!" As it follows Hamlet's pacing in this tiny space, the camera is able to pick out theatrical masks, a globe, a ticking clock, and finally an elaborate model theater—all of which speak to Hamlet's histrionics. He is "acting" here—indulging his emotions, rather than concentrating them. This builds to Branagh's exaggerated banging against the window as he curses Claudius and then sinks to the floor on "Why, what an ass am I."

With a paradox central to Shakespeare's conception of Hamlet, "acting"—the very element he despises in himself and others—is what repeatedly rescues him from his own self-absorption. Branagh's Hamlet spies the model theater that sparks his imagination and reanimates his spirit. The camera follows him as he rises from his defeated slump and moves to the rear of the model for the soliloquy's climax: he bends down so that the camera can catch his face framed in the model as Branagh dispatches the king, through the trap, to the "other place." Again the entire sequence is shot without a cut; its emotional rhythms are entirely dependent on the relationship between actor and camera.

Branagh's handling of the four major soliloquies is alert to their differences in tone and mood and subject. The first and last trace his progress from a son privately angered at his mother's remarriage to a prince publicly shamed that he has not yet cleansed the corruption of the Danish state. In the first, Branagh allows Hamlet's anger to erupt in the empty court, where his military posture and frank confession might lead us to believe that here is a man capable of opposing and exposing his corrupt stepfather. In the fourth, Branagh gives us the same figure, still dressed in black but now completely dwarfed and dominated by the land-scape. In the two intervening soliloquies, we see how his world and op-tions have been circumscribed. He has become, in many ways, a man trapped between two powerful fathers. In "O what a rogue," he damns himself for being his father's opposite: a man who unpacks himself with words rather than deeds. He's confined, first within his room and then within that model theater—the only world in which he can imagine tak-ing action. In the "To be or not to be" soliloquy, he is trapped by his own reflection and Claudius's penetrating presence on the other side of the mirrored door.

Branagh's Hamlet is certainly tougher, less erratic and neurotic, and more powerful than those of his immediate contemporaries, reaching back as far as Jonathan Pryce in 1980 to Mark Rylance and Adrian Lester in 2000, but his only weapon remains words. Those words are his glory as well as his enemy. They allow him to express a dazzling range of emo-tions, a keen intelligence, a cutting irony and sometimes brutal wit—even, in isolated moments, to express, with Ophelia, Gertrude, and Horatio, tenderness and a genuine concern for others. What they do not allow him is the ability to construct a unified personality. His identity is shattered by his mother's remarriage, his father's murder, and his loss of love and power: Ophelia and the crown. The play explores his heroic at-tempt to survive that disintegration and then to rebuild a new sense of self from its shards.

Though as the twentieth century came to a close and turned into the twenty-first, psychoanalysis had lost much of its impact as a therapy and as a mode of literary interpretation, it remains a powerful explanatory paradigm of human development, and for a century *Hamlet* has been its text. From Freud and Jones to C. L. Barber and Richard Wheeler and Peter Donaldson and Janet Adelman, *Hamlet* has been the Shakespearean work that most naturally opens itself up to the central concerns of ego psychology. Ernest Jones's reading of Freud and *Oedipus* heavily influ-enced Olivier's *Hamlet* film, and Donaldson has used Freud to provide an intriguing reading of the film through the lens of Olivier's own psycho-logical development.[23] Olivier made manifest his Hamlet's oedipal strug-gle by casting a Gertrude (Eileen Herlie) thirteen years younger than himself and by investing their moments together with a sexual tension not replicated in Hamlet's power struggle with Claudius.

Forty-two years later, Zeffirelli directed another *Hamlet* film heavily flavored with psychoanalytic insights—one more in keeping with Adelman's Kleinian reading of the play. In Zeffirelli's hands, the play becomes very much a family romance, rather than a political drama, and Glenn Close's Gertrude usurps Alan Bates's Claudius as the center of Hamlet's and the film's attention.

Branagh's approach, however, is closer to Barber and Wheeler's in seeing the play as dominated by fathers and brothers rather than mothers and lovers. Most productions, on stage or film, cut lines sparingly from Gertrude or Ophelia, but whole swatches of text from Ghost, Horatio, Rosencrantz and Guildenstern, First Player, and Fortinbras are left on the cutting-room floor. Branagh's full-text script automatically heightens Hamlet's relationship with the ghost and Claudius and also makes more evident the way that that script forces us to absorb Hamlet's personality as it is revealed by being embedded in a host of young male alter egos and two powerful fathers. Branagh's film then heightens several of these relationships, primarily the ghost's and Fortinbras's, by providing them with a visual power and presence in excess of their textual origins. Blessed's Ghost is a huge, bearded, dominating, demonic figure with piercing ice-blue, bloodshot eyes, several times captured in immense close-up. Blessed's vital, demanding Ghost is the antithesis both of Olivier's shadowy, helmeted figure (who speaks in Olivier's own voice, slowed several speeds in recording), and of Paul Scofield's drained and exhausted figure in Zeffirelli's film.

In his previous Shakespeare films, Branagh has used Blessed to portray aggressive paternal roles. As Exeter, in Branagh's *Henry V*, Blessed was the king's burly champion urging him vigorously into the French campaign. When Exeter waddled into the French court, his armored girth reminded me of Welles's Falstaff at Shrewsbury, and suddenly I realized that for Blessed (and Branagh), Exeter was a fantasy version of Falstaff, transformed from Hal's slippery subversive companion of the revels to Henry V's staunch military ally. Similarly, and less appropriately (because too massive and threatening), Blessed's Antonio in Branagh's *Much Ado About Nothing* loomed as a protective paternal figure, presiding over the women at the opening picnic while the men are away at war and eagerly challenging Claudio and Don Pedro after their shaming of Hero.

Branagh conceives of Hamlet's father as a huge, powerful military figure. His giant statue, situated just outside Elsinore's gates, frames the film. In the opening sequence, the ghost seems to emanate from that statue, and in the film's closing shots the statue is being razed by Fortinbras's troops. Branagh's film makes visually clear the ways in which Hamlet has mistakenly idealized his father, for Blessed's old Hamlet bears a much greater resemblance to Hamlet's description of Claudius than that of the dead king. Both as the ghost and, in several flashback sequences, as the king, Blessed is boisterous and overbearing, wearing a wide, lecherous grin resembling more a braying satyr than the graceful, protective Hyperion of Hamlet's memory. Jacobi's brilliant Claudius is by far the more attractive and subtle man. Branagh must be aware that his blond Hamlet bears an uncanny physical resemblance to Jacobi's Claudius, while it is Rufus Sewell's dark, swarthy Fortinbras who seems more naturally the son of Blessed's ghost and who completes this fatal quartet of fathers and sons.[24] In the film, Fortinbras looms; always in the background and on the move, he is closing in on a world crumbling from within. It's as though he and Hamlet were two sides of the same revengeful son: one pale and precise, moving against the establishment from within, the other dark and intense, closing in from without. Fortinbras is the monster that Branagh's Hamlet and *Hamlet* creates, and the film might be amusingly retitled *Dr. Hamlet and Mr. Fortinbras.*

Deflected perhaps by the surface glow of the late nineteenth-century world that the film depicts, critics have been slow to see how devastating Branagh's critique of the play's politics really is. The failure of nineteenth-century dynastic Europe to reform itself, his subtext reads, led directly to the tyrants who dominated the political landscape in the twentieth century. Robert Willson perceptively sees both the private linkages at work here ("Fortinbras qualifies as a reincarnation of the prince's father") and the public echoes of nineteenth-century Europe ("Here is Napoleon at the gates of Moscow, ready to strike"), but I think he misreads these images to believe that Branagh's film uncritically elevates Fortinbras to be the play's hero ("By privileging Fortinbras' figure and fortune, Branagh's *Hamlet* becomes not the story of the prince's tragedy but the heroic tale of Fortinbras' inexorable rise to power").[25] The politics of Branagh's film are more cautionary: Fortinbras is Shakespeare's contribution to the law of unintended consequences. He achieves power as the result of an internecine, corrupt, family dynastic struggle. Branagh's film echoes Shakespeare's text in the ambiguity of its ending. Willson rightly sees that when Fortinbras and his army break through those sparkling mirrored doors to discover the ravages of carnal, bloody, and unnatural acts, Fortinbras does not "take the actual throne. The slaughtered Claudius is still in it. Yet he assumes a chair near the middle of the room, imposing a presence that is reinforced by his strategically deployed soldiers."[26] Branagh, by so positioning Fortinbras, suggests the shift from the nineteenth century's monarchy to the twentieth century's military tribunal as the source of power.

While Branagh sets his film in the nineteenth century, he realizes that its final image of old Hamlet's statue being toppled and destroyed brings the film decisively into our own age: "The image at the end of the statue being pulled down was obviously one that was familiar to us from Eastern Europe."[27] Branagh's further explanation of the film's historical setting allows him to link up his version of the play's public politics with the private psychological struggle of its hero. If, as I have argued, Hamlet's identity is under intense pressure and forced to redefine itself constantly in relationship to the women in his life, two powerful fathers, and a host of attractive alter egos, then Branagh imagines a similar fate for the play's political entity, Denmark. He comments: "The story of the nineteenth century when it came to wars was one of constantly shifting boundaries: countries being created and then being obliterated and empires constantly shifting their borders. There was a volatility to the fate, the expansion, the diminishing of nations across that time."[28]

As Claudius and the ghost exert their psychological pressure on Hamlet, so in turn Hamlet and Fortinbras, those unruly sons, exert a political pressure on Claudius, and through him on the Danish state. The public and private, the political and psychological layers here are rich and deep. Branagh senses these connections, and his film, especially in its unusual privileging of Claudius, makes them explicit: "There was an unease and increased tension, particularly for Claudius, with the mounting difficulties of dealing with the Hamlet crisis and the understanding that the security of the nation [at Fortinbras's advance] itself was in a volatile state."[29] Had Claudius survived the threats from the two powerful forces moving against him, internally and externally, and written his political memoirs, "The Hamlet Crisis" might well have been an apt chapter heading.

Jacobi's Claudius not only resembles Branagh's Hamlet in appearance, subtlety, and good manners, but he also is given a similar latitude by the camera in his major scenes. The most stunning example is the filming of Claudius's reaction to Hamlet's murder of Polonius. In one continuous shot, Claudius learns of the murder from Gertrude, leaves his room and crosses to hers, kneels by the pool of blood where Polonius tumbled to the floor, rises, returns to the hall to send Rosencrantz and Guildenstern to seek Hamlet, and returns to his rooms to comfort his dazed wife. All of this action and movement is achieved in the process of shooting two pages of dialogue (forty-six lines of the filmscript) without a single cut. The camera tracks and circles in a manner reminiscent of its treatment of Hamlet, revealing both the director's confidence in Jacobi's abilities and his association of them with his own.

Because Branagh's film avoids making explicit the oedipal subtext of Hamlet's relationship with Gertrude, it may appear to have placed itself closer to Kozintsev's study of the play's public politics than to Olivier's and Zeffirelli's explorations of *Hamlet*'s psychoanalytic family romance. Such a reading fails to see the way in which Branagh's film, by focusing on the struggles between fathers and sons, manages to merge the psychological with the political.[30] Branagh's visual insistence on the ghost's centrality to Hamlet's tragic dilemma echoes Barber and Wheeler's understanding of the way in which Hamlet's inability to bury his father and move beyond him into his own mature personal and political identity is at the core of his psychological and social struggle:

> *Hamlet* dramatizes a crisis centered on identification with the murdered, heroic father who returns to demand that the son vindicate his heritage. Everything hinges on the protagonist's struggle to inherit, his effort to identify himself totally with his father's command. But identification with the father, instead of leading Hamlet out into the vengeful action to which he dedicates himself, blocks his purpose. In *Hamlet* Shakespeare sets up the problem of the transmission of heritage in a radically disruptive way, in a way that blocks its own full expression, so that the play exemplifies the crisis it sets out to dramatize.[31]

Branagh also understands Hamlet's psychological dilemma, caught as he is not just between heaven and earth but between two fathers, both "alive" in troubling, destabilizing ways. His desire to identify with the ghost and his command is blocked by his subconscious identification with the other father whom he has been asked to murder.

As I indicated earlier, Branagh not only fashions his Hamlet to share a startling physical resemblance to Claudius, he repeatedly links or twins them through the use of the mirrored doors in the "To be or not to be" scene, the way in which they are similarly treated by the camera, and in

Claudius's attempt at repentance ("O, my offense is rank, it smells to heaven"). Branagh shoots this moment with Claudius seated in his chapel's confessional, with Branagh's Hamlet slipping in on the other side of the screen to play scourge and minister. These two scenes link Hamlet and Claudius at their most vulnerable and reflective moments. Branagh's film makes manifest Hamlet's oedipal identification with Claudius. As Barber and Wheeler argue:

> Hamlet cannot kill a ghost. Nor can he realize that the destructive force of his effort to serve the Ghost, to retrieve the heritage of his lost father, has its roots in the filial bond he struggles to keep intact by making it the entirety of his life. The given situation, Claudius' murder of the elder Hamlet, demands absolute loyalty to the memory of the idealized father and permits the diversion of the son's murderous wish from father to uncle. But since this repressed wish is unconsciously tied to the assumption that its enactment means death, Hamlet's hatred cannot be directed at Claudius without being deflected back onto himself as well.[32]

Branagh's Hamlet is trapped between a demonic ghost and a super-subtle stepfather. The ghost is the terrifying father, Claudius the puzzling one. As I have indicated, Branagh's film repeatedly twins and mirrors Jacobi's Claudius with Branagh's Hamlet. Jacobi's polite, proper Claudius denies Branagh's Hamlet the opposition he would like to make between his own "spiritual manners" and Claudius's "ostentatious, crass, and overbearing" behavior.[33] Jacobi's Claudius repeatedly gives Hamlet reflection, not difference. Following Barber and Wheeler, Hamlet's hatred of Claudius is repeatedly deflected back into himself, and internalized. Branagh's Hamlet is distinguished not just by his good manners and clever wit but by a biting anger at himself that, in Branagh's take on the character, never gets released at its true objects—the father who won't stay dead and the stepfather who refuses to carouse—but only at their substitutes, Ophelia and Gertrude.

Branagh, instinctively, captures the ways in which contemporary critics as diverse as Harold Bloom and Marjorie Garber see the psychoanalytic traces of ghostly fathers at work in Hamlet's personal and social history. Branagh, through his conceptions of Ghost and Claudius, reveals his own creative struggle with the anxiety of influence as he engages them not only as actor but as artist. Blessed, as Branagh's youthful stab at autobiography reveals, is the brassy, imposing friend urging him to risk all by taking on the establishment—doing so by appropriating roles (actor, director, Henry V, Hamlet) definitively inscribed by others (primarily, Olivier).[34] Jacobi, on the other hand, represents that establishment itself: a product of Olivier's legacy as a member of the first company Olivier created at the founding of the National Theatre in 1961, he was the most famous Hamlet of his generation—the one Branagh remembers being thrilled by when he was seventeen; Jacobi also directed Branagh's stage *Hamlet* for his Renaissance Theatre Company in 1988. Branagh's *Hamlet* and his Hamlet embody these crosscurrents of cultural and personal forces that are not formally released and resolved until his Hamlet sends his rapier whizzing through Jacobi and Fortinbras comes crashing into Elsinore, smashing its mirrors and toppling its icons.

Branagh, like all artists, destroys even as he creates, and all the rush and energy of his career has come to a shattering head in his film of *Hamlet*. Burnett, the first critic to claim auteur status for Branagh, reads the film's politics and especially its final images in a similar fashion: "At the close, the imposing statue of Hamlet Senior is toppled to the ground, and any spectator attuned to the collapse of the communist countries in the 1990s will not miss the parallel. Branagh's *Hamlet* is an eloquent disquisition on the perils of aristocratic and royal authority; it is also a 'cunning' celebration of the plebeian forces that contest the ownership of power and privilege."[35] The destruction wrought by Hamlet and Fortinbras at the film's climax reveals Branagh exploding those powerful ghosts in the tradition of filmed Shakespeare, even as he echoes their achievements. That image of the fall of old Hamlet also reminds us that this extraordinary decade of Shakespeare films owes much to its historical moment. As the end of World War II led to the explosion of cultural festivals across continental Europe and England, often featuring—as in Avignon and Verona—productions of Shakespeare, so the end of the cold war has contributed to the commercial film's embrace of Shakespeare as material for an international audience. Only in this context, largely created by Branagh's artistic and commercial successes with his films of *Henry V* and *Much Ado About Nothing*, could a project as audacious as a four-hour, full-text, epic film of *Hamlet* have been contemplated and achieved.

Bankside Shakespeare

Edzard's As You Like It *and* The Children's Midsummer Night's Dream

In charting Shakespeare's translation into film, I have loosely used the symbolic landscapes of Stratford and Hollywood to suggest the continuing tension between these two powerful centers of Shakespearean activity in the last decade. In doing so, I have ignored potential sites of resistance to these two dominant institutions. For example, Michael Almereyda's *Hamlet*, completely shot on location in Manhattan, is a film that champions its "otherness" from either Stratford (it has an American cast, most with little or no experience of performing Shakespeare on stage) or Hollywood (the film takes the outcast Orson Welles as its model, rather than Branagh or Zeffirelli). It must be conceded that Almereyda's film, partially financed and distributed by Miramax, became the surprise art-house Shakespeare "hit" in 1999/2000, more than recuperating its production costs and making a name for its young director in Hollywood.

The filmmaker most removed from the Stratford-Hollywood axis is Christine Edzard, whose tiny Sands Films Studio, paradoxically, is located in two restored warehouses along the banks of London's River Thames, in Rotherhithe, less than three miles downriver from the site of Shakespeare's Globe. Her two Shakespeare Films, *As You Like It* (1992) and *The Children's Midsummer Night's Dream* (2001), are the most iconoclastic and radical films to emerge in the decade. Their subversiveness is all the more interesting for being expressed with a sweet but serious conviction. Edzard's films don't shout or show off or insist on sticking Shakespeare in your face, but both emerge from a deep commitment, something akin to Lilian Baylis's, her former fellow resident of the South Bank, that Shakespeare, like Dickens, is both a populist and a moralist.

Edzard was born in Paris, of German-Polish parents, both of whom were artists. She migrated to London via Rome, where she worked on Zeffirelli's film of *Romeo and Juliet*. In 1975 she and her husband, the film producer Richard Goodwin, restored two abandoned Rotherhithe warehouses and transformed them into the Sands Films Studio, where over the past twenty-five years she has made and directed six films, most prominently a four-hour version of Charles Dickens's *Little Dorrit* (1987). Her next venture was a further exploration of Victorian London, *The Fool* (1989), based on the works of Henry Mayhew, particularly *The London Rich and the London Poor*. Dickens and Mayhew readily lent themselves to the social critique Edzard wanted to explore. After all, George Bernard Shaw had rated *Little Dorrit* more seditious than *Das Kapital*.

From Dickens and Victorian London, Edzard then made a surprising shift to the world of Shakespeare's festive comedies. When I asked her about the links between the two authors, she replied, with a smile: "For someone who grew up in Paris there were only two English authors: Shakespeare and Dickens."[1] Her Victorian films had been noted for their painstaking attention to historical detail, especially in the period costumes, which all had been made by the studio's costume department. When she came to make her film of *As You Like It* (1992), she abandoned any attempt at historical representation and set the play in contemporary London. Edzard noted the problem of dealing effectively with the distance of Shakespeare's age from ours (an issue noted by most modern stage directors of the plays as well): "In the case of Dickens, the truth of the character is in the nineteenth century, and the truth does not materialize until you start putting in all the detail. The issue with *As You Like It* is completely different. First of all, I don't believe you can reach the sixteenth century in that sort of way. It's too remote: it would become an archaeological dig."[2] Of course, what Edzard says about Dickens is what Greenblatt would say about Shakespeare, but she understands that a modern English audience still has an access to Dickens's London and its social stratifications that is not readily available to it for Elizabethan London.

Edzard takes a bold approach to *As You Like It*, seizing upon those idealistic strains in Shakespeare's pastoral romance to fashion a Dickensian social critique of Mrs. Thatcher's London. Edzard is noted, in her Dickens and Mayhew films, for the design miracles she and her production crew wrought in transforming their tiny studio into a version of Victorian London. For her *As You Like It*, she cleverly uses several sets of French doors and windows, a wall of mirrors, several massive stone columns, and a revolving door to create an urban court world that is gaudy, shallow, and transparent, glimpsed often only in reflected flashes. Her Arden is an urban pastoral—an abandoned Rotherhithe construction site that becomes a precious open space not yet enveloped by Mrs. Thatcher's Docklands high-rises, which loom in the background in many of Edzard's shots. Amelia Marriette is quick to perceive several parallels between Edzard's film evocation of Dickens's London and Mrs. Thatcher's metropolis: "Both highlight the city as metaphor; both consider the complexities of viewing circumstances from double perspectives; and both center upon observing societies at work."[3]

Doors and mirrors, the liminal and the reflected, are the design keys to Edzard's approach to Shakespeare's text. She uses James Fox's gentle and persuasive Jaques as a narrator and guide to the court world, as well as to Arden, by opening her film with Fox delivering the "Seven Ages of Man" speech as he moves through the court landscape. Her camera captures him through windows, in reflection, and pausing in doorways to underline Jaques's ambiguous relationship to the society he both shuns and seeks, embodies and critiques. Edzard's *As You Like It* shares with many recent Shakespeare films an opening that announces its intentions to reshape Shakespeare's text into a screenplay that recognizes the film imperative—that it must find a way to express Shakespeare's words and images through its own language. The one constant that runs through these recent films, from Branagh and Luhrmann to Almereyda and Taymor, is the shared necessity to create an opening that invites the viewer into the Shakespearean material through the language of film.

Though formalist criticism taught us well that Jaques's famous set speech, like Polonius's advice to Laertes, is not the "World According to Shakespeare" but the cynical commentary of a melancholy libertine, Edzard understands that it is the one element in *As You Like It* that reaches out beyond the text into the general cultural consciousness. Her opening gambit is to present us with the doubly familiar Fox and the Ages of Man speech to lull and lure us into the more radical landscape that follows. I think she also wants to underline the words of Jaques's dismissive view of man to prepare us for the unexpectedly contemporary social critique that her film uses the play to explore and reveal. Edzard confessed to me that she now has reservations about her decision to foreground the "Seven Ages" speech: "In hindsight, I'm not sure I don't regret putting the 'Seven Ages of Man' speech in the beginning. It felt like a very nice introduction when I was thinking of doing it, but then you must have it again when it appears in its natural place in the play, and I'm not sure that was a good idea—doing it twice like that."[4]

Mirrors, reflections, and doublings are all essential to her project. This is revealed in her casting decisions, where Shakespeare's court/ country, good Duke/bad Duke, good brother/bad brother contrasts are captured by a series of effective doublings: Andrew Tiernan plays Orlando and Oliver; Don Henderson plays Duke Senior and Duke Frederick; and Roger Hammond, in two wonderfully nuanced performances, appears as both LeBeau and Corin. Emma Croft's Rosalind arrives in Arden wearing jeans, hooded sweatjacket, and watch cap—an outfit that exactly mirrors Orlando's scruffy attire. When Fox gives the reprise of the Ages of Man speech, now in its original context, with the exiled court and urban dispossessed huddled about an oil-drum brazier, the effect humanizes both Jaques and his reading of the human condition.[5]

The mirror theme is picked up visually in the ways in which Edzard contrasts court and country. Although Edzard badly fudges the wrestling match between Orlando and Charles, it is because she is more interested in the lavish party for which the contest serves as the climactic entertainment. Edzard's camera will not let us forget that this is a world of overabundance. She lingers over a buffet table groaning with rich treats. She underlines the Sloane Ranger-esque qualities of Croft's Rosalind by repeatedly shooting her insipidly licking a huge chocolate eclair (this is before Rosalind's imagination is galvanized by her love for Orlando and her banishment from Duke Frederick's court). By contrast, the exiles in Arden, rather than feasting on the local venison, are seen sharing packaged food rescued from a grocery store's garbage bin. The glittering mirrors of the court are contrasted with the sheets of polyurethane that help cover the cardboard huts that the homeless share with the exiles. Everyone at court, most notably Celia and her father, smokes elegant cigarettes; in Arden, it's roll-your-own joints.

The superfluity of the court world is further highlighted in the scene where Celia and Rosalind determine to flee to "liberty and not to banishment." Edzard shoots their exchange in Celia's enormous clothes closet—one rivaling Jay Gatsby's. The women seem momentarily paralyzed about what to pack: matching outfits of brightly colored hats, dresses, and shoes bulge from its racks and shelves. The idea of disguise comes as their first imaginative act of liberation from the materiality that has surrounded and defined them, though Celia Bannerman's pert, older Celia never abandons, even in Arden, a smashing hat. The relationship between Celia and Rosalind here is played more as aunt and niece than as cousin contemporaries. Edzard cast the young Croft right out of drama school, seeking youth and a fresh face rather than the established comedienne or romantic heroine we are accustomed to seeing as Rosalind (Maggie Smith and Gwyneth Paltrow span the normal range of casting choices). H. R. Coursen finds the combination of Edzard's choice and Croft's performance a winning one;[6] for me, its youth and vitality are attractive, but I miss the rich humor a more experienced actress often finds in the part (Juliet Stevenson's Rosalind for the RSC in 1985 springs immediately to mind). Edzard's casting decision was dictated by her medium: the camera would mercilessly expose the aging ingenue (as it does Elisabeth Bergner in Paul Czinner's 1935 film of the play). Edzard is more interested in Rosalind's spunk and dare than she is in her witty self-consciousness. And Croft's scenes in Arden with Tiernan's mop-haired Orlando have the genuine quality of two kids exploring and deflecting their first serious encounters with romantic emotions. In these scenes, the film reminded me more of such contemporary films as *Sammy and Rosie Get Laid, Trainspotting,* and *My Own Private Idaho* than of previous films of a Shakespearean comedy. These counterculture films explore with a Shakespearean vitality private worlds of hope and possibility created by the young surviving on the edges of the detritus of modern urban culture.

Croft's Rosalind is a work-in-progress; her tomboy, Orlando-inspired disguise liberates her from the social limitations placed on her gender. Rather than being offended by the gritty reality of the film's Arden, she discovers there a space to move in: a landscape of play. Croft's Rosalind, in the first great wooing scene, is repeatedly captured in a series of long-shots, skipping and dancing in delight about her confused but amused lover as she revels in the magnificently colorful graffiti Orlando has spray-painted in her honor on the building site's fence. She tosses out her knowing teases about women and wooing with the same natural ease with which she matches Orlando in lobbing stones off into empty space.

Clearly Edzard knows that her Arden is the most radical element in her film. Coursen has a point when he complains that by placing "the Forest of Arden in the London docks" her film "can't see the trees for the concrete."[7] But Edzard is hoping that, as the pastoral was a literary

metaphor for Shakespeare, we will see her Arden as a spatial metaphor—
a symbolic landscape of the imagination, not some slice of the Warwickshire countryside. In fact, I think her Arden works least well when she
jokingly tries to have it both ways—for example, having Corin lead a
sheep about on a leash (why not give him a Border collie as a companion,
which would make the joke without introducing the incongruity of a
sheep?) and transplanting several overgrown bushes into her urban
wasteland so that she can shoot some of Ganymede's and Orlando's exchanges against a more fertile background. Edzard is on better footing
when she translates Shakespeare's snake and hungry lioness about to attack the sleeping Oliver into urban muggers whom Orlando puts to
flight.

Marriette makes a bold attempt to link Edzard's use of *As You Like It*
to provide a social critique of Thatcher's London with "other modern and
dystopian films, such as Ridley Scott's *Blade Runner* (1982), Terry
Gilliam's *Brazil* (1985) and, especially, Oliver Stone's *Wall Street* (1987)."[8]
But the analogy, particularly with *Wall Street*, will not hold: it places too
great a strain on Shakespeare's use of the pastoral convention and denies
the huge cinematic stylistic gulf between Edzard's evocation of Docklands London and Stone's representation of lower Manhattan. As
Michael Hattaway rightly perceives, one of the film's visual failures is its
"strident over-determination of the setting."[9] What Edzard's film and
Marriette's analysis fail to convey is that in *As You Like It*, Shakespeare is
not only indulging the release of the festive imagination through the pastoral conceit, he is also providing, in the figures of Jaques and Touchstone, a counterbalancing critique of the sentimentality associated with
the convention. A stunning example of the film's misappropriation of
Shakespeare's tale is in its uncritical treatment of Jaques's "Seven Ages of
Man" speech. Shakespeare's stagecraft exposes Jaques's easy cynicism by
having Orlando enter with Old Adam in his arms after Jaques has just dismissed man's final age as "sans everything." Adam is a vibrant representative of seniority's loyalty, commitment, and wisdom, which totally escapes
Jaques's worldly posturing.

Fox's gentle performance, even when misjudged, is one of the film's
strengths, and Edzard, revealingly, has Fox's Jaques clearly taken with
Croft's Ganymede. To underline their relationship, Edzard's screenplay
reverses the narrative in act 4, scene 1 so that the Ganymede-Jaques exchange *follows*, rather than precedes, her mock wedding to Orlando. Thus
her dismissal of his ingrained melancholy is given an added poignance.

Edzard shoots Fox in handsome profile against a gold-red setting sun, as he gently tips his hat to this mysterious youth sitting on a wall, framed by a rich, blue sky. Past and future, age and youth, experience and innocence, ennui and vitality are neatly captured here. Edzard reminds us of these contrasts at the end of her film when she cuts from the multiple weddings to a shot of Jaques moving off, once again alone, along the Rotherhithe embankment.

The Jaques-Ganymede subtext was heightened by the playing of Orlando's relationship with this "pretty youth." Tiernan's Orlando repeatedly registered his own inner amazement at his willingness to play along with Ganymede's project. Because his Orlando was presented in the mode of modern youthful alienation, rather than as the heroic outcast of romance tradition, he was naturally more skeptical of Ganymede's advances. He joined the game almost in spite of himself. His conflicted responses to Croft's aggressive tomboy came to a climax in the mock wedding scene—the moment in the text when Rosalind is at her most audacious and subversive in usurping the civil and religious powers of the patriarchy. She picks her mate, comes unescorted to the altar, creates her own wedding text, and has the ceremony performed by a woman.

Edzard, however, is less interested in these social and political issues than she is in the gender complications of the moment, particularly their impact on Orlando. The scene begins in the construction site shrouded in fog and then moves into Orlando's plastic-draped cardboard hut for the mock ceremony itself. Croft's Ganymede gives Orlando an impulsive kiss when he says "I do," and the film pauses to measure his reaction. Here Edzard is exploring Valerie Traub and Stephen Orgel territory in a fashion similar to Trevor Nunn's handling of the Orsino/Cesario relationship as Feste is singing "Come Away, Death." Coursen astutely comments that Croft's "androgynous Ganymede" insists "that Orlando go through a homoerotic emotional experience—loving the male in Rosalind—before he can love the woman."[10] Coursen is right about this moment, though I think that by lingering on Orlando's response to the kiss—in which Tiernan repeats, in a flash, the pattern of his Orlando (skepticism, followed by acceptance)—it is Edzard, more than Croft, who is ultimately manipulating the stages of Orlando's emotional growth through and beyond gender.

The film never lets us forget that Rosalind and Orlando are kids. Here they are more closely associated, in body language and cultural style, with Valerie Gogan's Phebe and Ewen Bremner's Silvius than other film or stage productions of *As You Like It* that I have seen. This foursome might just as likely pop up in *Trainspotting* as in Arden. Gogan and Bremer perform something of a miracle in transforming Shakespeare's pastoral lovers, more literary conceit than flesh-and-blood creatures, into recognizable members of the current generation. My students recognize them in a flash.

The film's greatest failure is its inability to find a contemporary equivalent for the Touchstone and Audrey humor. Both Miriam Margolyes (Audrey) and Griff Rhys Jones (Touchstone) are fatally miscast.[11] Jones fails to locate a modern form of clowning to fit his character and relies rather exclusively on facial mugging to suggest that what he is saying about "the mustard and the pancakes" or the virtues of "If" is funny. Branagh's choices of the American comedians Michael Keaton, Billy Crystal, and Nathan Lane to play Dogberry, Gravedigger, and Costard looks inspired compared with Jones's floundering. The burlesque humor of Touchstone's bawdy relationship with Audrey is not capitalized upon because Margolyes (wonderful in Edzard's *Little Dorrit*, Martin Scorsese's *Age of Innocence*, and Baz Luhrmann's *Romeo + Juliet*) cannot be imagined as an object of Touchstone's lust.

Edzard's filmic imagination cannot find a place for Shakespeare's mocking humor in her landscape of the socially displaced and romantically alienated. Shakespeare, through Jaques and Touchstone, provides voices who, in their differing fashions, present a critique of Arden as a social and romantic paradise—a place where "men fleet the time carelessly as in the golden world."[12] Where Shakespeare displays a light-hearted ability to send up some of the very things he clearly cherishes, Edzard is more serious and dogged. Russell Jackson provides a tough-minded appraisal of the ways in which Edzard's ideology keeps concealing rather than revealing Shakespeare's: "The play's mixture of pastoral vagueness and social precision is lost, to be replaced with modern pieties rather than analysis and argument. Money-dealers are bad, destitution is a blight, so we should throw into neglect the pompous court. What occupation can Corin and Touchstone have in this landscape?"[13]

Edzard's film takes interesting chances with Shakespeare's text. For me and my students, it has proved a more interesting work to debate than to enjoy. Its virtues have emerged as it takes its place in the context of the recent proliferation of Shakespeare films precisely because it was never headed to the cineplex. It says no to Hollywood and Shakespeare's potential commercial appeal as strongly as it says no to Mrs. Thatcher's London.[14]

Almost ten years later, on the eve of Midsummer Day 2001, Edzard released her second Shakespeare film, *The Children's Midsummer Night's Dream*. Even though her *As You Like It* did not impede the continuing development of the Docklands project and the increasing gentrification of her Rotherhithe neighborhood, her own commitment to Shakespeare as a force for social cohesion had not waned. In 1998, Sands Films began a collaboration with the local Southwark Education Authority to produce a film of *A Midsummer Night's Dream* using, as cast and crew, students, ages eight to twelve, from a variety of racial and ethnic backgrounds, from eight nearby primary schools. Shooting began in January 2000 and lasted for six months, followed by four months of postproduction work. For the students, the film was their first introduction to Shakespeare. "Some of them couldn't even read," remarked Edzard.[15] Except for two sequences—when Hermia and Lysander discuss their plans to elope with Helena and when the lovers awake from their dream, which were filmed in the garden of the church next door—the entire film was shot in the Sands Films Studio, in a space measuring less than fifty by twenty-five feet.

If, as I will argue in the next chapter, Adrian Noble's film of *Dream* wanted to infuse the play with a child's sense of wonder, play, and curiosity about the adult world, Edzard's takes the further step of literally embodying Shakespeare's fantasy in the voices and bodies of children. It takes as its cue Helena's painful reflections on the relationship between the inconstancies of love and puberty:

> And therefore is Love said to be a child,
> Because in choice he is so oft beguil'd.
> As waggish boys in game themselves forswear,
> So the boy love is perjur'd every where.
>
> (1.1.238–41)

At its best, the film's use of children to body forth the forms of things unknown has something of the flavor of a cross between Michael Apted's *7* and *14 Up* films and *The Little Rascals*.[16]

The film's structure has an ingenious premise that allows Edzard to merge and mingle the play's metatheatrical dimensions with her own metacinematic interests. The film begins in a lovely reconstruction of a seventeenth-century puppet theater that might have been designed by Inigo Jones. It is a simple, neoclassical rectangle with a second level running around three sides and stairs leading up to the balcony in each corner. Several elaborate candle chandeliers are suspended from a beautiful ceiling that is largely constructed from painted glass panels. The film begins in the theater: a group of schoolchildren, the audience, are sitting on benches or perched in the balcony overlooking the scene, watching a scaled-down, puppet version of the play. Derek Jacobi's and Samantha Bond's distinctive voices are heard speaking Theseus's and Hippolyta's lines. The camera is as interested in the audience as in the puppets, cutting back and forth between them but lingering on the faces of the kids, some of whom are transfixed, others bored; some are restless, others share whispers. It is a typical audience of the young experiencing a dose of culture.

As the first scene builds, a girl suddenly rises from her bench in the audience and begins to recite a portion of Hermia's challenge to her father: "I would my father looked with my eyes." For the next fifty lines or so, the play shifts back and forth between the audience and the stage, as first a Demetrius and then a Lysander join with the still-standing Hermia to wrest control of the play away from the puppets. It is particularly apt that the child speaking as Hermia is the first to rise and speak, because it is Hermia's resistance to the patriarchal order that provides the play with its organizing energy, and Hermia, when all the lovers' vulnerabilities are exposed in the woods, is the one who is most self-conscious about her stature and wounded about being regarded as a "puppet." Hermia challenges her father's control over her and then comically (but painfully) suffers her loss of control over the affections of Lysander, Demetrius, and even Helena.

By the moment of Theseus's exit with Hippolyta, Egeus, and Demetrius, the play has been claimed by the audience. With the theater empty, Edzard cuts to Lysander and Hermia, still in their school clothes, framed in an open window lamenting true love's rocky road and planning their flight to the woods. Helena appears on the path below, and a quick cut soon has the trio discussing their fates in the garden. This location shot (repeated when the lovers awake) serves as a transitional space between the artifice of both theater and woods. This brief scene of three of the four lovers together does, however, help to capture some of the realities of puberty beyond the reach of mature actresses. The girls are ahead of the boys, both physically and mentally. They are taller and more self-possessed, though not yet fully at home in their bodies. Helena, especially, exhibits a wonderfully gawky body language, whether standing with her right knee bent nervously back against her left thigh or sprawled out on her bed clutching a stuffed toy animal as she gazes at a photo of Demetrius. Her pangs of rejection are so powerful that she can't resist phoning him to "tell him of fair Hermia's flight."

The same physical relationship holds between Titania and Oberon; she is taller than he, but this Oberon, though small of stature, has such a serious command that he and Titania seem well matched. They are the film's (and the play's) exotics, and here they are played by an Anglo-Indian girl and an Anglo-African lad. Puck, costumed as something of an Irish folk figure, seemed out of place to me, not quite belonging to either the fairy world or the mortal realm. The girl who played Puck gave him a wistful, melancholy expression, perhaps suggesting Puck's role as the intermediary between the fairies and the mortals. Perhaps, too, Edzard meant to glance at Puck's English origins somehow transported and out of place in an Ovidian, Mediterranean fantasy land.

To present Bottom and company, the film cuts from Helena's bedroom back to the now-deserted theater. The boys playing Peter Quince and Bottom are among the most animated in the cast. Quince, particularly, seems to have a real relish for the sport. When Bottom, near the end of the scene, fluffed a line, he momentarily broke into a big grin before recovering and moving on with the speech. I felt the film could have profited from retaining more of such moments. With one or two exceptions, the cast approached the speaking of their parts with such seriousness that some of the spontaneity, the play, the magic of the undertaking was threatened. Unlike the Children of the Chapel, those "little eyases" that Shakespeare grumbles about in *Hamlet*, Edzard's schoolchildren had no previous dramatic experience—only the brief training she could provide for them before shooting began. Under the circumstances, their achievement is considerable, but what the film misses, again with isolated exceptions, is the experience of watching a child be captured and absorbed by what he or she is saying. Mickey Rooney, for instance, was little older than these children when, at fourteen, he played Puck in the Reinhardt/Dieterle *Dream* in 1935. He was, of course, a professional child-actor by that time, but the crazy energy he brought to Puck is missing from most of the performances in Edzard's film.

As I suggested earlier, much of the film's magic is provided by Edzard and her director of photography, Joachim Bergamin. As Quince distributes the parts and makes his rehearsal plans, the camera occasionally cuts away to a scrim, painted with a forest scene, on the puppet stage. On the last of such cuts, we are made aware of a figure lurking behind the skrim, which turns out, appropriately, to be Puck. When the mechanicals exit, we notice that some of the supports for the theater's balcony have become wreathed in green vines sprouting white and yellow blossoms. Gradually the theater is taken over by the forest, and we hear the giggles of the fairies (echoing the giggles of the school audience at the film's beginning) and the sounds of the Fairy Band (all film *Dreams*, except Noble's, find the idea of a fairy band irresistible) playing ancient horns, recorders, and lutes as the film completes its journey into the woods.

The fairies are costumed in Elizabethan dress and equipped with little lanterns made from the glass teardrops (dewdrops?) of a chandelier. Oberon and Titania are extravagantly dressed in elaborate costumes of lavender and deep purple, studded with natural elements. Oberon's, in particular, is a thing of beauty—leaves sewn on his doublet, acorns for buttons, and the dried stamens of flowers sprouting from his crown. Both are stunningly presented as "creatures of a rarer sort." Titania has a willowy beauty, Oberon a serious intensity. Titania, however, keeps tripping over the verse's rhythms, looking for pauses in all the wrong places, while Oberon has a remarkable command for a child. Even his problem with the "*th*" sound, transforming "vile thing" into "vile fing," for instance, he manages to make charming, rather than grating. As Edzard had a host of children eager to participate in the project, she is able to fill her forest with fairy spirits. And because these kids are free to enjoy themselves without the pressure of having lines to memorize and recite, they often appear to be having the most fun, and they help establish the quirky, prankish nature of Shakespeare's woods, where how easily is a "bush supposed a bear."

When the lovers begin to tumble into this environment, they, too, have entered into the dream. No longer dressed in their school clothes—coats and ties, sweaters and slacks or skirts—they arrive decked out in the handsome red-and-green velvet outfits of the landed gentry. Lysander and Demetrius sport broad-brimmed hats with lots of long feathers (to my eye, they seemed more Cavalier than Elizabethan). Helena is particularly striking in her tailored outfit that is topped by an elegant green-and-red pillbox hat, worn at a jaunty angle. The mechanicals are similarly transformed. The floppy straw hat that Bottom had brought with him, perhaps as a prop, in act 1, scene 2 now sits on his head festooned with several pheasant feathers, anticipating his further transformation into the animal world by Puck.

Edzard's forest is more enchanting garden than frightening wood.

Picking up on elements in the text, it features a fountain, brook, and pond. The pond is used on several occasions to reflect a golden crescent moon, heralding, I take it, the old moon's waning. The forest floor is strewn with flowers, primarily in yellows and purples. The fairies, holding their lamps and surrounded by flowers, kept reminding me of John Singer Sargent's great painting "Carnation, Lily, Lily, Rose," even though Sargent's garden scene took place three hundred years later. In keeping with the spirit of her benevolent woods, Edzard does not inflict on her pair of lovers anything like the indignities experienced by the lovers in Michael Hoffman's recent film of the play, where they all end up in a muddy pond, or in Peter Hall's famous film version, shot on location in Warwickshire in the cold, wet September of 1967. The agonies of puberty, especially the sexual fears of possession and rejection experienced by Hermia, and the sadomasochism that underlies Helena's worship of Demetrius, are largely lost in the playing of the roles here by Edzard's youngsters. The one moment when the forest confusion comes most alive is in Helena's great speech about her schoolgirl friendship with Hermia. Daringly, Edzard has Helena produce a photo of the two in their present-day school outfits, their two heads inclined together as in those photos that school kids love to take, crammed into an instant-photo booth. There is the real comprehension of sisterly betrayal in Helena's delivery of these lines about the double-parted cherry, and Hermia responds with confused indignity. The scene reaches its climax here on Helena's withering delivery of "She was a vixen when she went to school."

After decades of *Dreams*, including the recent films by Noble and Hoffman, where the director cannot resist adopting Jan Kott's fierce, bestial reading of Titania's encounter with Bottom, the innocence of Edzard's treatment of their relationship became an ounce of civet to sweeten the imagination. This was child's play, rather than the imposition of a coarser, adult understanding on their entanglement. Titania, perhaps echoing Hermia, even lies "further off," rather than snuggling up to her gentle beast.

The move from night to day, from dream to wake, from woods to world was not as smoothly handled as the film's initial transition into the forest. Edzard had the problem of getting Theseus and Hippolyta from their stage incarnations into the woods to awaken the lovers. She accomplished this by cutting much of Theseus's long evocation of those Spartan hounds and by keeping her camera fixed on the awakening lovers while Theseus's lines were delivered off-camera. This also meant that the lovers had to be reabsorbed into the puppet world for the film's version of act 5. Bottom's awakening, and his dream analysis, take place, appropriately, in the empty theater. Edzard had the rest of the mechanicals bemoaning the loss of their leader and sixpence-a-day while knocking about in the costume-and-prop shop that appeared to be located underneath the stage.[17] Edzard cross-cuts between Bottom and the lovers to reinforce the way each hits upon the key term *dream* as a means of capturing and understanding the tricks of strong imagination.

Bottom's determination to "make a ballad of this dream," to turn his fantastic experience into art as a means of sharing it with others, completes the film's transition back into the world of the theater. Now, however, we have two playing spaces: the conventional proscenium stage dominated by the puppets and the floor of the auditorium, now cleared of its benches—like the democratic impulse behind the British proms at Covent Garden and the Albert Hall, where all the orchestra seats are removed to create a standing yard as in the Globe—to make room for "Pyramus and Thisby." The audience, too, has been reconfigured: it now surrounds the action on four sides. Those who are seated on benches in front of the stage are repeatedly (and amusingly) caught by Edzard's camera turning to shush the play's puppets when they interrupt the action of "Pyramus and Thisby" with their own attempts to embarrass the actors or offer lame witticism at the expense of the play. This playful moment reveals, on several levels, the film's proletarian, communal longings. Edzard's audience of schoolchildren has sided with its amateur colleagues against the professional puppets; they have become absorbed by the workingman's (the workingkid's!) version of the dramatic experience; they instinctively reject aristocratic attempts to show superiority to the rude mechanicals' efforts; and they enjoy turning the tables on the customary experience of the school "culture" outing in which it is the adults (their teachers) who impose the shush of silence on their giggles, whispers, and interjections.

Edzard is aware that Shakespeare's *Dream* provides rich material for her experiment: it isn't just child-friendly—it is child-inspired. The text abounds in references to children: winged Cupid painted blind; schoolgirls; waggish boys; and the little changeling boy. Love, imagination, and the creative spirit are all linked with that prelapsarian state we associate with childhood. Dreams are the adult's pipeline back to innocence and delight. So, as Bottom instinctively understands, is art. But there is a problem: *A Midsummer Night's Dream* depends, for its magic to work, on both states of consciousness: both that of child and adult. Bottom's beauty is not that he is a child but that he is a wonderfully childish adult. By literally making him a child, an important part of the play's charm is lost: something essential has been removed from the equation that makes the play so remarkable. A similar point can be made about the lovers: their confusions *are* childish, but our experience of the comedy of their pain depends precisely on their being not children, but young adults.

To acknowledge what, in our experience of the play, gets lost in Edzard's film is not meant to diminish the innocence and charm of her achievement. There's a bit of Dr. Johnson's (politically incorrect) analogy between a woman preaching and a dog walking on its hind legs at work here: we should quibble less about whether Edzard's schoolchildren can fully inhabit Shakespeare's text and admire more the simple fact that they can do it at all. One can tell that all her actors are working hard to deliver the language, and if that often impedes their ability to enact and embody it as well, that is the price her brave experiment willingly pays. Edzard's film is cleverly structured, handsomely costumed, sweetly scored, and often a delight to hear.

Edzard's *As You Like It* and *The Children's Midsummer Night's Dream* are unique in this generation of Shakespeare films. They are the work of a fiercely independent filmmaker whose Sands Films Studio is as far removed from Hollywood (or even Shepperton) as is aesthetically and financially possible. Edzard is less interested in popularizing Shakespeare for the world of mass entertainment than in using his art to make, or make a statement about, community. Her artistic impulses are social, rather than commercial, which explains why the common thread that runs through her work from *The Tales of Beatrix Potter* to her first films based on several stories by Hans Christian Andersen, from her Dickens's *Little Dorrit* to her Shakespeare films, is their interest in the child. Building community begins with the young, and Edzard has begun on the ground floor. In her iconoclastic, contemporary-Bankside way, she is keeping alive an important aspect of Shakespeare's art on film.

Shakespeare and Hollywood Revisited

The Dream*s of Noble and Hoffman*

I f Christine Edzard's Shakespeare films seem oblivious to the historical tension between Stratford and Hollywood in the genre's long history, two other recent films of *A Midsummer Night's Dream* illustrate it quite revealingly. Adrian Noble has been the director of the Royal Shakespeare Company for more than decade. Like his distinguished predecessors Peter Hall and Trevor Nunn, he has fashioned a unique style, which many critics have called cinematic, of producing Shakespeare on stage. His film of *A Midsummer Night's Dream* (1996) was, however, his first venture into the newer medium. Michael Hoffman, on the other hand, is something of a Hollywood veteran, having directed eight films—including *Soap Dish* (1991), *Restoration* (1996), and *One Fine Day* (1996)—and having worked with such major Hollywood actors as Sally Field, Kevin Kline, George Clooney, Robert Downey Jr., and Michelle Pfeiffer. If Noble was a Shakespeare veteran but a film novice, Hoffman was his mirror opposite. Their two films exhibited both the continuing strain and the new rapprochement between Stratford and Hollywood in the Shakespeare films released in the long decade.

Noble's film emanated from the Royal Shakespeare Company, the home of institutional, repertory Shakespeare, located in Stratford-upon-Avon, the capital of Bardworks. He was following in a tradition begun by Hall and Peter Brook, who respectively each transformed successful RSC stage productions of *A Midsummer Night's Dream* (1968) and *King Lear* (shot in 1969; released in 1971) into what seemed then radical and inventive films. More recently, this tradition was revived by Kenneth Branagh, whose film of *Henry V* (1989) was inspired by the RSC stage production of that play that was directed by Noble. All three of those films had featured RSC actors who, for the most part, had appeared in the stage versions of the plays. None of them, with the exception of Paul Scofield (who played Brook's Lear and who had won the Academy Award for best actor in 1966 for his performance as Sir Thomas More in *A Man for All Seasons*), were established film actors.

Noble's *A Midsummer Night's Dream* followed in this tradition. It was based on his highly successful 1994 stage production, which extended over two Stratford seasons, a London run, and a United States tour. Several of his actors, most notably Alex Jennings (Theseus and Oberon), Barry Lynch (Philostrate and Puck), and Desmond Barrit (Bottom), had been with the production from its inception. Noble's company of experienced Shakespearean actors (like Hall's and Brook's and Branagh's before him) were, however, largely novices when it came to working in film.

Hoffman's film, on the other hand, more resembled the Hollywood Shakespeare films of the 1930s, dotted with stars from the big studios. In fact, as I will later argue, Hoffman's film, in style and spirit, more resembled the 1935 Warner Brothers *A Midsummer Night's Dream*, directed by William Dieterle and Max Reinhardt, than any of the reinvented Hollywood Shakespeare films of the 1990s. Unlike Zeffirelli and the later, post–*Henry V* Branagh, Hoffman eschewed a mix of established English stage Shakespeareans and American film actors; he peopled his *Dream* exclusively with film and television stars: Michelle Pfeiffer, Kevin Kline, Stanley Tucci, Calista Flockhart, Sophie Marceau, and Rupert Everett.[1]

While, as I mentioned in my opening chapter, several of the films of the 1990s were inspired by stage productions (all four of Branagh's films and Loncraine's *Richard III*), they all labored hard to disguise their stage roots.[2] They made their devil's bargain between Stratford and Hollywood largely in the casting mix of experienced Shakespeareans (Branagh, Dench, Stephens, McKellen, Jacobi) with established film stars (Keaton, Washington, Williams, Downey, Bening). Noble attempted to straddle Stratford and Hollywood by openly retaining cast, costumes, and set design from his stage production, but then interweaving those details with film conceits about childhood dreams and fantasies created by filmmakers as varied as Ingmar Bergman, Walt Disney, and Steven Spielberg. The seams showed. In a revealing paradox, the elements in the stage production that had seemed most magical—the confusions of the lovers in the woods—translated onto film as the most earthbound and static, while the play's most solid and grounded characters—Bottom and his crew of hempen homespuns—took flight in the film.

Noble's *Dream* was shot on a tight, five-week schedule on a sound stage in Bray, just up the Thames from London. Hoffman, on the other hand, followed Branagh to Tuscany for his location shooting, and Fellini to Rome's Cinecitta Studios for the scenes in the woods. If Noble's film reveals its humble stage origins and tiny budget in every sequence, Hoffman's revels in its Hollywood opulence. If Noble's film often seems underdone, Hoffman's is almost always overheated. Following the extravagant early attempt by Reinhardt and Dieterle in 1935 to apply the language of film—from spectacle to montage to special effects—dramatically to Shakespeare's *Dream*, Hoffman, much in the manner of his *Restoration*, finds that his road to Shakespeare runs through the palace (and woods) of excess. His film, at its best, has a giddy visual overload. He does not bombard the viewer, like Baz Luhrmann, with slam zooms and jump cuts, but he creates a sensuous spectacle-Shakespeare quite in harmony with his Victorian setting and his operatic subtext and musical score. Luhrmann assaults our visual and auditory senses, Hoffman drowns them.

Noble's tenure as the director of the Royal Shakespeare Company has been a rocky one as he tries to realign the company's work with contemporary theatrical practice. Russell Jackson, writing in the *Shakespeare Quarterly* in summer 1999, summarized the complaints about the company often heard in the English press: "One can justly complain that in recent years the RSC has lacked a prerequisite of all these virtues [national subsidy, actors on long-term contracts, repertory seasons of production, multiple playing spaces in Stratford and London]: artistic vision. Beyond mere survival, it is hard to see what policy the company has."[3] Jackson fails to recognize that Noble's strength as a director—a vital, bold eclecticism—is one that is difficult to translate into a unified, recognizable company policy for producing Shakespeare. Of the RSC's directors over the last two decades, Noble has been the only one to consistently produce mainstage Shakespeare productions that work both as vivid storytelling and as critical commentary.

His long collaboration with the designer Bob Crowley, over almost fifteen years, produced a string of interesting productions that were unmatched by any other director/design team in the RSC's history. Among those productions, I would include *King Lear* (1982), *Henry V* (1984), *As*

You Like It (1985), *Macbeth* (1986), *The Plantagenets* (1989), *Henry IV* (1990), and *Hamlet* (1992). He also directed similarly outstanding productions that were designed by Anthony Ward: *The Winter's Tale* (1992), *King Lear* (1994), *A Midsummer Night's Dream* (1994), and *Cymbeline* (1997). The richness of these productions rests in their variety. Noble has a strong visual imagination and of the RSC artistic directors is the one who has been most influenced by film. His style, unlike Hall's severe formalism, cannot be easily cloned or copied. He rarely repeats himself (although he did indulge a midcareer fascination with balloons, umbrellas, and highly stylized and choreographed battle sequences), and has both nurtured stunning performances from relatively young unknown actors (Anthony Sher and Kenneth Branagh) and helped revive the careers of established older ones (Michael Gambon and Robert Stephens). Noble's strengths and flaws were all evident in his stage production of the *Dream.*

Noble's *Dream* was, in part, a response to the two most radical productions of the play in our time: Brook's legendary white circus for the RSC in 1970 and Robert LePage's muddy splash for the Royal National Theatre in 1992. Both productions emphasized the imaginative metatheatricality at the heart of Shakespeare's play—Brook's by releasing the play's exaggerated romantic emotions into aerial magic, LePage's by immersing those same emotions in a primordial ooze. Brook's production was in Technicolor; LePage's in black-and-white. Brook gave us trapezes for the lovers, LePage a stunning acrobat—a Puck who dangled above the action much like the single bare lightbulb from whose suspended cord she hung. Brook gave us a white box with rear and side doors through which the lovers and mechanicals could storm; LePage gave us a mud pond for the lovers to swim in and a bedframe that, when propped on its side, provided a gate through which the lovers could enter the forest and a perch from which Oberon and Puck could oversee the night's confusions.

Noble took Brook's white-box set and washed it in a deep blue. He dressed his principals in loose, satin outfits—vaguely Gandhian in design—and splashed them with bold colors: blue, purple, green, red, and yellow. He took Brook's two side doors and added them to the two in the rear to heighten the farce atmosphere of the lovers' experience in the woods. Following LePage, he created two door frames from which Oberon and Puck could observe the action—but in this case, the frames rose up out of the stage floor. He took LePage's bare white lightbulb and multiplied it into twenty or more yellow ones hanging from the flies to create a starry welkin, and he brought Lynch's Puck down from the heavens suspended from a huge green umbrella. Titania's bower was a similar upturned umbrella, but in hot red. Peter Quince arrived on a bike, Bottom on a motorcycle, complete with helmet and goggles, and, as his own addition to Brook's famous doubling of Theseus and Oberon, Hippolyta and Titania, Philostrate and Puck, Noble doubled the rude mechanicals as Titania's fairy band.

In chapter 1, I discussed Jack Jorgens's three basic modes of Shakespeare films: the theatrical, the realistic, and the filmic. Jorgens finds potential strengths and weaknesses in each approach; he does not, for instance, privilege the filmic over the theatrical.[4] Noble's *Dream* obviously belongs to Jorgens's first category since it incorporates the basic design and costume elements of his stage production, but Noble adds a crucial new device—a dreaming child—to serve as a frame and an internal linking mechanism to interweave the connections between Shakespeare's four plot levels.

The film opens with a pan shot that descends through a layer of clouds and enters the window of a child's bedroom, where it lingers over its contents: cricket bat, rocking horse, teddy bear, sailboat, Pierrot doll, and a Victorian toy theater. The camera finds a sleeping boy (Osheen Jones) with an open copy of *A Midsummer Night's Dream*, illustrated by Arthur Rackham, on his bed. The boy rises, leaves his room, walks down a long hallway, and peeks in through a keyhole to observe, if not quite the primal scene, then its anticipation—Theseus and Hippolyta's exchange about desire and restraint that opens the play. Throughout the film, Noble continues to use the boy as a silent observer: he falls, Alice-like, down a long shaft that brings him to the mechanicals' clubhouse; he peers at Oberon and Puck through the back of the toy theater, rides across the moon in Bottom's motorcycle's sidecar, and watches the lovers be put to rest by Puck in suspended cocoons at the end of the night's vexations; he pulls the curtain for "Pyramus and Thisby"; and finally, he joins Puck for the epilogue.

The film's most sympathetic and perceptive critic, Mark Burnett, is alert to the many ways the boy's perspective supports Noble's own visual and conceptual purposes. Burnett sees Noble's use of the boy as allowing the director to create "less an experience of Shakespeare . . . [than] an intertextual rehearsal of familiar children's stories, past and present. In this way, Noble's *A Midsummer Night's Dream* pushes back the perimeters of what constitutes 'Shakespeare,' combining elements from 'high' and 'low' cultural traditions and mixing 'old' and 'new' representational materials."[5] This access to cultural eclecticism, typical of Noble's work, is what the boy provides the film's form with. Within the narrative itself, as we have seen, he keeps popping up in both mortal and fairy worlds to earn, like Enobarbus, a place in the story. Again, Burnett sees that the boy's multiple roles, including that of "the little changeling boy" assigned to him by the text, are meant to heighten issues relating to expanse and impasse, fantasy and reality, passivity and power at work in Shakespeare's *Dream*. At one moment, as Burnett notes, when the toy theater is "magically transported to the forest, the Boy must struggle with Oberon for ownership of the puppets' strings. Oberon's seizure of a model figure from the theatre implies that he has no qualms in usurping the Boy's imaginative privileges. Power in Noble's conception of things is a matter of contest, and no one is permitted to exercise a secure and unchanging control."[6]

Shakespeare's *Dream* is a paradoxical mixture of classical Ovid and native Warwickshire, sexual nightmare and social vision, wanton green and liquid pearl, fierce vexation and shaping fantasy. It is, along with *Hamlet* and *Henry V,* his most metatheatrical work, and it surpasses them both in the intricate delicacy of its architecture. The play radiates out in a series of overlapping layers, all emanating from Titania's seduction of Bottom in the play's central scene: we are shown the mingling and merging of implacable reality and exotic imagination—of unaccommodated man and fairy queen, of beauty and the beast. Shakespeare's handling of his folk and classical material mirrors the story of the night as it is experienced by Bottom and the lovers, in which fancy's images are transformed into something rich and strange. Noble's film attempts to create a similar magical intertextual hybrid. By using children's stories, ranging from *Alice in Wonderland* to *Peter Pan,* and modern films about childhood such as *The Wizard of Oz* and *ET,* Noble seeks to translate his Shakespearean material into a contemporary milieu.

The use of the boy allows Noble to evoke echoes of childhood that stretch from Carroll and Rackham to Disney and Spielberg. Use of the boy originated from Noble's desire to make a Shakespeare film that would open itself up to the child's imagination, but it also serves to remind us that the play is about the quarrels and disruptions that flare up over two changeling boys: the boy-child at the center of a parental dispute between Titania and Oberon that has caused such a breach in nature

and the man-child (Demetrius) who has changed his affections from Helena to Hermia and caused a similar upheaval in the social world. As
Noble has remarked, "I remembered that I had said to the actors when we
were preparing the RSC [stage] production that they had to find the
child-like in themselves because . . . the logic of the *Dream* is experienced
by the characters in an extraordinarily intense way."[7] When Noble came
to prepare the film script, he was looking for "a point of purchase . . . an
overall camera angle" that would open up the text for the cinema:

> So when I was at an early moment in the script development stage
> I thought we should look at literally making it a dream—a child's
> dream; someone through whom we could relive the story . . . [a
> dream that would allow us] to quote in quite a saucy and playful
> way a wide range of childhood fictions. And that was joyful too as
> it seemed quite in keeping with the spirit of Shakespeare's text.[8]

To conceive of the film as the changeling boy's dream added weight to the
doubling of Theseus/Oberon (Alex Jennings) and Hippolyta/Titania
(Lindsay Duncan) since now they could be conceived as parents as well as
the sponsors of the brawls that have disturbed the natural world.

Noble's eclectic imagination was obviously stimulated by working in
film, but I think he came to discover that film magic is often harder (and
certainly more expensive) to achieve than its stage equivalent. He was
clearly intrigued with using the toy theater as a reminder of the play's
metatheatricality, but he couldn't find a way to make it metacinematic as
well. Having the fairies float down, contained within balloon-like bubbles, did attempt to use film dazzle as old as Billie Burke's great entrance
in *The Wizard of Oz*, but he did not fully integrate those bubbles with the
dangling light bulbs and great umbrellas carried over into the film from
the stage production. To get his special effects, Noble used what he calls
the "fox gloves," and he learned that creating such effects was both expensive and time-consuming: "We spent hours and hours with what we
call the 'fox gloves,' the digitalizers. A four-second shot can cost you
twenty thousand pounds. A blue screen shot. And you get nothing. You
get a tiny bit of nothing for your twenty thousand pounds. You need millions and millions and millions to do serious special effects."[9] Borrowing
the bicycle-across-the-moon shot from *ET* was clever, used once, but it
lost its magical impact when repeated. In contrast, the film's capturing of
"the watery moon"—a great yellow oval swimming precariously above

the sea—was a lovely visual film image that did borrow from those suspended yellow light bulbs doubling as stars and tears. Noble used his watery moon well when he shot Titania and Bottom floating off in her lush umbrella bower, bobbing out to sea toward that huge moon low on the horizon, rather than having them elevated toward the heavens as the stage production had done.

If the boy opened up fresh avenues for Noble, he also created problems. How much of the lovers' pubescent agonies might we expect to occupy the dreams (or nightmares) of a small boy? How much of what is sexually provocative and playful in Noble's handling of Titania's relationship with Bottom flows from a child's imagination? What boy, falling asleep with Rackham's illustrations dancing in his head, would dream up fairies as coyly disguised adults? In his *The Uses of Enchantment,* Bruno Bettelheim gives a provocative account of the therapeutic powers of fairy tales, and Burnett makes interesting use of Bettelheim to sanction Noble's presentation of the explicit sexuality contained in Bottom's encounter with Titania.[10] Genital sexuality in fairy stories, however, is almost always implicit, rather than explicit, a matter of dream work rather than literal representation.

Shakespeare's *Dream* is too often at odds with Noble's dreamer. Noble's idea might have been better served if he had just allowed the boy to be used as a framing device. As it is, the boy keeps popping up within the narrative itself, where his presence is not always fully integrated with the performance he finds himself observing. Branagh's and Nunn's way, it seems to me, is more successful: they appropriate an element from within Shakespeare's text (the songs "Sigh No More" and "The Wind and the Rain," for example) and use it as a frame, rather than imposing the device from without. Even Shakespeare found the use of a frame a risky practice, as witness the critical debates that still swirl around the Christopher Sly material in *The Taming of the Shrew.*

Key energies from the text are lost in the film. These energies (which were captured in the stage production) concern the bittersweet comedy about the agonies of puberty experienced by the quartet of lovers. Noble's screenplay excises too much of Helena's (Emily Raymond) two great explorations of her friendship with Hermia (Monica Dolan) and their puzzling clash of fortunes in romance.[11] The film retains, for the forest scenes, the stage production's line of four rear doors and the frames of two more doors that popped up from the floor to provide perches for Oberon and Puck to oversee the lovers' confusion in the woods. The multiple doors are a theatrical signal that we are in the world of farce—and in the theater, because our field of vision encompassed the entire landscape, we become swept up in the farce-like atmosphere of the lovers using the doors for comic entrances and exits: the ins and outs underline their emotional confusions and tantrums. Little of this comic energy is captured on film. Noble does not find a corresponding cinematic rhythm of cutting and editing to capture the comedy here, and as a result we lose our involvement in the genuine emotional turbulence experienced by Helena and Hermia as their lifelong friendship is rent asunder.

Noble was aware that the forest scenes with the lovers failed to make the transition from stage to film successfully. He has commented, "Everything in the forest was compromised by resources. Had I known that, I would have done everything differently."[12] He learned that it is less expensive to shoot on location, for instance, than to fill the screen with compromised special effects. This led him to conclude, thinking back on his work, "I'd . . . reconstruct the forest completely. I would . . . go outside to do that; provide another dimension to the multiple layers of reality the text and film represent. All those elements like the lake I could develop more fully—a Yeatsean Lake Isle of Innisfree sort of thing. I'd create a strange world of forest and water."[13] Noble became so enamored with his use of the young boy that he seems to lose interest in the text's other adolescents, and he even left their awakening from the night's dream on the cutting-room floor.

The Bottom comedy works better. Barrit is a natural comic, but he also found a way to show the human beneath the ham. A revealing bit of business retained from the stage production has Titania, sprawled sinuously on the floor in front of Bottom, using her bare foot to massage his thigh as she purrs "Thou art as wise as thou art beautiful." Barrit's plump Bottom, clearly a sexual novice, finds that the initial pleasure of this activity quickly dissolves into blushing embarrassment, and he gently lifts her foot and moves it away from his groin. Barrit's Bottom is shy, and Barrit was at his most winning when finding ways, as in the above example, to find that quality in the character.

The film does not find a smooth or intelligent means of making the transition from woods to palace, from dream to wedding, from "Bottom and Titania" to "Pyramus and Thisby." The wedding feast is too gaudy, with too much visual emphasis on the lavish spread (as though we are back in Edzard's version of Duke Fredrick's court) and not enough on the human reaction to the miracles of the night. Noble kept all of Theseus's neat rationalization of the lovers' experiences in the woods, but he inexcusably cut Hippolyta's crucial (and winning) five-line reply that starts with "But all the story of the night told over." In a film at pains to demonstrate the liberating and lasting powers of the imagination, it seems a shame to have eliminated the text's collaboration with that view, while giving voice to Theseus's rational skepticism.

This omission was a part of a larger pattern of the film's devaluation of the female experience central to the text. Noble's silencing of Hippolyta here joins with his earlier evisceration of Helena's two great laments about her relationship with Hermia and his complete elimination of Titania's rich and potent evocation of her relationship with the Indian vot'ress, whose changeling boy she now protects. All Shakespeare films, with the notable exceptions of Hall's *Dream* and Branagh's *Hamlet*, cut and shape the text to suit the director's interpretive slant and the demands of the film genre. My critical preference is to emphasize what the screenplay retains from the text, rather than to lament what it omits. But Noble's insistence on gendering his *Dream* as exclusively male leads to a radical and puzzling elimination of issues of sisterhood and the clash of female power with the patriarchy—elements that seem to me to be at the heart of the text's dramatic concerns.

For "Pyramus and Thisby," Noble moves the action into a life-sized version of the Victorian toy theater that he repeatedly uses as a prop. Here he creates one stunning shot that suggests a metaphor his film might have developed more consistently and imaginatively. At the end of the Bergomask dance, the aristocrats join Bottom and company on stage to congratulate the actors. When the iron tongue of midnight tolls, Noble creates a series of shots flashing us back through key moments in the narrative and then has his camera peer out through the back of the theater to discover Oberon, Titania, Puck, and their fairy band floating toward us on the water, silhouetted by an enormous moon. In this shot, we move literally and metaphorically from stage to film. Noble appears to be suggesting an exciting contrast here between stage and film as an imaginative means of presenting the text's clash between the worlds of day and night, court and fairyland, reality and imagination, onstage and backstage, but it proves to be "brief as the lightning in the collied night" (1.1.145) since he does not sustain the distinction.

Noble's film is bold and vivid. It presents the viewer with a series of suggestive ideas about the text, but it never fully integrates those ideas into a coherent form. Knowing Noble's admiration for Ingmar Bergman,

I imagine he had Bergman's wonderful film *The Magic Flute* (1975) in mind when he set out to make a film of the *Dream* that would appeal to the child in us, as Bergman did by presenting Mozart's magical opera through a child's eye.[14] But Bergman made his *Flute* when working at his zenith, whereas Noble's *Dream* repeatedly reveals the hand and eye of a film apprentice.[15]

If Noble's *Dream* was Stratford-conceived and child-centered, Hoffman's emanates from Hollywood and gives pride of place to Kevin Kline's Bottom. As Hoffman reports, his original casting intention was to have Kline play Oberon, but the more he studied the play, the more he decided to center it on Bottom—to make the film be "Bottom's Dream." When Hoffman shared his vision with the actor, Kline initially resisted switching parts: he finally relented by proposing a way in which he could play Oberon, Bottom, *and* Theseus: "I breathed a sigh of relief. He'd already begun his work. He was Bottom volunteering to play Thisby, the lion, the wall—everything."[16]

Hoffman's approach was to set the text in what he terms a "late Victorian setting," which turns out to be in Tuscany, thus echoing Shakespeare's daring and playful mixture of Ovid and English folklore in the *Dream*. Bottom lives in Monte Athena, where he is conceived as a melancholy chap with an eye for the ladies. The lovers (Calista Flockhart, Anna Friel, Christian Bale, and Dominic West) are buttoned-up Victorians on the verge, via the bicycle and the phonograph, of bursting out into the less-rigid social conventions of the new century.

Hoffman's lush, visually stunning, approach treats the play as a feast, a perspective underlined by the montage in which his camera lovingly lingers over piles of tomatoes, onions, garlics, and roasting birds and boars in the film's opening sequence. He cannot resist the temptation to crowd the screen with ripe images that, all too often, do not link up imaginatively with anything in the text. He attempts to open his film with a visual sequence as potentially inviting as Branagh's in *Much Ado About Nothing*, but he fails to understand how cleverly Branagh used the words of Balthazar's song about the inconstancy of male wooers as a textual license for his approach. Hoffman has a fertile cinematic imagination, but his art is only fitfully in control of his Shakespearean material. As H. R. Coursen indicates, "Hoffman introduces a village square in Tuscany, early Twentieth Century technology [the phonograph], Etruscan ruins, and Woody Allen effects from the delightful *Midsummer Night's Sex Comedy* that collide with each other, confusing rather than clarifying."[17] Hoffman, surely, took his liberty here from Shakespeare's own wild amalgam of sources, but too often he produces jarring discords rather than unexpected harmonies.

His treatment of Bottom provides a revealing example. In a brilliant and daring move, in consort with Kline, the film creates a Bottom who is both something of a dreamer and a dandy. Kline's performance is exquisite, with delicate, subtle shadings that demonstrate American film Shakespearean acting at its best (Brando's Marc Antony is another example from the deep past). As David Denby remarks, "The role of Nick Bottom, the weaver and amateur actor, allows Kline's talents to exfoliate into the richest comic work he's done yet."[18] There is not a trace of a rude mechanical in Kline's Bottom, but often a sweet suggestion of Marcello Mastroianni a bit lost in one of Fellini's cinematic dreams. This Bottom is neither ass nor ham, but the lost soul who comes into focus through his attempts to transform himself in art.

Kline finds a genuine discovery and thrill, rather than the usual hyperbolic bombast, in his delivery of Bottom's "the raging rocks / And shivering shocks." Kline's delivery of the lines, in Denby's fine account, is "grandiloquent and preening, his eyes afire, his head thrown back. He seems to be parodying styles of theatrical flamboyance which no longer exist—bits of legendary hamming, perhaps from Nineteenth Century road companies."[19] My own sense, given the film's Italian setting and strong operatic flavor, is that Kline was imagining himself as a great tenor pouring forth his soul through an inadequate lyric. But Hoffman can't resist giving his actor some "help." First, he introduces him sitting at a café on the town square—the camera discovering him just as a local tradesman leads his donkey across the frame in front of him. Then he provides him with a shrewish wife who scorns his artistic pretensions (an idea that Jackson has recently revealed is as old as the screenplay for the Warner Brothers Dream, and one that, fortunately, ended up there on the cutting-room floor).[20] And finally, after Kline has transfixed his fellow thespians (and much of the crowd from the town square that has gathered to watch his act) with his "roaring as gentle as any sucking dove," Hoffman has two kids scamper up a scaffolding to dump several bottles of Chianti over Kline's head and down his white suit. Some actors playing Bottom may deserve such a treatment, but not Kline, and not after the performance he has just treated us to. This moment is inexplicable; it doesn't link up with other moments of despoiling in the film, unless we are to imagine the little pranksters as harbingers of Puck, who will later crown Bottom in another fashion. Our relish in Kline's Bottom is suddenly turned to pity—a sentimentality that radically undermines the character's wonderful sweet obliviousness.

Another potentially attractive idea that gets overwhelmed and lost in the film is Hoffman's handling of the spirit world. In the opening "feast" sequence, the camera spies several dwarfs filching plates and bowls and silverware (and most importantly a phonograph) from Theseus's bustling kitchen and trundling them off in a small cart. Of course, these items are headed to fairyland, where they eventually materialize. Neat notion. Hoffman, with a nod to the Brothers Grimm and Reinhardt and Dieterle, picks up on Shakespeare's incorporation of Puck and English household sprites into Ovid's classical landscape. But Hoffman then does not connect these creatures with Puck but with Titania's retinue of nubile beauties worthy of a Howard Chandler Christy mural. In fact, Hoffman's woods are crammed with a multinational cast of fairies that ranges from Disney fireflies to a motley crew of monsters and over-the-hill nymphs hanging out at a grotto fairy bar, straight from George Lucas, from an all-blue changeling boy to a dwarf band left over from the 1935 *Dream*, and an Oberon and Titania out of *The Clash of the Titans*. Hoffman's teeming imagination just doesn't know when to stop. He becomes so stimulated by Shakespeare's fine frenzy that he can't bring his own under control. He is a bit like Bottom; he wants to be the lunatic *and* the lover *and* the poet.

The film's opening sequence is laced with healthy doses of the familiar Mendelssohn, but Hoffman, because of his decision to set the film in late-nineteenth-century Italy, embraced the opportunity to get opera onto the soundtrack as well. Here I think his musical excess yields rewards. When the rude mechanicals arrive in the woods to rehearse, the soundtrack associates opera with them, breaking into the festive "Libiamo" from *Traviata*. Later, Bottom brings the lyric strains of bel canto (not quite the tong and the bones) to Titania's bower as he instructs the fairies in how to make the purloined phonograph release its magical spell. The aria that swells on the soundtrack is the "Casta Diva" from *Norma*, and although Pfeiffer's Titania is soon to be a very unchaste goddess, the bel canto voice and style fits the moment in its ravishing and romantic intensity.

In a film overloaded with detail, the phonograph, stolen by the dwarfs in the opening montage, is Hoffman's most inspired device. The prop languishes in Titania's fairy bower, its horn being used as a vase for flowers, as the spirit world is technologically challenged. Bottom, of course, knows how to make it work. As Coursen wittily remarks, the fairies's "'Hail mortal!' is a tribute to his facility." This is a moment, Coursen goes on to observe, "where human technique is superior to pagan power."[21] But Hoffman's use of the phonograph suggests even more than that. The phonograph and the film medium grew up together; both became a part of a twentieth-century technological revolution that brought the power and passion of what had come to be regarded as high or elite art (the opera, let's say, and Shakespeare) back into popular culture; a high culture transported, via the phonograph, radio, television, and now the VCR and computer, into every man's bower—Bottom's bower, now liberated from being the exclusive province of the social and cultural gods.[22]

Hoffman's representation of the woods (constructed on Fellini's old sound stage at Cinecittà), gives us a less-successful mingling of iconographic ideas. A portion of the woods appears to have overgrown a deep pagan past, with vines and vegetation covering huge carved stone faces that to Hoffman suggested Etruscan temples but to Coursen looked like "the ruins of the Mayan City of Tula north of Ciudad Mexico."[23] Titania's bower was suspended above a decidedly neoclassical gazebo that might have served as an adornment to the garden of an old Hollywood mansion. Perhaps Hoffman meant to suggest a connection between Ovid's ancient randy gods and our own film stars, but if so I wished he had given us a few more definitive clues—an abandoned swimming pool, perhaps, to go with the gazebo. But instead he gives us a mud pond (stolen from Le-Page's very slippery *Dream* at the National Theatre in 1992 and quite out of keeping with the film's lush woods and late-Victorian setting), and into it, with none of LePage's imagination and humor, he plops the four lovers. This is another example of Hoffman's hoping that excess will lead to clarification, to modify C. L. Barber's formula for the structural logic of Shakespeare's festive comedy. But it doesn't happen. The film, in its studio forest, reverts to being an updated version of the Warner Brothers *Dream*. Here the fairy world does not appear as a heightened nocturnal version of either Theseus's grand villa or Bottom's Monte Athena but as a highly artificial echo of other movie fantasy worlds (Jabba the Hut's bar out of *Return of the Jedi*) or of stage versions of the woods (Brook's suspended red-feather bower for Titania or LePage's mud hole for the lovers).

When Hoffman's camera is roaming Theseus's estate and capturing various stages of the lovers' determination to flee to the forest, it often shoots them in Theseus's garden framed against classical statues carved to resemble Tucci's Puck, Everett's Oberon, and Pfeiffer's Titania. Here was a potentially witty idea for linking the classical world with the nineteenth-century setting: Oberon with Theseus, night with day, rigidity with fluidity, and reality with the tricks of strong imagination. But the statues are not brought to life. They do not preside over the night's errors and revels; they never make it into Hoffman's studio-constructed forest setting. They remain simply another visual idea, exploited for a moment and then abandoned.

Eclectic treatment of landscape is reflected in acting styles as well. The performances that work best come from Kline, Everett, Tucci, David Strathairn (Theseus), and Bale (Demetrius), who let Shakespeare come to them rather than feeling they have to chew hard on all the riches of the poetry. The performances that are less successful, Flockhart (Helena), West (Lysander), Bernard Hill (Egeus), and Friel (Hermia), think that the way to emotional intensity in Shakespeare is to ignore his natural rhythms by plucking out every juicy word to underline. On screen, less is always more with Shakespeare, which is nowhere made more evident than in Sam Rockwell's brilliant, moving Flute. I did not think I would ever see a better Flute (and Thisby) on film than Joe E. Brown's, but Rockwell gives us a heartbreaking Thisby, and he makes his delivery of "his eyes were green as leeks" as tragically moving as Juliet's "thy lips are warm." Here Hoffman does help his actor: he allows his film to pause for several beats while the aristocrats absorb and respond to Thisby's grief. Again, however, Hoffman allows his actor to become self-conscious about his big moment, which works against the grain of Shakespeare's conception of the mechanicals and their performance. Flute, Snout, Starveling, and Bottom are always peeking out from behind Thisby, Wall, Moonshine, and Pyramus. They aren't professionals; they can't lose themselves in the characters (or objects) they are playing; that is their comic genius and their imaginative limitation. Rockwell's Thisby genuinely grieves for her Pyramus—something Shakespeare's Flute is incapable of conceiving or enacting. We are given a brilliant moment, but one that runs against the grain of the comedy.

Something similar happens at the end of the film, when Hoffman follows Kline's Bottom back to his barren flat in Monte Athena. As he stares forlornly out of his window, Bottom is clutching a jewel that Titania has given him. Bottom's wonderful exuberance, his triumph with the play, his memories of the fierce vexation of his dream—all this is drained from Kline's countenance. This sad, melancholy moment is another version of his being doused with wine; it puts an unnecessary layer of sentimentality over his unique genius. Hoffman tries to rescue the moment by having Bottom spy one of those cute Disney fireflies that danced to Mendelssohn's score over the opening credits of the film. As the firefly darts about the darkened town square, a small smile appears on Kline's face, signaling the revival of his spirits. But this is to turn Shakespeare's Bottom into Barrie's Peter Pan; this is Tinkerbell coming to Ovid's rescue.

Hoffman's film, while glancing back to Hollywood's ancient *Dream*, also wants to draw its energies from the most commercially successful film of a Shakespearean comedy in the past decade: Branagh's *Much Ado About Nothing*. From Branagh, he takes his lush Tuscan setting and an Anglo-American, all-star cast. What he does not retain from Branagh is a confidence in his Shakespearean material. As Stanley Kauffmann complains, Hoffman's film falls prey to an attitude that says to its audience, "We know it's Shakespeare; but see how we're trying to keep it from being dull."[24] This subtext is at work, of course, in the Reinhardt/Dieterle *Dream*, but that film contains a daring, darker visual approach to the text (particularly Victor Jory's Oberon) much ahead of its time: it has a cinematic exuberance in trying to fashion a film language to parallel Shakespeare's. As Kauffmann notes:

> Very few Shakespeare films have been free of this subtext—most notably Branagh's work—but Branagh's passion for the plays, and his experience with them, flowed from the stage to the screen to produce new incarnations rather than cultural obeisance by movies to classics. And for the most part Branagh was supported by actors who relished the chance to do in a new form what they had always loved doing; they weren't entering a strange, intimidating obstacle race. Hoffman's film shows no sign of the (let's call it) Branagh attitude.[25]

What Kauffmann, importantly, understands is new in Branagh's work is its genuine desire to create a bold, modern, commercial film style for Shakespeare that carries with it the actor's pleasure in the text rather than swamping the words with lush images or showy film dazzle. But Hoffman's own pleasure in film's power to be visually overwhelming works against his efforts to match what Kauffmann calls the "Branagh attitude." Only Kline brings Branagh's actorly sense of the power of Shakespeare's language to the film, and, as I have argued, Hoffman binds him with a conception of Bottom that is contra-intuitive and counterproductive. As David Denby comments, "Hoffman has a weakness for schlock excess, and he doesn't bring much rhythm, or even momentum, to the material . . . the entire production is neo-Victorian in its clutter."[26] That excess and clutter finally sink the film's more interesting achievements. Hoffman, to his credit, pays homage to both Hollywood's *Dream* and to Branagh's Tuscan romp, and his attempts at synthesis are often bold and not without momentary pleasures, but too often they are "swift as a shadow, short as any dream," and the film, full of quick, bright, unassimilated things, comes to confusion.

These two recent *Dream*s make an instructive contrast: they reflect two important traditions in translating Shakespeare into film. Noble's film is too often pulled back toward its stage origins. It never quite finds the film language it seeks to give vigorous expression to the play's metatheatrical elements and its metacinematic potential. It makes intelligent and inviting use of the young boy as a framing and linking device, but, in the process, Shakespeare's ferocious and funny tale of the young lovers, lost in the woods and in all the agonies of puberty, fails to materialize. To adopt and adapt one of the film's own key literary devices, it's a bit like Winnie-the-Pooh stuck in Rabbit's hole: it's caught halfway in its journey from the stage to the other, honey-world of film.[27]

Hoffman's *Dream* is a Hollywood creation. Pfeiffer and Kline are film stars who rival Glenn Close and Mel Gibson. Hoffman's film, at its best, cleverly invokes in casting and style the Warner Brothers *Dream* and Hollywood's first flirtation with appropriating Shakespeare for film's cultural and commercial purposes. Hoffman's film, along with Zeffirelli's *Hamlet*, Luhrmann's *William Shakespeare's Romeo + Juliet*, and Branagh's *Much Ado About Nothing*, found the cineplex audience that most of these recent Shakespeare films sought, but even though it opened widely on screens across the country, it did not generate the box-office interest of the other three films. One might have concluded, given its example, that the Shakespeare-on-film revival was at an end—destroyed by an excess of what it fed on: Hollywood stars and lavish production values. But the revival still had enough energy left to produce two of its most inventive and challenging creations: Michael Almereyda's *Hamlet* and Julie Taymor's *Titus*.

The Prince of Manhattan

Almereyda's Hamlet

f Baz Luhrmann's *William Shakespeare's Romeo + Juliet* (1995) took the Shakespeare film triumphantly from the urban art house to the suburban cineplex, Michael Almereyda's equally radical and daring *Hamlet* (2000) snatches it back again. Both films are dominated by their landscapes—Luhrmann's, a virtual reality city, mixing elements of Miami, Los Angeles, and Mexico City, Almereyda's, a glinting, glistening, Manhattan that is discovered by his camera rather than digitally constructed in the editing room.

Almereyda's film of *Hamlet* shares Luhrmann's postmodern perspective, but is even more radical and interesting in its use of its Shakespearean material. As we have seen, Luhrmann's *Romeo + Juliet* is saturated by media images from consumer culture. Almereyda's film works a similar territory. Here is the director responding to early reviews complaining about "product placement" in the film:

> The undignified, all but unbelievable truth is that we paid for the privilege of parading certain logos and insignias across the screen. "Denmark's a prison," Hamlet declares early on, and if you consider this in terms of contemporary consumer culture, the bars of the cage are defined by advertising, by all the hectic distractions, brand names, announcements and ads that crowd our waking hours. And when, in this independent film, the ghost of Hamlet's father vanishes into a Pepsi machine, or Hamlet finds

himself questioning the nature of existence in the Action aisles of a Blockbuster video store, or Shakespeare's lines are overwhelmed by the roar of a plane passing overhead—it's meant as something more than casual irony. It's another way to touch the core of Hamlet's anguish, to recognize the frailty of spiritual values in a material world, and to get a whiff of something rotten in Denmark on the threshold of our self-congratulatory new century.[1]

Both filmmakers find the crush and visual overload of postmodern urban life a rich, contemporary cultural equivalent for the political and familial claustrophobia that threatens both Romeo and Juliet and Hamlet and Ophelia. Luhrmann's film, with its rock soundtrack (even the religious music features a Prince lyric) and rapid-fire editing, bursts out of the world of MTV and John Woo action films; Almereyda's film, however, has a very different legacy.[2] His ragged, jagged, inventive film is haunted by the substantial shadow of Orson Welles, oddly missing (except for Branagh's Agincourt sequences in his *Henry V* and the mirrored doors in his *Hamlet*) as a looming presence in the current revival of the Shakespeare film genre. With a competitive nod to Luhrmann's film (and the Zeffirelli-Branagh visual aesthetic), Almereyda credits Welles and his film of *Macbeth* (shot in twenty-one days) as his inspiration and model: "Welles described his film as a 'rough charcoal sketch' of the play, and this remark, alongside the finished picture, provoked in me a sharp suspicion that you don't need lavish production values to make a Shakespeare movie that's accessible and alive. Shakespeare's language, after all, is lavish enough."[3]

Almereyda shot his film "fast and cheap" in Manhattan in super 16 mm (later blown up to 35 mm format for release) "to make everything as urgent and intimate as possible."[4] The film has that marvelous Wellesian quality of the spontaneously discovered landscape, shot from an odd camera angle that provides an imaginative fit with the surprise twists and turns of Shakespeare's verse. I am thinking of Welles's bug-eyed Macbeth, shot in close-up against the dripping walls of his Inverness cave ("then comes my fit again"); of Gielgud's Henry IV, shot from below on that high, cold platform in the abandoned cathedral in Cardonna in *Chimes at Midnight* ("So shaken as we are, so wan with care"); of MacLiammoir's Iago, swinging from his cage in *Othello*, finally himself entrapped in the net meant to "enmesh them all."

Almereyda's film has a dozen such shots. The most memorable include Sam Shepard's Ghost dissolving into a Pepsi dispenser; Ethan Hawke's Hamlet reflected in the glass window of a tumbling laundromat dryer, cleaning his blood-stained clothes after the murder of Polonius; Claudius, Gertrude, and Ophelia framed in long-shot as each appears on a different level of Frank Lloyd Wright's Guggenheim Museum; Polonius caught in the refracted light of Claudius's penthouse swimming pool; and, especially Wellesian, the mirrored closet door in Gertrude's bedroom shattered by the bullet Hamlet fires into it—the bullet that kills Polonius. These examples illustrate Almereyda's working aesthetic: "My main job, anticipating work behind the camera, was to imagine a parallel visual language that might hold a candle to Shakespeare's poetry. There was no wish to illustrate the text, but to focus it, building a visual structure to accommodate Shakespeare's images and ideas."[5] His remark about not wishing to "illustrate the text" is, perhaps, intended to distinguish his film from Branagh's, which often has the intentional feel of a nineteenth-century illustrated edition of the play. Almereyda acknowledges that his movie is "an attempt at *Hamlet*—not so much a sketch but a collage, a patchwork of intuitions, images, ideas."[6] His film is American movie Shakespeare at its most interesting: in its relentless slashing and repositioning of the text and its radically imaginative film style, it might well be regarded as the anti-Branagh *Hamlet*.

Elvis Mitchell gave the film a glowing review in the *New York Times*, calling it "vital . . . voluptuous and rewarding."[7] He also found it useful to contrast Almereyda's achievement with Luhrmann's, and perceptively noted:

> The *Romeo and Juliet* director Baz Luhrmann fired his camera out of the barrel of a gun, and the over directed velocity was a movie maker's equivalent of nervous tics; Mr. Almereyda's audacity comes in problem solving . . . whereas Mr. Luhrmann's dazzle is all from the outside, Mr. Almereyda goes to the heart of things and has given Shakespeare a distinctively American perspective. *Hamlet* is a movie about urban isolation and the damage it causes, using corrupting wealth as a surrogate for stained royalty.[8]

Mitchell is right to see that his Manhattan landscape is central to Almereyda's conception: "The city's contradictions of beauty and squalor give the movie a sense of place . . . and New York becomes a complex character in this vital and sharply intelligent film."[9] David Denby also seizes on the visual importance of Manhattan to the film: "The black towers of Times Square, fretted with neon, tessellated with ledges, balconies, and catwalks, make a sinister and elegant setting for the power struggles within the Denmark Corporation."[10]

Denby understands that Almereyda's Manhattan, unlike Woody Allen's, is soulless and sinister. It looms, from the film's opening frame of its glass-and-steel towers shot through the sunroof of Claudius's stretch limousine to the final penthouse balcony confrontation between Hamlet and Laertes. The city, through Almereyda's camera, becomes one huge, glittering mirror, refracting light and reflecting images. His camera captures Hamlet reflected in the window of the limo, the glass walls of his apartment in the Hotel Elsinore, and the offices of the Denmark Corporation, the mirrored doors of his mother's bedroom, and the aforementioned laundromat dryer; he shows us Ophelia framed in the ripples of Claudius's penthouse pool, in the waterfall fountain where she drowns, and the high windows of the Guggenheim overlooking Fifth Avenue; and Shepard's weathered Ghost is first caught on the security camera of the Denmark Corporation, then through the windows of Hamlet's apartment, and again vanishing into the bright surface of the Pepsi machine—one corporate giant swallowed up by another.

Denby's use of the phrase "fretted with neon" echoes Hamlet's disillusioned description of the world to Rosencrantz and Guildenstern: "I have of late—but wherefore I know not—lost all my mirth; forgone all custom of exercise; and indeed it goes so heavily with my disposition that this goodly frame, the earth, seems to me a sterile promontory. This most excellent canopy, the air, look you, this brave o'erhanging firmament, this majestical roof fretted with golden fire—why, it appears no other thing to me than a foul and pestilent congregation of vapors" (2.2.293–301). The sparkling Manhattan skyline becomes in the film a sterile promontory; and Hawke's Hamlet, who in his morose slouch has clearly forgone all custom of exercise, finds himself trapped in the prisonhouse of those enormous skyscrapers, fretted with a most modern form of golden fire: neon ads and stock quotations.

The film never breaks free of Manhattan's hold until Hamlet's ride, on the back of Horatio's motorcycle, to Ophelia's funeral. Almereyda intends this scene to signal a return to a more natural and honest landscape—earth and death—presided over by the wit and wisdom of the gravedigger, the one character in the play unsullied by Claudius's corruption and Hamlet's efforts to challenge and expose it. But the exchange

between Hawke and Jeffrey Wright's Gravedigger was cut in the editing
process—a victim, Almereyda reports, of his own "failure to get it right
. . . the tone and timing were off, and the whole episode seemed to side-
track Hamlet's response to Ophelia's death."[11] The scene at Ophelia's
grave, like the final duel, is stilted, and ends up with Hamlet and Laertes
rolling through the leaves down a small embankment in an awkward embrace. Almereyda's visual imagination is sparked by the built landscape of
glass and steel and not by dessicated autumn leaves.

If Hawke's Hamlet is trapped in a monolithic, malevolent Manhattan,
he is also defined and circumscribed by a host of modern technological
gadgets, most significantly a pixel camera on which he records a video
diary of his experience. This Hamlet is an amateur filmmaker (Ophelia,
similarly, is a photographer) who thinks art may provide the answer to
life. Kyle MacLachlan's Claudius is conceived as the CEO of a multime-
dia corporate giant; his stepson is a member of the Danish Dogme 95 film
movement. Claudius is Hollywood; Hamlet is cinema verité.

Technology is everywhere: television screens blink with violence in
the background of many shots; Hamlet carries his camera with him
everywhere, making and then editing the endless home movie; phones
and phone-answering machines are ubiquitous (Hamlet blares out "Get
thee to a nunnery. Go, farewell!" over Ophelia's answering machine and
calls his mother from the basement of the Hotel Elsinore, where he has
deposited Polonius's body to continue their exchange—"One word more,
good lady"); a security camera captures the "fishmonger" insult; Ophelia
is rigged with a wire; the news of her death is communicated to Gertrude
by telephone; Hamlet's cheeky letter to Claudius ("High and mighty") arrives by fax; Hamlet discovers Claudius's instructions to his English
counterpart by invading Rosencrantz and Guildenstern's laptop; "The
Mousetrap" is a video/film directed by "Hamlet, Prince of Denmark";
Rosencrantz's "Never did the king sigh, but with a general groan" comes
over the speaker phone in Claudius's limo, as its television screen projects
an image of President Clinton about to deliver that day's State of the
Union address; and, in another of the film's all-too-few touches of humor,
Hawke delivers the "To be or not to be" soliloquy while wandering the
Action Movies aisle at a Blockbuster video store, while images from *Crow
II: The City of Angels* flicker on the store's television monitors.[12]

These examples illustrate how cleverly (and almost seamlessly)
Almereyda translates *Hamlet* into a contemporary visual idiom: "The chief
thing was to balance respect for the play with respect for contemporary

reality—to see how Shakespeare can speak to the present moment, how they can speak to each other."[13] The echoes of Jan Kott, linked to post-modern notions of interpenetrating textualities, are intended. The film repeatedly explores issues about alienation, paranoia, spying, self-absorption, communication, and generational conflict that are alive in Shakespeare's text. The film reminds one yet again how plastic and re-silient the play is. Here is a somber *Hamlet*, without 60 percent of the text, the players, Yorick's skull, the pictures of the two fathers in the closet scene, and the gravedigger—and it still works. By setting the film in late October against the Halloween season, Almereyda does manage to give us skeletons, goblins, and ghosts; by making Gertrude's full-length mir-ror (rather than her bed) the focal point of the closet scene, Almereyda does present potent reflections of mother and son; and by his own, clever use of landscape and cross-cutting, Almereyda provides some of the humor missing from Hawke's Hamlet and Bill Murray's Polonius.

The movie's greatest contribution to the ever-lengthening list of *Hamlet* films, and its most interesting quality, is its metacinematic aware-ness. Almereyda provided Hawke with a pixel camera and a clamshell ed-iting machine, and these gadgets are his constant companions; Hamlet's video diary becomes a film-within-the-film. In fact, the two films—Almereyda's, shot in color, with a wonderfully glossy surface, capturing the sleek look and feel of Claudius's Manhattan world, and Hamlet's, shot in grainy black-and-white, getting at the texture of his inner agony—compete brilliantly with one another during the first two-thirds of the master narrative. The film loses some of its disjointed immediacy after Hamlet screens his film/video of "The Mousetrap" for Claudius and Gertrude, for that signals the culmination of his experience as a film-maker. The last third of Almereyda's film misses the internal visual voice of Hamlet's diary as an alternative vision to the power of Claudius's cor-porate culture. It would have been an interesting idea for Hawke's Ham-let to have passed his pixel camera to Karl Geary's street-savvy Horatio to allow him to record Claudius's reaction to "The Mousetrap" (providing yet another metacinematic layer to the film), Hamlet's arrival at Ophelia's funeral, and the final confrontation with Laertes. This would have added an important visual dimension to Hamlet's final request that Horatio "Absent thee from felicity awhile, / And in this harsh world draw thy breath in pain, / To tell my story" (5.2.347–49).

In fairness, Almereyda allows a mix of several images from his film and Hamlet's video diary to flash through Hawke's mind as he dies—

among them, Ophelia at her waterfall, his father's face, and the tumbling dryer at the laundromat. He also returns to the idea of competing visual records of Hamlet's experience for the final beat of the film.

Without directly introducing the character, Almereyda has made Fortinbras a presence in his film by having Claudius wave a copy of *USA Today* with a screaming headline and picture about Fortinbras's takeover bid to the assembled members of the Denmark Corporation in the film's equivalent of act 1, scene 2. To the delight of his audience, MacLachlan rips the newspaper in half on "So much for him." Later, when Claudius, Gertrude, and Hamlet are on their way to a movie premiere, Claudius proudly displays another edition of the paper showing him ripping the front page under the headline "Denmark Thwarts Fortinbras." When Hamlet is on the plane to England, he sees a picture of Fortinbras on the news, and that image provokes the "How all occasions do inform against me" soliloquy, delivered as he roams the plane's aisles and finds himself in the lavatory, searching his face in the mirror for the answer to his hesitancy. Almereyda's idea—and perhaps the motivation for setting the Hamlet-Laertes duel on a high, cold balcony, which makes the scene unnecessarily crowded and clumsy—was to have Casey Affleck's Fortinbras arrive by helicopter to observe the final chaos and pronounce the closing lines of the film.

Almereyda had pressed hard, in his discussions about the play with Hawke, about Fortinbras's importance. For Almereyda, Fortinbras is a "doppelgänger, a proud, fatherless prince like Hamlet, but deprived of Hamlet's melancholy, his self-loathing, his talent for introspection. Fortinbras is decisive and active; a warrior, a winner. He's also the embodiment of history—history's bloody bootprint, stamping remorselessly among the corpses of all the over complicated young men, the ones who hesitate, who stun themselves by looking into mirrors, the poets, the losers."[14] Almereyda is playing devil's advocate here, of course, but he also might well be describing the impact of Rufus Sewell's Fortinbras in Branagh's film of the play.

Though Hawke resisted this idealized view of the character, it remained in the plan to include Fortinbras in the final scene. As Almereyda acknowledges, it is a commonplace in movie culture that every film is made or imagined three times: in the screenplay, in the shooting, and in the editing. In this instance, as with the gravedigger, the editing triumphed. Almereyda was unsatisfied with the Fortinbras scene as it was shot; Miramax refused additional funds to reshoot; and Casey Affleck had another film commitment. Necessity's sharp pinch again proved the mother of invention as the production team, to replace Fortinbras, enlisted the aid of Robert MacNeil—the former coanchor of PBS's *News Hour*—to provide a newscaster's summary of the final slaughter. Inspired by Harold Bloom's use of the lines as an epigraph to his *Shakespeare and the Invention of the Human*, Almereyda lifted the Player King's lines: "Our wills and fates do so contrary run / That our devices still are overthrown; / Our thoughts are ours; their ends none of our own" (3.2.211–13) as a choric summation of MacNeil's news report.

While this device resembles Luhrmann's use of a newscast to frame his *Romeo + Juliet*, Almereyda's does have a different impact. For one, his film does not, like Luhrmann's, also begin with a newscast. After the opening shots of the Manhattan skyline, Almereyda cuts to Hawke's grainy face peering out at us from his video diary, as he mumbles lines from the "What a piece of work is a man" speech, intercut with scenes of contemporary violence and the ghostly shadow of a Stealth bomber.[15] In this context, we see that the film begins in a free verbal and visual space—free from our textual expectations of encountering the ghost rather than lines from deep within the narrative, and free from the film's master-camera (coded, color) to float in Hamlet's visual imagination (coded, black-and-white). The use of MacNeil to conclude the film does become a fitting modern media equivalent for Fortinbras's political function in the text. Both take control and provide an ironic "official" voice (and image) of closure on the Hamlet narrative that, of course, refuses to close or be contained.

In another stroke of happenstance, MacNeil suggested that Almereyda feed him his lines on a teleprompter, which gave the director the idea to shoot those rolling words themselves as the film's final image: "It made perfect sense to end this image-saturated movie with a final shot of—*words*. Shakespeare's words, ascending a glowing screen. Safe to say they'll survive a deluge of further adaptations."[16] And those final words that close the film, like those that opened it, have been lifted from elsewhere in the text, so even if Hawke's Hamlet and his inner film have been silenced, Almereyda's movie manages to get the last word, as well as image.

As I have indicated, Hawke's video diary reflects the fractured and tormented state of Hamlet's soul and imagination. It's a thing of shreds and patches he repeatedly tinkers with on his editing machine. Images of his father and Ophelia are prominent, and there is an extended sequence of his father and mother ice skating, which visually underlines Hamlet's voice-over memory: "[He was] so loving to my mother / That he might not beteem the winds of heaven / Visit her face too roughly"[17] (1.2.140–42). As this example indicates, Hamlet's video is used primarily as a device for recording and reflecting the bits and pieces of his early soliloquies retained by the screenplay. It functions much as that line of mirrored doors does for Branagh's *Hamlet* to suggest the degree of Hamlet's narcissism. There's a morose (and often sullen) self-absorption to Hawke's conception of the character; he seems to be able to find himself only on the screen, in reflection. Suicide is a genuine option. Several times he puts a gun to his head or mouth, and we are never quite sure what prevents him from pulling the trigger.

As the players are cut, it is the image of James Dean, in a clip from *Rebel without a Cause*, that spurs the "O what a rogue and peasant slave am I" soliloquy. Dean's famous haunted and alienated melancholy becomes a rich cultural icon for Hawke's Hamlet. There's something very 1950s-ish about his performance: the sensitive, brooding, inarticulate soul caught in a world whose values (whether of *Rebel*'s middle class or *Giant*'s Texas) he despises. He is caught in an adolescent battle with Polonius for Ophelia's affections, pulling her away from her father at the end of the first beat of act 1, scene 2 and bolting from her East Village photographer's pad (where he has come to deliver the poem he's been struggling to write to her) when Polonius unexpectedly shows up.[18] Hawke's Hamlet takes no pleasure from his ironic wit. He gets no secret charge from making a fool of Polonius in the "fishmonger" exchange, nor from tossing off the crack about the "funeral baked meats" coldly furnishing forth the "marriage tables" to Horatio; he doesn't get off on calling Guildenstern a "sponge," from humiliating Claudius about searching for Polonius, or from ripping into Ophelia in the nunnery scene. This Hamlet fully realizes that his wit's diseased; it, too, is a part of his soul sickness, and not an aggressive release from its debilitating melancholy.

Hawke's performance of Hamlet matches the American feel and rhythm of Almereyda's visual imagination. Hawke's shy, sensitive, melancholy Hamlet is on an existential errand—another echo of the 1950s. His eyes are always lowered (seeking for his father in the dust?); he slouches through the film, hidden behind a pair of shades, buried beneath a sea of troubles and a Sherpa's wool cap, and sipping innumerable Carlsbergs. He sports the stubble of a goatee, which he has shaved off when he flies back from England, an indication of the sea (or sky) change that journey has made in his development. The strength of Hawke's performance is that he never drops the mask he has created for his Hamlet. He plays to the camera, but never intentionally to the audience beyond. His age helps. He was twenty-seven when the film was shot, and he looks it, feels it, acts it. He has remarked that "Hamlet was much more like Kurt Cobain or Holden Caulfield than Sir Laurence Olivier,"[19] and that 1950s judgment is captured by his refusal to make his Hamlet winning through his wit or his vulnerability.

Hawke's performance fits the landscape and context of the film; he's not superior to it or to his fellow players. There's nothing bravura about his performance, an often irresistible temptation for any actor playing the part on stage or film. He does not appear to take a particular relish in Shakespeare's language, but his low-key delivery makes it seem almost natural, even in the film's Manhattan setting. Almereyda's filmscript and editing help him enormously: all the soliloquies except the "To be or not to be" are either greatly reduced or broken into various segments, shot both on camera and via the video diary, and with a clever mix of voice-over and spoken delivery, so that Hawke never has to sustain the demands of a single-take shooting of these massive chunks of verse that distinguishes Branagh's film and performance.

Hawke's youth is more than matched by that of Julia Stiles, who was seventeen when the film was made and already something of a Shakespeare-on-film veteran, having played Kat in Gil Junger's *Ten Things I Hate About You*, an updating of *The Taming of the Shrew* to a contemporary high-school setting, and Desi Brable in *O*, a similar treatment of *Othello*.[20] Stiles's Ophelia shares some of Kate's independence and stubbornness. She is genuinely puzzled by the intensity of both her brother's and her father's concern for her reputation in her relationship with Hamlet. Liev Schreiber's Laertes is significantly older than his little sister, and in their early scenes together there is none of the casual humor or horseplay that often marks their relationship in performance. Stiles resists her brother and father, but the price of her resistance is repression. She is clearly angry with Murray's Polonius when he waves Hamlet's poem to her under the noses of Claudius and Gertrude, and she tries to snatch it away from him. As her father prattles on in this scene, she walks the edge of Claudius's penthouse pool and imagines diving into it to drown her embarrassment. She weeps as Polonius rigs her with a wire for her encounter with Hamlet. Since Hamlet's letters to her fill a sizeable pink-and-white box, that scene reveals that her relationship with Hamlet has been of long standing. The box also contains a little rubber ducky, surely Almereyda's witty glance at Aki Kaurismaki's *Hamlet Goes Business* (1987), a modern mock-heroic treatment of the Hamlet story in which Claudius is a smooth businessman trying to corner the world market in rubber ducks.

As did Baz Luhrmann's visual expression of the relationship between Romeo and Juliet, water plays a crucial symbolic role in Almereyda's conception of Ophelia. Her imagined plunge into Claudius's pool returns her to the landscape the film has created for her: an urban fountain/waterfall. The film twice finds her alone in this spot after she has fled the confines of her family. And it is, of course, the site of her suicide. Almereyda gives her a sensational setting for her mad scene: an art exhibit opening at the Guggenheim. Her anguished screams ricochet down Frank Lloyd Wright's long, spiral ramp and echo in his atrium. She drowns with Hamlet's letters floating around her body, as if to say, Here lies one whose name was writ in water.

Almereyda surrounds Hawke and Stiles with a strong quartet of adults, rivaling the performances of Jacobi, Christie, Briers, and Blessed in Branagh's film. MacLachlan provides an interesting take on Claudius, making him old Hamlet's baby brother. He's young and sleek, exuding a powerful enjoyment of playing the CEO and possessing Gertrude. Manhattan is his element; he strides its streets and commands its boardrooms (even a red-neon PaineWebber sign is reflected in his hotel apartment's window) as if to the manner born. Hamlet does shock him into a painful moment of self-awareness, but when MacLachlan emerges from his limo after his silent, voice-over confession, Almereyda's camera captures him in a low-angle shot framed against a yellow-neon ticker tape of stock quotations circulating above, and we immediately grasp that his internal crisis has passed: this Claudius is back in business.

MacLachlan is well-matched by Diane Venora as Gertrude. With more to work with here than she had as Gloria Capulet in Luhrmann's *Romeo + Juliet*, Venora is a bright, alert, stylish Gertrude who positively glows in Claudius's company. This Gertrude is defined by her closely trimmed raven hair and the bold, red slash of her lipstick—the brightest color in a film dominated by black, blue, burgundy, and gun-metal gray; she is handsome and subtly sexy. The only time Venora's performance flirts with cliché is in her retreat into alcohol after Hamlet murders Polonius. This does provide her, however, with a keen eye for Claudius's stoup of wine, and, like Eileen Herlie in Olivier's film of the play, she clearly suspects that the drink has been poisoned. She rushes to take it from her husband's hand as he moves to offer it to Hamlet. The two are seated so closely together that when she takes a big sip, Almereyda wisely cuts Claudius's line "Gertrude, do not drink."

Murray's Polonius belongs to a different generation than MacLachlan's Claudius. He's a bit rumpled and scruffy, with a potbelly, and in need of a haircut. Lacking their lean and hungry look, he does not seem to emerge from the same corporate world as either old Hamlet or Claudius. Murray gives a wonderfully nuanced performance, refusing the part's invitation to seek caricature and resisting his own talent for deadpan self-mockery. He plays Polonius with a genuine, if misguided and fatal, concern for his children. He surreptitiously tucks a wad of bills in Laertes's jeans jacket as he sends him off to Paris, and he can't resist tying the shoelaces on Ophelia's sneakers as he scolds her about Hamlet. He shows up at Ophelia's apartment bearing balloons and a cake (the film-script tells us it's her birthday) at just the wrong moment: discovering Hamlet delivering his "Doubt that the stars are fire" poem he immediately confiscates it, which sends Hamlet rushing out into the night. Though outfitting Ophelia with a wire for the nunnery scene (an idea evidently suggested to Hawke courtesy of Linda Tripp), certainly fit with the film's fascination with technology, it didn't seem natural, coming from Murray's Polonius, and might better have been left to the Secret Service type (MacLachlan's single Switzer) who was always hovering at Claudius's ear and elbow.

Murray's scene with Claudius and Gertrude, in which he diagnoses Hamlet's melancholy as love sickness, gives the actor ample room to work, and his reading of the word *declension* in "Then to a lightness, and by this declension / Into a madness wherein he now raves / And we all mourn for" (2.2.149–51), capturing Polonius's pedantry in language, thought, and gesture, is a little miracle. The film here makes a stunning cut: from Murray's self-satisfied (and unintentionally ironic) pronouncement "I will find / Where truth is hid, though it were hid indeed / Within the center" (2.2.157–59) to Hamlet delivering the "To be or not to be" soliloquy as he wanders the aisles of the Blockbuster video store.[21] The center of the play's poisoned truth is, of course, Claudius, whom Polonius will never discover: that task belongs to Hamlet. Almereyda's skillful cut contrasts the blind with the bland. Hawke's Hamlet still can't shake free of his debilitating existential angst to concentrate on his quest to uncover the corruption at the play's center.

That quest is of course dictated by Hamlet's father, and Shepard's

Ghost is harrowing in his intensity. His performance is chiseled and chilling, in look and language. Shepard's sad, craggy face and his long torso, wrapped in a black leather greatcoat, create an indelible image. He savors Shakespeare's language as if it were his own, finding a powerfully insistent vocal rhythm that stresses the early beats in Shakespeare's pentameters. Some words and phrases—"burnt," "purged," "curse," "seeming virtuous," "wretch," "imperfections"—are given special emphasis: this ghost radiates ruined authority.[22] Almereyda's camera circles, tracks, zooms in, and pulls back, as the ghost keeps backing Hamlet into dark corners, a perfect visual image for their relationship. The intense, furious glint in Shepard's eye also carries the hint of the crazy, demonic father Hamlet both fears and idealizes. Shepard never removes his penetrating gaze from his son, but his right hand repeatedly presses a tightly folded handkerchief to his ear, reminding us of that primal wound.[23] Shepard pulls Hawke into a vise-like embrace on "Remember me" and leaves his son as shaken as he is committed by his father's command for revenge.

Almereyda keeps Shepard's presence alive throughout the film: Hamlet slumps against the wall beneath his father's framed photograph in the Denmark Corporation's auditorium where Claudius announces his marriage and dispatch of Fortinbras; Shepard's image flickers out at us repeatedly in segments from Hamlet's video diary; he makes his customary appearance in act 3, scene 4, where he sits calmly in a chair, intently scrutinizing the emotional chaos of Hamlet's encounter with Gertrude; then Almereyda brings him back to stare balefully at Hamlet during the "readiness is all" exchange with Horatio, and again—for the final time—his image flashes into Hamlet's mind as Claudius dies.

If Orson Welles is the external ghost who haunts the formal texture of Almereyda's film, Shepard's Ghost is its internal conscience and demon. He grips the film as he does his son, with a hold that is as fierce as it is frightening. He is the powerful father who will not die or be denied. The film repeatedly makes us see that Hawke's Hamlet is trapped by several fathers: one who challenges (Claudius); one who chatters (Polonius); and one who commands (the ghost). And only the ghost refuses to die. One of the strengths of Almereyda's direction is that while he makes imaginative use of Hawke's video diary to provide fragmented images of Hamlet's fractured consciousness, he holds his camera steady and his cutting to a minimum when working with MacLachlan, Venora, Murray, and Shepard. He gives them space to work as actors, rather than constructing their performances out of dizzy camera angles and fussy editing. He holds shots, especially in Murray's farewell to Laertes and Shepard's welcome to Hamlet, so that his actors can attune their physical gestures and movements with the torrent of language they contain and release. There is much to listen to as well as to observe in Almereyda's adaptation, and he is particularly generous to his older actors in allowing them a remarkable freedom of movement and expression.

Because the most striking formal element in Almereyda's film is its metacinematic quality, incorporating several films within the master narrative, one can be in danger of overlooking another effective formal device he brings to bear on scenes not dominated by Hamlet. If Hamlet's video diary is one means of breaking the frame of the conventional film, Almereyda's interest in breaking or cutting the frame on the horizontal is another. Though the Manhattan skyline looms, and though scenes are shot in penthouses and on rooftops, Almereyda is more interested in the horizontal line than the vertical. The first, and most stunning, example of this device comes in the continuation of act 1, scene 2, when it spills out onto Park Avenue as Claudius and Gertrude question Hamlet about his excessive mourning duties for his father. As Gertrude enters the waiting limousine, its tinted windows looking like dark mirrors, Almereyda's camera catches the images of Claudius and Hamlet reflected by the car. As Claudius scolds his stepson for his unmanly grief, the rear window lowers about half-way, and the shot continues to give us the two men in reflection while Gertrude's inviting face confronts the camera directly. The lowered window severs the frame in two; the mother who peers out from above that line is radiant in her happiness, but the men in her life, caught in reflection on the lower half of her window, are locked in battle. This family is as fractured and disjointed as the slashed frame of Almereyda's shot.

The horizontal line is apparent again in the shooting of the play's other troubled family triangle. Polonius's apartment is a modernist gem overlooking the East River. The floor levels are cantilevered so that when in one room, one can see the shoes of those moving across the floor above—another disturbance of the horizontal. The apartment is constructed with metal railings cutting the horizontal and lined with rows of white bookshelves. It is against this backdrop that Almereyda films his version of act 1, scene 3, in which we see Ophelia trapped between the members of her family as Hamlet was by his in the preceding scene. Here the handsome horizontal lines disturb the frame, as first Laertes and then

Polonius complicate Ophelia's natural affections for Hamlet. Increasingly, these myriad lines are transformed into Ophelia's prison as she comes to discover that her value and identity are predicated, for brother and father, on her chastity.

After the lover she rejected has murdered the father she reluctantly obeyed, Stiles's Ophelia releases her repression in her bawdy, defiant songs. As mentioned earlier, Almereyda sets this scene in the Guggenheim Museum, with Ophelia, Gertrude, and Claudius captured in long-shot appearing on different levels of Wright's great spiral ramp. Again the strong lines of that ramp cut across the horizontal as Stiles's screams pierce the landscape. Wright's once radical building no longer belongs to the young: it has been absorbed by the corporate culture of Claudius's world of movie premieres and art-exhibition openings. Surrounded by the art of late modernism, Stiles's Ophelia can only offer her sad, bitter songs and her Polaroid photos of leaves and flowers: these she distributes as her version of rosemary and rue.

The film loses much of its energy and invention in its concluding segment. Hamlet's flight to England on American Airlines is clumsy and ill-conceived. The in-flight delivery of the "How all occasions" soliloquy could well have been jettisoned (and more of "What a piece of work is a man" retained), its spirit running so counter to Hawke's passive, even pacifist, Hamlet. His Hamlet speaks volumes about why "man delights not me," but is unconvincing when declaring "O from this time forth, / My thoughts be bloody, or be nothing worth!" (4.4.65–66). The loss of the gravedigger to the cutting-room floor is regrettable because his humor, along with Hamlet's acceptance of death as a part of life, helps restore a welcome sanity to both play and prince. Hamlet's tussle with Laertes at Ophelia's grave is awkwardly blocked and shot, and the final duel between the two is repeatedly hindered by the cramped space on the forty-eighth-floor balcony on which it is shot. The duel does have one nice film-insider touch. Paul Bartel, playing Osric, appears only in this scene and thus is freed from carrying any of the character's "waterfly" baggage. As Almereyda indicates, Osric "directs" the duel, an appropriate designation for Bartel, an older actor who is the director of such film-cult classics as *Eating Raoul* and *Death Race 2000*.[24]

Almereyda's film is a Wellesian hall of mirrors, containing layers of reflecting images, and Hawke's Hamlet is a brooding narcissist. The film is willing to take risks with its Shakespearean material, and many of the risks—particularly the metacinematic elements—pay handsome dividends.

The film, along with Baz Luhrmann's *Romeo + Juliet* and Julie Taymor's *Titus*, is the most radically inventive of the many major Shakespeare films of the decade. It has the essential quality—imagination and respect, but not reverence—for its source. It keeps Welles's legacy alive in this fertile renaissance of Shakespeare as material for film and will speak to those adventuresome students who find Welles's way of working with Shakespeare more stimulating than Olivier's. It will send them to some provocative corners of the text, and its relationship to their cultural moment, and will make a stunning teaching contrast with Branagh's epic version of the play.

A Wilderness of Tigers

Taymor's Titus

I opened this investigation of the recent revival of Shakespeare on film by exploring some of the textual and visual resonances between Kenneth Branagh's film of *Henry V* (1989) and Steven Spielberg's *Saving Private Ryan* (1998). I close it by examining a similar series of correspondences between Julie Taymor's *Titus* (1999) and Ridley Scott's *Gladiator* (2000).

Branagh's film was of course compared with Olivier's famous bright and bustling film of *Henry V,* released in 1944 just as the Allies were launching the invasion of Europe. Olivier's Henry was cut in the heroic mode; Branagh's darker version of the same character was dubbed "Dirty Harry." Olivier's film was a brilliant use of Shakespeare in the war effort, certainly the best-scripted propaganda film ever made. Branagh's seemed more in the antimilitarist mode created by the response to the conflicts in Vietnam and the Falklands. A mere decade after its release, Branagh's film now seems less a critique of the Vietnam War than a gritty celebration of the collapse of the Berlin Wall and the end of the cold war. Branagh's film seems less a radical revision of Olivier's and more like its natural successor.[1] Both films, and their cultural moments, inspired the two most fertile periods in the twentieth century's long infatuation with Shakespeare as a source for films.

Following the end of the decade and the dawn of the new century, the issue was no longer the survival of the United States and the West but the danger of their internal collapse from triumphalism. No surprise, then, that parallels with Rome and its empire should begin to surface in the work of post–cold war historians and analysts of foreign affairs as diverse as Paul Kennedy and Robert D. Kaplan.[2] And no surprise that ancient Rome should return, absent since Anthony Mann's Vietnam era's *The Fall of the Roman Empire*, to the world of film.

Ridley Scott's *Gladiator* begins with a Roman general's careful scrutiny of his legions about to unleash their awesome power on a mass of hairy barbarians somewhere in Germania. Scott's camera slowly pans down the line of mud-laden, battle-scarred, scowling faces of the general's troops. These are not the well-scrubbed legionnaires of *Quo Vadis* or the hardy English of Olivier's *Henry V* but distant military cousins of Branagh's muddy crew in his version of Agincourt.

After a prologue set in the contemporary world, Taymor's *Titus* begins with a long parade of Roman troops, home from the wars, into the Colosseum (actually shot in the ruins of the Roman arena in Pula, Croatia). At first glance, Taymor's mud-caked warriors, seen as emerging from some primal ooze of male competitive violence, might be mistaken for *Gladiator*'s legions. But the parallel is as deceiving as it is intriguing. Scott's film cannot sustain the stylized horror of its opening spasm of violence, shot as a beautiful light show begins to sprinkle down on the mayhem, while every precisely choreographed clanking step of Taymor's Roman army creates an indelible image of the Age of Iron. Scott's film quickly deserts the originality of its opening to snuggle back happily into its genre—the epic Roman melodrama made familiar by films such as *Ben Hur* and *Spartacus*.

Taymor's *Titus*, of course, has its source in Shakespeare's early, and youthfully excessive, experiment with an established genre: the Renaissance version of the revenge play. Shakespeare, true also of his early ventures into the genres of romantic comedy and the English history play, is alive to his material in fresh and outlandish ways. He begins his dramatic career by challenging Lyly, Kyd, and Marlowe at their own game and on their own genre territory. He finds fresh ways, in style and structure, in plays like *Henry VI*, *Love's Labour's Lost*, and *Titus Andronicus* to imitate their work in such a brash manner that he ends up transcending what he set out merely to emulate.

Taymor's *Titus* provides some of the same filmic pleasures. *Titus* is her first feature film, and its $25 million budget makes it, along with Michael Hoffman's *Dream*, the most expensive of this generation of Shakespeare films. Like Scott, Taymor wants to establish resonances between ancient

Rome and the contemporary United States, but unlike Scott she is willing to take chances to impose her own imaginative design on her Shakespearean material. Though *Titus* was her first feature film, she had
worked with the play before in a heralded production at the small (off-
off-Broadway) Theater for a New Audience, and her most famous stage
work, Disney's *The Lion King*, was a tale deeply embedded in the Hamlet
myth.[3]

Taymor signals her bold intentions with the framing device she creates for her film. The film opens and closes with two scenes of Taymor's
invention centering on young Lucius (Osheen Jones), whom she elevates
to the status of silent (with one key exception) witness to the events of the
narrative. In the opening scene, Lucius is a contemporary child, playing,
with growing violent abandon and gobs of ketchup, with his toy soldiers
on a kitchen table. Suddenly the external world begins to echo his imaginary violence as bombs begin crashing into his home and he is swept up
by an oddly dressed figure who floats with him, Alice-like, down a great
vortex into the world of *Titus*.[4] At the film's end, young Lucius unlocks
the small cage in which Aaron's baby son has been imprisoned, cradles the
infant in his arms, and walks slowly out of the Colosseum into the dawn,
as Elliot Goldenthal's score swells on the soundtrack. Lucius is the key
device through which Taymor dramatizes her desire to see *Titus* speaking
to us about the violence in our own world as well as that of ancient Rome.
And Lucius is the figure through whom she overlays an optimistic, and
controversial, ending on the bloody carnage that litters the end of Shakespeare's brutal tale.

While I am not convinced that her film needs either of these moments to achieve its considerable impact, Taymor does make them consistent with her use of Lucius within the body of her film. Contrary to
Stanley Kauffmann, who thinks Lucius "virtually disappears once he gets
there [Titus's Rome]," Taymor's use of her young, silent witness is ubiquitous.[5] His opening mock war played out on the kitchen table is haunt-
ingly echoed when Titus leads Aaron through his home and into the
kitchen, seeking its butcher block and meat cleaver as the site and means
of chopping off his hand—an event witnessed through a crack in the
kitchen door by Lucius. And that same kitchen is, of course, revisited for
the slaying of Chiron and Demetrius, who are suspended upside down
above the cook's work table. Taymor's camera captures Titus (Anthony
Hopkins) through the links of the steel chain he used to suspend his
victims, as he absentmindedly wipes his knife clean against his white

terry-cloth robe (one of many brilliant mad details from Hopkins's performance) and their blood drips into Lavinia's pan.

The dining room, as domestic adjunct to the kitchen, is also linked to young Lucius. Taymor's screenplay gives Lucius Marcus's lines in the text about the killing of the fly at the heart of Shakespeare's sad, absurdist version of the family dinner-table scene.[6] Shakespeare's fly-killing episode is what provides Taymor with the warrant and inspiration for her opening sequence of toy-soldier destruction: young Lucius becomes her vehicle for moving beyond violence by moving through it as symbolic participant and silent witness. As Taymor has indicated, "The development of the child from innocence through knowledge to compassion is, to me, the essentially most important theme [of the film]."[7]

Taymor's intentions are further underlined by costume and set design. Lucius wears a T-shirt with an image of a female wolf on its back—meant to remind us, I gather, of the she-wolf who nursed Rome's founders Romulus and Remus. This image of a potentially nourishing Rome is placed in contrast to the immense throne she builds for Saturninus, over which looms a giant iron head of a savage wolf. There are no high-flying eagles in her conception of Rome—only her wolves and Shakespeare's ravenous tigers.

Taymor's visual expansion of young Lucius's role is an intelligent attempt to mirror and modify key elements in Shakespeare's text. Shakespeare's play is literally and figuratively about parents devouring children. As C. L. Barber and Richard Wheeler point out, Shakespeare in *Titus Andronicus* has not yet fully developed his startling ability to link the personal with the social and political that will distinguish later tragedies like *Hamlet*, *King Lear*, and *Macbeth*.[8] When the play opens, Titus has sacrificed his sons (twenty-one of twenty-five of them) for Rome; he will later kill another for opposing him; and the subtext of the tragic action surrounding his daughter Lavinia concerns his repressed incestuous longings for her.

Shakespeare hints at these turbulent psychological waters by having the early action of the play focus on the tomb of the Andronici, where Titus's sons are buried, and the wild pit that Aaron digs, in which to ensnare two more of Titus's sons. What Shakespeare does not create is the larger sense of Rome as the patriarchal state that demands of Titus such blind sacrifice—of his own sons and those captured in Rome's service. The brutal sacrifice of Tamora's eldest son, Alarbus, which initiates the revenge motion of the play, does not spring from something powerful be-

yond Titus's own insistence that the blood of his slain sons must be ritu-
ally honored by the blood of their enemy.[9] The play pits father against
mother in Titus's demand that Tamora's son be sacrificed, but nothing
seems at stake in their conflict beyond two stubborn egos. This, too, produces Shakespeare's most awesome house of horrors, but without the pity
and terror aroused by Lear's later journey through similar psychological
terrain.

Shakespeare substitutes for deep, tragic embeddedness a powerful
eclecticism in substance, style, and structure. The play's poetry mixes the
lyric (Tamora's pastoral seduction of Aaron) with the absurd (the fly-
killing scene), mixes the symbolic (Titus shooting his message-laden ar-
rows up at the gods) with the cruel and tender (Marcus's evocation of the
ravished Lavinia). Taymor's film restlessly tries to find visual equivalents
for Shakespeare's shifts of tone and atmosphere. I have already spoken of
how her film slides from the present to the past, from modern kitchen to
ancient Colosseum. Titus's mud-laden troops enter that Colosseum in a
highly stylized series of movements, and they are followed by an assortment of military machinery, from horse-drawn carts to motorcycles to
tanks. She then cuts from that arena to Saturninus and Bassanius cam-
paigning from the back of modern convertibles as they converge on Mussolini's EUR building, whose 1930s modernist architecture was meant to
echo the Colosseum's. The film's score makes parallel jumps in style and
tempo: from the symphonic for Titus and his troops to jazz and a raucous
sax for the battling politicians. From the EUR building, Taymor plunges
us into the bowels of the Roman baths, which also serve as the tomb of
the Andronici. Here her film captures massive masculine bodies, exposed
and naked, being doused by water flowing from huge pipes and washed
by streaks of light filtering down from above.

These abrupt visual and musical shifts are Taymor's way of not just
mingling past and present but of finding filmic equivalents for similar
startling transpositions in Shakespeare's textual atmospherics. Taymor
daringly incorporates dream sequences in the flow of her film—what she
calls "Penny Arcade Nightmares"—taking us (as Kenneth Rothwell has
pointed out) back to the origins of film in England's music halls and
penny gaffs and America's vaudeville and nickelodeons.[10] The first of
these nightmares visualizes the sacrificial flames licking up around Alarbus's entrails framed between the profiles of Hopkins's Titus and Jessica
Lange's Tamora. Taymor senses that *Titus*'s violence leaps beyond realism
into the symbolic and surreal. She describes her efforts as a means to

"portray the inner landscapes of the mind as affected by the external actions. These stylized, haiku-like images appear at various points throughout the film counter-pointing the realistic events in a dreamlike and mythic manner. They depict, in abstract collages, fragments of memory, the unfathomable layers of a violent event, the metamorphic flux of the human animal and the divine."[11]

As Shakespeare keeps his material alive by shifting styles as he piles horror upon horror, so Taymor's film never allows the audience to relax into the comforts of genre, whether that of Gothic horror, ancient epic, or decadent orgy. In fact, unlike the work of many of her Shakespearean film-director contemporaries, particularly Branagh, Parker, and Almereyda, Taymor's film is never in the grip (even playfully) of film history. The closest echo, in her handling of Saturninus's rule-by-orgy, is with Fellini's *Satyricon*. Such echoes are natural, given her location shooting, in Rome, and her use of Fellini's old studio, Cinecitta, for the interiors.

Interestingly, I find her use of Fellini as a model here the least successful element in her film. Like Stanley Kubrick in *Eyes Wide Shut*, Taymor does not do orgies well. They don't stimulate her visual imagination. Other than the wonderful, enlarged vase-frieze paintings that line the walls of Saturninus's pool, the orgy images she produces are stale and flat. Unlike her military images, Taymor's evocation of Saturninus's sexually decadent world does not catch contemporary parallels. Our world is still remarkably prudish (witness Clinton's impeachment). The West is on a shopping spree, not a sex spree: global consumerism is the defining appetite of the age. Her efforts are weakened further by her decision to cast Alan Cumming as Saturninus. Cumming came to *Titus* fresh from his award-winning performance in the revival of *Cabaret*, and one sees what must have struck Taymor about parallels between the demimonde world of 1930s Berlin and ancient Rome, but trying to link Saturninus with the Nazis and Fascists remains an idea poorly realized. The Nazis were cold, efficient killers; Cumming's Saturninus is an insipid brat who strikes poses.

Taymor does make a startling cut from the arrival of Titus's army in the Colosseum to the arrival of Saturninus and Bassanius at EUR. As the brothers approach this modernist version of the Colosseum, black banners are unfurled from the arches of its top floor. I thought Taymor had found an architectural image for her interrogation of modern power as potent as her use of the ruins of ancient Rome to capture the violence of Titus's blind patriarchy. But the film does not sustain this early image; her version of the Rome that abuses and opposes Titus degenerates into a pool party, rather than concentrating on that ravenous wolf suspended above Saturninus's throne.

Cumming's limp Saturninus also complicates Titus's early series of disastrous political and familial decisions that plunge the play into violence: his refusal to become emperor; his selection of Saturninus for that honor; his refusal to honor Lavinia's betrothal to Bassanius; and his ego-driven murder of Mutius: "What villain boy, / Barr'st me my way in Rome?" (1.1.290–91). Lear's stubborn vanity seems mild by comparison. By making Saturninus so obviously the real "villain boy," Taymor's film underlines just how blind Titus's devotion to his notion of Rome and the patriarchy is. As H. R. Coursen comments about Taymor's handling of these scenes, "Titus' sense of service seems incomprehensible, not just exaggerated";[12] as a result, her film momentarily loses its imaginative play between text and image, Rome and the twentieth century. Coursen is right to see that Taymor is searching for images, like Hopkins's Titus filling the empty combat boots of his dead sons with sand sifted from his hand, to convey that in "Shakespeare's late fourth century Rome, rituals have emptied of their meaning."[13]

The film regains its energy when it turns to focus on Titus and Aaron, when it moves from the public sphere into the private. Taymor's visual imagination is sparked by Titus and Aaron: Titus, the patriarchal insider who comes to discover he's the ultimate outsider, and Aaron, the proud outsider who prowls his way to the center by devouring everything in his path, only to discover that his rough nihilism melts in the face of paternity. Taymor understands that "Titus and Aaron are mirrors, absolute mirrors of each other. As you watch Titus become a monster, you watch Aaron become a father."[14]

Taymor repeatedly shoots Hopkins's Titus against the background of the ruins and remnants of the Roman civilization he honors. An ancient aqueduct stretches out behind the garden of Titus's house, and skeletons of classical buildings dot the landscape surrounding the great crossroads scene, where Taymor shoots the prostrate Hopkins recounting his sorrows to a stone as his sons (Quintus and Martius) are carted off to their execution. Harry J. Lennix's brilliant Aaron, with a visual nod to Welles's *Othello*, is associated with a variety of cages: the largest is in the bowels of Saturninus's palace, where Chiron and Demetrius have a version of the family game room; the smallest is the tiny iron cage from which Aaron's child is released by young Lucius in the film's final sequence.

The crossroads scene (3.1) is perhaps the film's finest; it is certainly pivotal. It comes at a moment when Aaron (through his use of the pit and the body of Bassanius to trap Quintus and Martius) and Tamora (through the rape of Lavinia by her sons Chiron and Demetrius) are at their zenith. At this moment, correspondingly Titus confronts his stunning fall from the center of the Roman world he has instinctively idealized. As her film moves through a series of real and stylized landscapes, Taymor is in full command of her considerable cinematic skills. As I mentioned earlier, the periphery of the crossroads is dotted with Roman ruins she has repeatedly associated with Titus. The slow progression of the cart and military entourage escorting Titus's sons to their executions recalls the opening procession of Titus's army into the Colosseum. Now, however, Titus is not at the head of this power, but at its feet. He is not the conqueror, but the conquered. Taymor's camera captures the prostrate Hopkins, his cheek pressed against the paving stones, through the spokes of the wheel of the cart bearing his sons to their deaths. The wheel of the tale has come half-circle: Titus has moved from top to bottom, and now it is he, not Tamora, who pleads for mercy:

> Hear me, grave fathers! Noble tribunes, stay!
> For pity of mine age, whose youth was spent
> In dangerous wars, whilst you securely slept;
> For all my blood in Rome's great quarrel shed;
> For all the frosty nights that I have watch'd;
> And for these bitter tears, which now you see
> Filling the aged wrinkles in my cheeks;
> Be pitiful to my condemned sons,
> Whose souls are not corrupted as 'tis thought.
>
> (3.1.1–9)

Through those bitter, and unanswered, tears, Taymor's Titus sees one of the film's Penny Arcade nightmares: on an altar, a sacrificial lamb with the head of Mutius, the son Titus killed for opposing his decision to give Lavinia to Saturninus. This surreal flash recalls the earlier nightmare sequence of the flames licking at Alarbus's limbs, caught between the frozen profiles of Titus and Tamora. Then it was Titus who had the upper hand and whose ears were deaf to a stricken parent's plea.

Titus picks himself up from the ground to be greeted by his two remaining children. The son, Lucius, reveals that he has been banished; the daughter, Lavinia, tells Titus that she has been raped and maimed. The Andronici are now the outcasts. In the film's most tragically beautiful shot, the faces of the remnants of this ruined family—Titus, Lavinia, Lucius, and Marcus—are captured reflected in a puddle, where they have knelt to join Titus as he says, "[Look how we] sit round about some fountain / Looking all downwards to behold our cheeks / How stained like meadows yet not dry, / With miry slime left on them by a flood?" (3.1.123–26). Taymor's camera holds their reflected images in the water as rain begins to beat against the puddle's surface, obliterating the outlines of their faces.[15] In this remarkable sequence, Taymor (and Hopkins) have found a way to express in the melding of performance and landscape the myriad, eclectic shifts of Shakespeare's tone and style in *Titus Andronicus*.[16]

The crossroads scene is set up not just by Titus's public humiliation in having his sons charged with Bassanius's murder, but by the private devastation of Lavinia's rape and mutilation by Tamora's sons Chiron and Demetrius. Scholars, most notably Jonathan Bate, searching for Roman sources for *Titus Andronicus*, rightly conclude that Shakespeare raided Ovid's *Metamorphosis* more vividly than any other known historical material. Bate comments: "I believe that the play was composed out of a series of precedents in the dramatic repertoire of the period and a series of patterns in Shakespeare's reading of the classics. Aeneas, Hecuba, Virginius, Coriolanus and Seneca's Hippolytus are among those patterns, but the two most significant are the two exemplary classical stories of rape."[17]

Shakespeare made his own Ovidian patterning by mingling elements from the tales of Tereus's rape of Philomel (and Progne's revenge against her husband for his brutal treatment of her sister) and Jupiter's rape of Io. In the play's most difficult scene to stage effectively (2.3), Shakespeare has Marcus discover the raped and ravaged Lavinia, who has had her tongue cut out and her hands cut off by her attackers so that she cannot reveal their identities. The scene is difficult, not just because of the audience's encounter with the physical reality of Chiron's and Demetrius's savagery, but because Shakespeare provided Marcus with an agonizingly long, and often lyrical as well as lurid, account of Lavinia's mutilation. The scene, like many in *Titus*, by its shocking and excessive overlaying of word and image, can invite a nervous and queasy laughter from an audience unprepared for such a radical representation of human vulnerability and transgression—a laughter even more probable from a film audience trained in the largely realistic conventions of the genre.

With her film's opening images, Taymor has already announced her intention to challenge those conventions. Here she faces the daunting imaginative task of bringing us inside Lavinia's horror and suffering (and Marcus's verbal description of it), rather than to respond to it with the defensive laughter prompted by its admittedly Grand Guignol effect. Taymor has helped prepare us for this moment by the way her film has relentlessly focused on the human body, from those soldiers caked in mud to their naked bodies being washed by water streaming down on them from gigantic pipes, from the sinuous tattoos that line Tamora's arms and back to the giant marble body parts—hands, feet, torsos—that create a unique sculpture garden outside Saturninus's palace. Now Taymor again combines the real and surreal by having her camera—from Marcus's perspective—discover Lavinia in long-shot. She is poised on a stump on the edge of a swamp, dressed only in a flimsy white slip. In a surreal master stroke, merging text and design, the stumps of her hands are represented by a series of gnarly twigs. Here Taymor is boldly making literal Marcus's description: "Speak, gentle niece, what stern ungentle hands / Hath lopped and hewed and made thy body bare / Of her two branches" (2.3.16–18). The camera moves closer to Lavinia as Marcus's description becomes more graphic: her stationary position, fixed on the pedestal of her charred stump, reminds us that her body is an object made (or at least refashioned) by the culture of violence that defines Titus's world.

This is another of the film's indelible images. The only false note in the scene is Taymor's treatment of Chiron and Demetrius. When the camera first discovers Lavinia on the edge of the swamp, it pivots to catch her tormentors as they scamper away. Taymor has each actor pull down his pants to moon his victim. The crime is horrendous; the response infantile. Taymor, I imagine, wants the image to be a contemporary parallel to Shakespeare's "braving," evoking a modern Central Park "wilding," but their action diminishes the impact of the visual tableau Taymor has so brilliantly organized. This moment epitomizes the film's inability to find a visual language for the world of Saturninus, Tamora, and her progeny as compelling as the one it imagines for Titus's family and, eventually, for Aaron.

I have already commented upon Cumming's highly stylized performance as Saturninus, accomplished by repeating two or three artificial poses: a tilt of the chin; a toss of the head; a twist of the torso. His performance comes from another world and tradition than that of Lange's Tamora: they come out of radically different acting traditions and training. Lange is all breathy naturalism and does not possess the steely qualities to make a vengeful seductress convincing. Her breathing problems punctuate all her extended encounters with Shakespeare's blank verse, and her costumes—from a red riding habit to a metallic-gold version of a Madonna bustier—do not fit or flatter. Lange's Tamora is enervated, rather than energized, by her revenge. Even her encounter with Aaron in the woods is limp and passionless, not charged and sexy. Lange is an intelligent actress, but she is more skilled at being fey and languorous (better qualities for Eugene O'Neill and Tennessee Williams than for Shakespeare), than quick and treacherous.

Taymor's problems imagining Tamora extend to Tamora's sons Chiron and Demetrius, who are conceived as two hypercharged brats. Their idea of being shocking is, as mentioned before, to moon Lavinia after ravishing her. In the film's dream sequences, they are represented as tigers, but in reality they are a pair of cubs constantly pawing one another.[18] Their evil is banal, not rapacious. The film's costume designer, Milena Canonero, worked on Stanley Kubrick's *A Clockwork Orange*, but she doesn't find a visual style for Tamora's sons to equal the one she created in *Clockwork* for Alex and his droogs in order to capture their mindless violence. I realize that Taymor's varied treatment of Saturninus and Tamora is part of the eclectic style of her film, inspired by her response to Shakespeare's text, but her film reveals that her imaginative powers are more alive when concentrating on the play's second odd couple, Titus and Aaron. The film makes us care about the fates of these two fathers, but fails to find a spark of sympathy (or interest) in what motivates Tamora's revenge.

Every scene that Hopkins and Lennix are in brings out the best in Taymor's sense of design and camera work. In a fine cut from Titus's image being washed by the rain at the end of the crossroads scene, Taymor's camera finds young Lucius's face staring out of a window streaked with rain at Titus's house. Aaron arrives in a black Fiat convertible, sporting a handsome umbrella: the rain is just a nuisance for him, not the symbolic metaphor it has become for Titus and his family. The two men encounter one another, and Hopkins's eyes narrow when Lennix informs him that chopping off his hand as a token of loyalty will move Saturninus to spare Quintus and Martius. An energetic traveling shot follows Titus and Aaron as they make their way to the kitchen for cleaver and chopping block. Hopkins's eyes gleam with the perfect reasonableness that characterizes the logic of the mad, something like the wild gleam that must have danced in Shakespeare's eyes as he spun out his relentless puns on hands in the text.

From this moment on, Titus and Aaron, Hopkins and Lennix,

dominate the film. When Lennix picks up Titus's hand from the chopping block, he drops it into a plastic ziplock baggy; and as he drives off, with a saxophone riff wailing on the car's radio, he affixes the baggy to his car's rearview mirror. The baggy works—in contrast to the mooning of Lavinia—because it catches at the absurdist elements that increasingly dominate Shakespeare's treatment of his brutal and violent material. After all, when the messenger (played by the same Fellini-esque clown figure who rescued young Lucius in the film's opening scene) later arrives with the heads of Quintus and Martius as well as Titus's "warlike hand," the moment signals a crucial turn in Titus and the text. Titus's response, because he does not have "another tear to shed," is laughter. He's been pushed beyond reason into a realm without rules. As they move off into the house, he picks up one head, instructs Marcus to pick up the other, and to Lavinia says, "Bear thou my hand, sweet wench, between thy teeth" (3.2.282). As Bate remarks, catching Shakespeare's dramatic spirit here: "This is a visual joke, for it shows that she has become the *hand*maid of Revenge (a role which will later involve her in dexterous work with a basin between her stumps)."[19]

Taymor's imagination can conceive of Titus's hand dangling in that baggy from Aaron's rearview mirror, but it cannot dwell permanently in the absurdist mode. She offers her own corrective to Lavinia's exit with her father's hand gripped in her teeth by the creation of a silent scene in which young Lucius seeks out the stall of a woodcarver and brings back to Lavinia two wooden doll's hands to use as prostheses. Taymor cannot resist wanting to help even when Shakespeare's text is moving beyond such humane concerns. Taymor sees that if those stumps can be represented by bent twigs, so, too, can they be refashioned by another kind of woodworking.[20] Unlike the film's director, once Hopkins moves his grizzled Titus into the world of the revenger's imagination, there is no turning back. His eyes squint, his mouth hangs open and then suddenly rolls into a grin, and his mind sharpens as revenge replaces Rome as the sole focus of his life.

Aaron, who has been the play's key revenger seeking retribution not for a single specific slight but for an entire history of ostracism, makes an opposite turn in his journey to self-discovery. Once Aaron has played his role in murdering Bassanius, framing Quintus and Martius for the murder, impregnating Tamora, and playing his cruel joke on Titus, he seems momentarily, in text and film, exhausted. The film finds him reduced to babysitting Chiron and Demetrius in their game room and video arcade in the depths of Saturninus's palace. What reinvigorates Aaron is, paradoxically, what destroys Titus: paternity. When the nurse delivers his baby to Aaron, Taymor's camera gives us repeated close-ups of the beautiful, wide-eyed child. Here is something, finally, that cannot be dispatched or dismissed. Aaron's nihilism is obliterated by that baby. Lennix proudly cradles the child in his arms as he quickly realizes that he, now, has something more important to treasure than his own desire to destroy.

The film cross-cuts between the two fathers to deepen the parallel. Titus usurps Aaron's role as the revenger as Aaron usurps Titus's role as the patriarch. Taymor's reading of Aaron is undoubtedly influenced and softened by the racial history of the United States, though her move to elevate Aaron to the status of the Good Father is not completely at odds with Shakespeare's text. When Demetrius attempts "to broach the tadpole on my rapier's point," Aaron provides a proud defense of his son and his color:

> Stay, murtherous villains, will you kill your brother?
> Now, by the burning tapers of the sky,
> That shone so brightly when this boy was got,
> He dies upon my scimitar's sharp point,
> That touches this my first-born son and heir!
> . . . .
> What, what, ye sanguine, shallow-hearted boys!
> You white-lim'd walls! ye alehouse painted signs!
> Coal-black is better than another hue,
> In that it scorns to bear another hue;
> For all the water in the ocean
> Can never turn the swan's black legs to white,
> Although she lave them hourly in the flood.
>
> (4.2.88–92; 97–103)

Aaron is unwilling to sacrifice his son for his own ambition or even to maintain his own position of power as Tamora's lover, while Titus, at the play's beginning, was honored to see his sons destroyed in the name of Rome. Aaron and his son are eventually captured by Lucius's army and brought to its encampment—shot by Taymor in an abandoned stone quarry. This is another example of the film's excellent use of external landscapes that match the internal motions of the text. In this road-warrior wasteland, Aaron is beaten and then made to climb a tall ladder, intended as the place of his lynching. Even in captivity, the text and film give Aaron a position of superiority from which to secure his son's life, even as the father snarls out his own continued defiance of the Roman world. Aaron's confession is accompanied by the full symphonic score earlier associated with Titus, rather than with the raucous jazz tune associated with Aaron earlier in the film.

To further underline the Titus/Aaron parallel, Taymor cuts from Aaron's echo of the fly-killing scene at Titus's dining-room table:

> But, I have done a thousand dreadful things,
> As willingly as one would kill a fly
> And nothing grieves me heartily indeed,
> But that I cannot do ten thousand more.
>
> (5.1.141–44)

The immediate next shot is of Titus, sitting in his tub, writing down his "bloody lines" of revenge. This is another of Taymor's stunning visual moments.[21] Hopkins is literally writing those lines in blood as he dips his quill into the wound from the stump of his amputated hand. The floor of his dank and steamy bathroom is littered with his "sad decrees." Again the expression on Hopkins's face catches precisely the concentrated focus of the obsessed. When Tamora calls from below, Taymor's camera does a reverse zoom to catch Hopkins's face framed in his foggy bathroom window. This moment recalls young Lucius looking out of the rain-stained window at Aaron's arrival in 3.1; it also positions Titus (like Aaron on his ladder) in control of the vertical. These parallels are all textually inspired: Titus immediately knows it is Tamora, not Revenge, who has come calling, "coming for my other hand." From this moment, the film rushes to its climax. Taymor even lets us see that Titus has baked his meat pie medium rare as Hopkins's Titus, dressed in a full chef's outfit, smacks his lips in tasty approval of his dish fit, if not for the gods, at least for the emperor and his wife.

At the outset, I presented the view that *Titus Andronicus* does not possess the layered resonances between the personal and political, the psychological and the social, the family and the state that characterize Shakespeare's mature tragedies. Perhaps sensing that gap, Taymor's film tries to provide its own visual images to compensate for those absent in the text. Taymor does so by linking the family's communal domestic space—the kitchen and dining room—with the space that has come to dominate our political understanding of the Roman Empire: the Colosseum. I have indicated how Taymor's film links the opening scene of the young boy playing war on his kitchen table with Titus's troops marching into the Colosseum; and there is also the kitchen scene in which we witness Aaron chopping off Titus's hand, and the dining-room table setting for the absurdist conversation about the killing of the fly. The ultimate site of Titus's revenge, too, is enacted in that same domestic space.

When the violent chaos erupts, Titus stabs Tamora in the neck, then is himself impaled with the table's candelabra. At this moment, the film dissolves from dining room to the Colosseum, from the domestic world to the political arena. The Colosseum is filled with silent witnesses to Titus's bloody revenge. Marcus and Lucius address the gathered multitudes through a microphone as the film equates the site of Titus's private revenge with that of Rome's for public entertainment. The Colosseum was the site of public executions as well as the battles of the gladiators. Shakespeare's text, in its final beats, seeks to restore Rome to a central place in the story: Shakespeare works "Rome" and "Romans" thirteen times into the play's last one hundred and thirty-five lines. His final lines attempt to restore Rome, while Taymor's final images surely seek to indict the city and its violent legacy.

Scott's *Gladiator* also closes in the Colosseum—in that case after the expected final clash between the evil Emperor Commodus and the film's hero, Maximus. Scott's computer-generated depiction of the Colosseum and its massive audience hungry for blood created a less compelling image of Rome's barren power than did Taymor's haunting evocation of the Colosseum as silent witness to Titus's fate. Interestingly, both films exit the Colosseum with a thumbs-up sign: Scott allows the wounded Maximus a dying reverie of escape to his family farm, while Taymor has young Lucius release Aaron's babe from its cage and cradle it in his arms as he slowly walks out of the Colosseum into the dawn.

Taymor's *Titus* failed to compete with Scott's in the modern entertainment arena—in the cineplex. Spurred by her success with *The Lion King*, Taymor clearly sought a mass audience for her film. When it opened in London at the ABC Cinema on Shaftesbury Avenue, it played opposite Jackie Chan's *Shanghai Noon*, but *Titus* did not lure a cross-over audience. A pity, for her use of Shakespeare's *Titus Andronicus* as a Roman fable for our time was finally more imaginative and compelling than Scott's more obvious attempt to use Marcus Aurelius's Rome as a parable for our own potential decline and fall.

Conclusion

The Abrupt Edge

The poet Stanley Plumly has mused on the rich, metaphorical densi-
ties inherent in the ornithologist's phrase "the abrupt edge." In bird
lore, according to Plumly in his prose poem "Field," the abrupt edge
signals an "edge between two types of vegetation . . . where the advan-
tages of both are most convenient." Plumly goes on to speculate that "the
advantage of the edge is that it allows the bird to live in two worlds at
once. . . . The edge is the concept of the doorway, shadow and light, inside and outside . . . when the density and variety of the plants that love
the sun and the open air yield to the darker, greener, cooler interior
world, at the margin."[1] Shakespeare on film provides an aesthetic version
of the abrupt edge. The convergence of the world's most famous dramatic
poet and the twentieth century's most popular art form provides a vivid
landscape in which high art mingles with low, Renaissance drama meets
Mad Max, lyric poetry competes with jump cuts and slam zooms, epic energies are contained by postmodern pastiche, overwrought rhetorical
embellishments meet narrative clarity, three-dimensional theatrical immediacy jostles with a vibrant flat surface, the singular experience becomes infinitely repeatable, word and image collide, crumble, and
recombine—all at twenty-four frames per second.

Film provides an abrupt edge where open-air and interior drama,
Shakespearean spectacle and intimacy, can meet and mingle. Kenneth
Branagh, for instance, can give us the intimacy of the domestic tragedy
unfolding within the false sparkle of his Elsinore's mirrored interiors and

he can then cut away to Fortinbras's inexorable and powerful military machine advancing on the Danish court from without. Julie Taymor's camera can close in on Titus's face pressed against those paving stones and can then pull back to give us the full image of Rome's crushing power as we watch Titus's sons being carted off to their executions. Here Titus's metaphorical lament at his entrapment in a "wilderness of tigers" is instantaneously literalized and generalized. Film provides an abrupt edge where Shakespeare's dense text can be captured and enriched by movie forms as bold as the gangster film or musical comedy or as subtle as noir and screwball.

The films of the Branagh era are distinguished by their embrace of popular film's codes, conventions, and genres. Most of Branagh's contemporaries are fearless (and unashamed) to create by incorporating Shakespeare into the forms of mass (and elite) entertainment that they have come of artistic age with. Baz Luhrmann's *William Shakespeare's Romeo + Juliet* gathers its energy and life from the incessant MTV pulse of its soundtrack and visual style; Michael Almereyda's *Hamlet* is as fascinated by modern communication technology as it is disgusted by a materialist society controlled by corporate advertising; Michael Hoffman's *A Midsummer Night's Dream* is dominated by an eclectic visual style, raiding images from twentieth-century films as disparate as *Peter Pan* and *Star Wars*, and it has a soundtrack awash in nineteenth-century operas as distinct as *La Traviata* and *Norma;* and Trevor Nunn's *Twelfth Night* moves deep into cinematic language in its opening plunge beneath the roaring waves to depict Viola's and Sebastian's separation by drowning; Nunn then uses the camera to establish more indirect dramatic tension by cross-cutting among the various groups of lovers at cross-purposes during Feste's singing of "O Mistress Mine."

Nunn, in his use of several Cornwall locations—especially Saint Michael's Mount—to establish Orsino's and Olivia's residences, creates a landscape that stimulates the imagination in ways possible only on film. Taymor's *Titus* does something similar with its use of Mussolini's EUR Building and the ruins of the Roman past as symbolic landscapes for the tragic clash between Tamora and Titus. I find Taymor's use of these sites much more apt and compelling than all the digitalized razzle-dazzle of Ridley Scott's Rome in his *Gladiator.* Branagh, Luhrmann, Almereyda, Nunn, and Taymor all use location shooting to do more than create "a local habitation and a name" against which to set their Shakespearean tales. Tuscany, Blenheim, Mexico City, Manhattan, Rome, and Cornwall

all become players, active agents in the way in which their films' actions unfold and language in the films resonates between character and landscape. Only film can provide the pressure of a vivid, insistent sense of place to the Shakespearean enterprise without compromising the speed and fluidity of the way in which the text opens up and out in time and space.

I grant that none of the films I have pointed to, with the possible exception of Branagh's *Hamlet*, can match the personal, autobiographical riches of Olivier's *Hamlet* or Welles's *Chimes at Midnight*, but almost all of the films of the Branagh era are more accomplished pieces of commercial filmmaking. Olivier's *Hamlet* is perhaps the most revered Shakespeare film in the canon, but it announces its "classic" status in every image, cut, and camera movement. Welles's *Chimes* is, to my mind, the greatest Shakespeare film ever made, but its brilliance speaks more to the Shakespearean student and cineaste than to the average moviegoer. By going, metaphorically, to Hollywood, the Shakespeare films of the long decade have brought Shakespeare's scripts closer to a mass audience than they have been at any time since their origins in the hurly-burly liberties of Elizabethan London's South Bank.

H. R. Coursen, trying to define what is uniquely Shakespearean in any modern production of a Shakespeare script, settles on the term *archetype:*

> An element of the script that becomes "momentarily essential" as historical circumstances allow us, with the director, to experience the way a script means . . . : Successful Shakespearean performance is oxymoronic. It contacts something that is for the moment timeless [though] our sense of what is "timeless" in Shakespeare quickly becomes—as we can tell when we look back at what was being said about Shakespeare fifty or a hundred years ago—a coincidence between our construction and some aspect of the script.[2]

What Coursen is driving at is that all productions are translations; the script is transformed from words on the page to bodies set in motion in space and time and reshaped by the cultural moment in which they are released. Shakespearean scripts have myriad, but not limitless, possibilities. Their robust mythic variety and vivid language are what make them so perpetually inviting to directors and performers. What opens them up for endless reinterpretation yet makes them recognizably Shakespearean is the way they circulate around core myths and ideas in a vibrant metaphoric language that opens up rather than closes off. Shakespeare's texts are clay, not plastic; their origins are in the earth, not the lab; they can be smoothed or roughened, but not transformed into something unrecognizable. They resist, even as they reveal themselves in performance as well as critical analysis.

In the Branagh era, the Shakespeare film genre has been not only revived but also revitalized. Even as these films have gathered energy from Hollywood, many—especially the films directed by Branagh, Nunn, and Taymor—have shown a remarkable respect for Shakespeare's language. The theatrical experiments in the past twenty-five years with performing Shakespeare in small, intimate venues like Stratford's Other Place, London's Cottesloe, and New York's Theater for a New Audience have allowed actors to emphasize the naturalistic, conversational potential in his verse, rather than its rhetorical flights and flourishes, and has led to the creation of a speaking style appropriate for handling Shakespeare's language on screen. This more intimate Shakespeare is the great contribution to the performance history made by the post-Olivier and Gielgud generation of classical actors. Taymor and Branagh, particularly, never allow their actors to back away from the dense delights of the subtle rhythms of Shakespeare's verse and prose. For them, that language, always the core problem in making the Shakespeare film, is an asset to be celebrated rather than a nuisance to be negotiated. In contrast to Olivier's anxious attempts to disguise Hamlet's soliloquies with a variety of devices from radical surgery to voice-overs, and from impressionistic images to fainting spells, Branagh attacks them with vigor and relish. Taymor faces an even greater potential problem in confronting the challenges of Shakespeare's audacious and often cruel bursts of poetic fancy in *Titus Andronicus*. She does so by taking that language absolutely seriously, rather than as the immature excess of a young poet just discovering his talent; we find startling Taymor images emerging from Shakespeare's metaphors (the stumps of Lavinia's hands imagined as twigs, for instance), without the film director trying to rival or replace them.

Language, so minimal and barren in the contemporary commercial film, is one of the joys of this revival of the Shakespeare film genre. These films remind us of the pleasure James Agee found years ago in Olivier's *Henry V*: "The one great glory of the film is this [Shakespeare's] language. The greatest credit I can assign to those who made the film is that they have loved and served the language so well."[3] Agee to the contrary, many, including Peter Brook, had thought, based on the brilliant Shakespeare films of Kurosawa and Kozintsev, that perhaps great Shakespeare films could be made only in the spare translations of another language so that Shakespeare's poetry did not have to compete with the language of film. Branagh, Nunn, and Taymor have given the lie to such thinking. All of the Shakespeare films in the past decade, unlike those of the post–World War II period, have been made by directors working from scripts in English. Even one of the most fascinating recent spin-off films—*The King Is Alive* (2001), directed by Kristian Levring, a member of the Danish Dogme film group, and featuring a mixed cast of American, British, and European actors—was made in English.

When these films stumble, it is almost always related to critical idea, rather than technical execution. Loncraine's *Richard III*, for example, is a lively and assured piece of filmmaking, and the virtual world he creates out of the wry juxtaposition of current London landmarks with Shakespearean settings is often wonderfully amusing. I am thinking specifically of his use of the Bankside Power Station (now the Tate Modern) as the Tower of London, where Clarence is imprisoned and its Thames-side partner, the gutted Battersea Power Station, as the site for the battle of Bosworth Field. But the film falters when Loncraine's parodic imagination, his head swimming with Hollywood genres like the gangster film, meets McKellen's script based on Richard Eyre's deadly serious stage production, with Richard III conceived as a fascist member of Britain's royal family in the 1930s. The two ideas, each potent for the play on its own terms, fail to cohere when piled on top of one another. In a different fashion, Nunn's melancholy, autumnal *Twelfth Night*—beautifully shot on location in Cornwall—allows Mel Smith to turn Sir Toby Belch into an ugly bore, thus completely sabotaging Shakespeare's clash between Toby's excessive twinkle and Malvolio's obsessive efforts to put a lid on holiday. Shakespeare's subplot just won't comfortably squeeze into Nunn's Chekhovian ideas about the script. Hoffman becomes so enamored with film's potential for potent landscape and lush soundtrack that Shakespeare's exquisite interweaving of strands of plot and theme in *A Midsummer Night's Dream* are obliterated, rather than enhanced, by score and image.

These Shakespeare films are distinguished by their raids on Hollywood, and Hollywood has been happy to return the favor. Shakespeare has become ubiquitous in the high-school teen flick. If such a film contains a scene set in an English class, you can be sure that the subject won't be Wordsworth or Dickens or Frost; it will be Shakespeare. The recent raunchy *American Pie* (1999), perhaps seeing Hal as an Elizabethan version of the male teen on the make, managed to include a discussion of *I Henry IV* in its brief visit to the classroom. But most commonly, from Steve Martin's *L.A. Story* (1991) to John McTiernan's *Last Action Hero* (1993) to Amy Heckerling's *Clueless* (1995), the Shakespearean work of choice for playful parody is *Hamlet*, both as text and film. Having fun with *Hamlet* is an American tradition as old as Mark Twain, and having fun with Olivier's film of *Hamlet* dates from *The Catcher in the Rye* and Holden Caulfield's skeptical assessment: "I don't see what's so marvelous about Sir Laurence Olivier, that's all. He has a terrific voice, and he's a helluva handsome guy, and he's very nice to watch when he's walking or dueling or something, but he wasn't at all the way D. B. said Hamlet was. He was too much like a goddam general, instead of a sad, screwed-up type guy." Forty-five years later, a postmodern version of Holden, *Last Action Hero*'s Danny Modigan found Olivier's Hamlet more passive wimp, in need of rescue by Arnold Schwarzenegger, than "goddam general." McTiernan's film, as Lynda Boose and Richard Burt suggest, is "one more version of the way that America, through the aesthetic medium that is as peculiarly American as the stage is English, tries to come to terms with its own, unregenerate fascination with the Bard of Avon."[4]

As I briefly mentioned in my second chapter, Branagh's *Henry V* helped to inspire the return of the genre of the good war film. As I argued there, Steven Spielberg's *Saving Private Ryan* is itself a spin-off from both Shakespeare's play and Branagh's film. Its success has spawned a spate of World War II films, including *The Thin Red Line* (1998), *Enemy at the Gates* (2001), *Pearl Harbor* (2001), and *Captain Corelli's Mandolin* (2001), to mention only the most obvious. In each instance, though, unlike a generation of Vietnam films, the good guys, whether Americans, Russians, or Italians, never become the bad guys. The enemy remains the "other" (the Germans or the Japanese), never ourselves. In almost all instances, but most especially in *Enemy at the Gates*, the good guys, like Branagh's dirty Harry, are distinguished by being covered in mud and grime. These are worker-soldiers, rather than sparkling heroes. The revival of the genre of the good war film—and its Shakespearean echoes—reached its apotheosis in the recent Royal Shakespeare Company staging of *Henry V* (2000) directed by Edward Hall, where the siege of Harfleur was reconceived as the landing at Omaha Beach, and in the BBC-HBO television series *Band of Brothers*, coproduced by Spielberg and Tom Hanks, which recreates in ten installments the Normandy invasion and the battle for Europe. If, as I suggested at the outset, some of the cultural energy that sparked this revival of the Shakespeare film genre emanated from the end of the cold war, perhaps the events of September 11, 2001, will signal the end of its flourishing.

As both a Hollywood insider (Al Pacino) and an outsider (Nunn) have acknowledged, Branagh made this revival of the Shakespeare film possible by demonstrating to commercial film producers that Shakespeare was not, as had been commonly accepted, box-office poison. The success of Branagh's *Much Ado About Nothing* was the key that unlocked the funding for two films that had the audacity to incorporate Shakespeare's name in their titles: Luhrmann's *William Shakespeare's Romeo + Juliet* and John Madden's *Shakespeare in Love*. The former film became the box-office champion in this renaissance of the Shakespeare film, and the latter became one of only four romantic comedies ever to win the Academy Award for best picture. Shakespeare was, for a moment in the late 1990s, so hot that national news magazines like *Time* and *Newsweek* ran major stories on the phenomenon, as did prestigious national newspapers—the *New York Times* and the *Christian Science Monitor*. The success of Branagh's *Much Ado* certainly helped to create a movie audience prepared to delight in a script as witty and rich as Marc Norman's and Tom Stoppard's for *Shakespeare in Love*, which, as Tony Howard rightly notes, "simultaneously debunks the Romantic deification of Shakespeare and takes it in rhapsodic new directions."[5]

The Shakespeare films of the Branagh era have created a dense and provocative abrupt edge where four-hundred-year-old scripts have helped to revitalize the twentieth century's most potent and popular art form. The interplay between those scripts, contemporary ideas about the Shakespearean agenda, and film history and technology have created, like the birds in Plumly's prose poem, something to sing about.

Notes

ONE

1. See Kenneth S. Rothwell, *A History of Shakespeare on Screen: A Century of Film and Television* (Cambridge: Cambridge University Press, 1999).

2. See Robert Hamilton Ball, *Shakespeare on Silent Film: A Strange Eventful History* (London: George Allen and Unwin, 1968).

3. Rothwell, *History of Shakespeare on Screen*, p. 246.

4. The first time a film appears in the text, I include its release date; thereafter, I include the date only if it is relevant to the context of my discussion.

5. I also do not include the films of *Macbeth, Hamlet,* and *King Lear* that were made in England during this period and shown on television but never released as commercial films. Nor do I include consideration of the three low-budget, cult horror-film versions of *Titus Andronicus,* directed by Lorn Richey (1996), Christopher Dunne (1999), and Richard Griffin (2000). For a consideration of the *Titus* films, see Richard Burt, "Shakespeare and the Holocaust: Julie Taymor's *Titus* Is Beautiful, or Shakesploi Meets (the) Camp," *Colby Quarterly* 37, no. 1 (2000): 78–106.

6. For an excellent discussion of the finances of the contemporary Shakespeare film and the impact of Zeffirelli's *Romeo and Juliet* at the box office, see Russell Jackson, introduction to his *Cambridge Companion to Shakespeare on Film* (Cambridge: Cambridge University Press, 2000), pp. 1–12.

7. Ibid., p. 5.

8. For details on film screenings and grosses, see boxofficeguru.com.

9. Branagh speaks nostalgically of *Henry V*'s financing, which came from the City (the London equivalent of New York's Wall Street), rather than from Hollywood and the movie industry: author interview, March 16, 2001, London.

10. See Michael Almereyda's introduction to his *William Shakespeare's Hamlet: A Screenplay Adaptation* (London: Faber and Faber, 2000), p. xi.

11. Jack Jorgens, *Shakespeare on Film* (Bloomington: Indiana University Press, 1977), pp. 7–16.

12. Ibid., p. 8.

13. Harold Bloom, *Shakespeare: The Invention of the Human* (New York: Riverhead Books, 1998), p. 4.

14. Jorgens, *Shakespeare on Film*, p. 9.

15. Ibid.

16. Richard Eyre had directed McKellen's stage performance of *Richard III* for the Royal National Theatre in 1991. Eyre was McKellen's first choice to direct the film, but other commitments prevented him from doing so.

17. Lynda E. Boose and Richard Burt, "Totally Clueless? Shakespeare Goes to Hollywood in the 1990s," in Lynda E. Boose and Richard Burt, eds., *Shakespeare, The Movie: Popularising the Plays on Film, TV, and Video* (London: Routledge, 1997), p. 14.

18. Jorgens, *Shakespeare on Film*, p. 8.

19. Ibid.

20. See Orson Welles and Peter Bogdanovich, *This Is Orson Welles* (New York: HarperCollins, 1992), p. 228.

21. Ibid., p. 10.

22. Ramona Wray and Mark Thornton Burnett, "From the Horse's Mouth: Branagh on the Bard," in Mark Thornton Burnett and Ramona Wray, eds., *Shakespeare, Film, Fin de Siècle* (London: Macmillan, 2000), pp. 167–68.

23. See Kathy Howlett's chapter on Zeffirelli's *Hamlet* in her *Framing Shakespeare on Film* (Athens: Ohio University Press, 2000) for a thorough analysis of the influence of the Hollywood western on the film.

24. Rothwell, *History of Shakespeare on Screen*, p. 231.

25. Marlon Brando, *Songs My Mother Taught Me* (New York: Random House, 1994), p. 204.

26. Ibid., pp. 204–5.

27. Jackson, *Cambridge Companion to Shakespeare on Film*, p. 1.

28. Robert F. Willson Jr., *Shakespeare in Hollywood, 1929–1956* (Madison, N.J.: Fairleigh Dickinson University Press, 2000).

29. Pauline Kael, *Movie Love* (New York: Dutton/Plume, 1991), p. 216.

30. Gary Taylor, "Theatrical Proximities," *Shakespeare Quarterly* 50, no. 5 (1999): 350.

31. Michael Hattaway, "The Comedies on Film," in Jackson, *Cambridge Companion to Shakespeare on Film*, p. 89.

32. See "Fathers and Sons: Kenneth Branagh's *Henry V*," in my *Shakespeare Observed: Studies in Performance on Stage and Screen* (Athens: Ohio University Press, 1992), pp. 165–74.

33. Kenneth Branagh, *Hamlet: Screenplay and Introduction* (New York: W. W. Norton, 1996), p. 73.

34. Michael Almereyda, *William Shakespeare's Hamlet: A Screenplay Adaptation* (London: Faber and Faber, 2000), p. ix.

35. Interview with Branagh, March 16, 2001.

36. Lorne M. Buchman, *Still in Movement: Shakespeare on Screen* (New York:

Oxford University Press, 1991); John Collick, *Shakespeare, Cinema, and Society* (Manchester: Manchester University Press, 1989); H. R. Coursen, *Shakespearean Performance as Interpretation* (Newark: University of Delaware Press, 1990), idem, *Shakespeare in Production: Whose History?* (Athens: Ohio University Press, 1996), idem, *Shakespeare: The Two Traditions* (Madison, N.J.: Fairleigh Dickinson University Press, 1999); Anthony Davies, *Filming Shakespeare's Plays* (Cambridge: Cambridge University Press, 1988); Peter S. Donaldson, *Shakespearean Films/ Shakespearean Directors* (Boston: Unwin Hyman, 1990); Barbara Hodgdon, *The End Crowns All* (Princeton, N.J.: Princeton University Press, 1991); Bernice Kliman, Hamlet: *Film, Television, and Audio Performance* (Cranbury, N.J.: Associated University Presses, 1988); Luke McKernan and Olwen Terris, eds., *Walking Shadows: Shakespeare in the National Film and Television Archives* (London: British Film Institute, 1994); Ace G. Pilkington, *Screening Shakespeare: From Richard II to Henry V* (Newark: University of Delaware Press, 1991); and Kenneth S. Rothwell and Annabelle Melzer, eds., *Shakespeare on Screen: An International Filmography and Videography* (New York: Neal-Schuman, 1990).

37. Anthony Davies and Stanley Wells, eds., *Shakespeare and the Moving Image* (Cambridge: Cambridge University Press, 1994); and Jackson, *Cambridge Companion to Shakespeare on Film.*

38. Michael Skovmand, ed., *Screen Shakespeare* (Aarhus, Denmark: Aarhus University Press, 1994); Boose and Burt, *Shakespeare, The Movie;* Robert Shaughnessy, ed., *Shakespeare on Film, New Casebooks Series* (Basingstoke, Eng.: Houndmills, 1998); Burnett and Wray, *Shakespeare, Film, Fin de Siècle.*

39. Rothwell, *History of Shakespeare on Screen.*

40. Douglas Brode, *Shakespeare in the Movies: From the Silent Era to* Shakespeare in Love (New York: Oxford University Press, 2000); Sarah Hatchuel, *A Companion to the Films of Kenneth Branagh* (Winnipeg: Blizzard, 2000); Howlett, *Framing Shakespeare;* and Willson, *Shakespeare in Hollywood.*

41. See Thomas A. Pendleton's review in *Shakespeare Newsletter* 50, no. 1 (2000): 18–23.

42. Three new studies, published too recently to be included in my survey, have joined the ever-burgeoning field: Stephen Buhler's *Shakespeare in the Cinema: Ocular Proof* (Albany, N.Y.: SUNY Press, 2001), H. R. Coursen's *Shakespeare in Space* (New York: Peter Lang, 2002), and Courtney Lehmann's *Shakespeare Remains: Theater to Film, Early Modern to Postmodern* (Ithaca, N.Y.: Cornell University Press, 2002).

TWO

1. Jorgens, *Shakespeare on Film*, p. 2.
2. Crowl, *Shakespeare Observed*, pp. 165–66.
3. Rothwell, *History of Shakespeare on Screen*, p. 246.

4. "Kenneth Branagh at the Quilting Point: Shakespearean Adaptation, Post-modern Auteurism, and the (Schizophrenic) Fabric of 'Everyday Life,'" *Post Script* 17, no. 1 (1997): 7.

5. Rothwell, *History of Shakespeare on Screen*, p. 247.

6. Kael, *Movie Love*, p. 216.

7. "Taking on Shakespeare: Kenneth Branagh's *Henry V*," *Shakespeare Quarterly* 42 (spring 1991): 60–71.

8. Kenneth Branagh, *Much Ado About Nothing: Screenplay, Introduction, and Notes on the Making of the Movie* (New York: W. W. Norton, 1993), p. x.

9. Ibid.

10. *New York Review of Books*, 6 February 1997, p. 12.

11. Norman Rabkin's chapter "Either/Or: Responding to *Henry V*," is in his *Shakespeare and the Problem of Meaning* (Chicago: University of Chicago Press, 1981). See Chris Fitter, "A Tale of Two Branaghs: *Henry V*, Ideology, and the Mekong Agincourt," in Ivo Kamps, ed., *Shakespeare Left and Right* (New York: Routledge, 1991), pp. 259–75; Curtis Breight, "Branagh and the Prince, or a 'royal fellowship of death,'" *Critical Quarterly* 33, no. 4 (1991): 95–111; and Donald K. Hedrick, "War Is Mud: Branagh's Dirty Harry V and the Types of Political Ambiguity," in Boose and Burt, *Shakespeare, The Movie*, pp. 45–66.

12. Michael Manheim, "The English History Plays on Screen," in Davies and Wells, *Shakespeare and the Moving Image*, p. 130.

13. These films include Austen's *Sense and Sensibility* (1995), *Persuasion* (1995), *Emma* (1996), and *Mansfield Park* (1999); James's *Portrait of a Lady* (1996), *The Wings of the Dove* (1997), and *The Golden Bowl* (2000); and Wharton's *The Age of Innocence* (1993) and *The House of Mirth* (2000).

14. Quoted in David Rosenthal, *Shakespeare on Screen* (London: Hamlyn, 2000), p. 215.

15. Breight, "Branagh and the Prince," pp. 95–96.

16. Rothwell, *History of Shakespeare on Screen*, p. 246.

17. Donaldson, "Taking on Shakespeare," p. 61.

18. Branagh wryly boasts, "The greatest tracking shot in the world. That was my theory, anyway. It was certainly bloody long": Kenneth Branagh, *Beginning* (London: Chatto and Windus, 1989), p. 235.

19. Branagh reports, "I'd heard the Ian Holm School of Acting described as follows: 'Anything you can do, I can do less of'": Branagh, *Beginning*, p. 235.

20. Donaldson, "Taking on Shakespeare," pp. 60–71.

21. Hatchuel, *Films of Kenneth Branagh*, pp. 142–63.

22. Branagh's other major stage Shakespeare roles include Laertes, Edgar, King of Navarre, Touchstone, and Peter Quince.

23. Quoted in Jon Naughton, "The Return of the Magnificent Eight?" *Premiere*, September 1993.

24. See Hatchuel, *Films of Kenneth Branagh*, p. 152.

25. Wray and Burnett, "From the Horse's Mouth," p. 169.

26. "About the Production," Miramax Press Packet for *Love's Labour's Lost*, p. 2.

27. "Film Reviews: Three by H. R. Coursen," *Shakespeare and the Classroom* 3, no. 1 (2000): 34.

28. Wendy Wasserstein, "Where I Seem to Find the Happiness I Seek," *New York Times*, "Arts and Leisure," Sunday, June 4, 2000, pp. 15–20.

29. Unless otherwise indicated, all Shakespeare quotations are from *The Riverside Shakespeare* (Boston: Houghton Mifflin, 1997), 2nd ed.

30. C. L. Barber, *Shakespeare's Festive Comedy* (Princeton, N.J.: Princeton University Press, 1959), p. 92.

31. A. O. Scott, "What Say You, My Lords? You'd Rather Charleston?" *New York Times*, June 9, 2000, p. B12.

32. Ibid.

33. Coursen, "Film Reviews," p. 34.

34. Ibid., p. 35.

35. Mark Caro, "Top Hat—and Tales," *Chicago Tribune*, sec. 5, June 22, 2000, p. 6.

36. Stanley Kauffmann, "Well, Not Completely Lost," *New Republic*, July 10 and 17, 2000, p. 32.

37. John Updike, *More Matter* (New York: Knopf, 1999), p. 666.

THREE

1. See Davies, *Filming Shakespeare's Plays*; Collick, *Shakespeare, Cinema, and Society*; Donaldson, *Shakespearean Films/Shakespearean Directors*; Buchman, *Still in Movement*; and my *Shakespeare Observed*. H. R. Coursen includes a brief treatment of Glenn Close's Gertrude in his chapter "Gertrude's Story," in his *Watching Shakespeare on Television* (Rutherford, N.J.: Fairleigh Dickinson University Press, 1993), pp. 70–79.

2. Charles W. Eckert, ed., *Focus on Shakespearean Films* (Englewood Cliffs, N.J.: Prentice Hall, 1972).

3. Jorgens, *Shakespeare on Film*.

4. See Ace G. Pilkington's "Zeffirelli's Shakespeare," in Davies and Wells, *Shakespeare and the Moving Image*, pp. 163–79; Robert Hapgood, "Popularizing Shakespeare: The Artistry of Franco Zeffirelli," in Boose and Burt, *Shakespeare, The Movie*, pp. 80–94; and Deborah Cartmell, "Franco Zeffirelli and Shakespeare," in Jackson, *Cambridge Companion to Shakespeare on Film*, pp. 212–21.

5. Hapgood, "Popularizing Shakespeare," p. 92. See also Howlett, *Framing Shakespeare*, pp. 20–51, for a recent extended and intelligent analysis of Zeffirelli's *Hamlet*.

6. Jorgens, *Shakespeare on Film*, pp. 74–75.

7. Hapgood, "Popularizing Shakespeare," p. 89.

8. *Zeffirelli: The Autobiography of Franco Zeffirelli* (New York: Weidenfield & Nicolson, 1986), p. 191.

9. Howlett, *Framing Shakespeare*, p. 21.

10. Janet Adelman, *Suffocating Mothers* (London: Routledge, 1992), pp. 14–15.

11. Julia Reinhard Lupton and Kenneth Reinhard, *After Oedipus: Shakespeare in Psychoanalysis* (Ithaca, N.Y.: Cornell University Press, 1993), p. 83.

12. The quotation of Claudius's lines is taken directly from the film; it corresponds to 1.2. 107–9. Cartmell makes an intriguing connection between this shot and Zeffirelli's focus on Juliet's hand opening in the Capulet's tomb in his *Romeo and Juliet*: "Hamlet thus begins where *Romeo and Juliet* ends": "Franco Zeffirelli and Shakespeare," p. 219.

13. Linda Charnes, "Dismember Me: Shakespeare, Paranoia, and the Logic of Mass Culture," *Shakespeare Quarterly* 48 (spring 1997): 1–16.

14. Wayne Koestenbaum, *The Queen's Throat: Opera, Homosexuality and the Mystery of Desire* (New York: Persea Books, 1993), p. 142.

15. Ibid., p. 151.

16. For a brilliant competing analysis of the poster configuration, see Barbara Hodgdon, "The Critic, the Poor Player, Prince Hamlet, and the Lady in the Dark," in *Shakespeare Reread*, ed. Russ MacDonald (Ithaca, N.Y.: Cornell University Press, 1994), p. 167.

17. Anthony Dawson, *Hamlet in Performance* (Manchester: Manchester University Press, 1996), p. 197.

18. Michael Skovmand, "Mel's Melodramatic Melancholy: Zeffirelli's Hamlet," in Skovmand, ed., *Screen Shakespeare*, p. 126.

19. See Donaldson, *Shakespearean Films/Shakespearean Directors*, pp. 31–67.

20. Howlett, *Framing Shakespeare*, pp. 20–51.

21. "Dismember Me," pp. 7–11. Charnes wants Zeffirelli's film to be father-centered, when, as I am arguing, it is relentlessly about mothers.

22. Hapgood quotes Zeffirelli as saying of Hamlet: "The problem of the boy is quite simply—whom to love? He did not really love his father; that was a secondary character in his life. Ophelia? No, there is no love-story possible there, he is always uncertain, ambiguous—because his heart is not come out of his mother's womb! Because there is no safer place in all the world": "Popularizing Shakespeare," p. 90.

23. On "Get thee to a nunnery," Skovmand argues that "leaving the nunnery injunction . . . out of the nunnery scene and shifting it to the play within the play gives it a more logical context, placing this rather definitive statement in what is effectively the last scene with Ophelia and Hamlet together, their only later 'encounter' being at Ophelia's funeral": "Mel's Melodramatic Melancholy," p. 118.

24. Adelman, *Suffocating Mothers*, p. 14.

25. Hapgood argues that "although the closet scene is the most powerful in the film, it does not sit well with the rest": "Popularizing Shakespeare," p. 91. My analysis is meant to demonstrate why the scene is both powerful *and* crucial to Zeffirelli's film. See also Murray Biggs's reading of the scene in "He's Going to His Mother's Closet," in *Shakespeare Survey* 45 (1993): 61–62.

26. Skovmand is excellent on Zeffirelli's use of tinting and filters in the film: warm amber for Gertrude, cold gray-blue for the Ghost; see "Mel's Melodramatic Melancholy," p. 127.

27. Donaldson, *Shakespearean Films/Shakespearean Directors*, p. 34.

28. Dawson, *Hamlet in Performance*, p. 205.

29. Adelman, *Suffocating Mothers*, p. 32.

30. Ibid., p. 33.

31. Ibid., p. 34.

32. Ibid.

33. Ibid.

FOUR

1. See Hapgood, "Popularizing Shakespeare," pp. 92–93.

2. See Fredric Jameson, *Postmodernism, or, The Cultural Logic of Late Capitalism* (Durham, N.C.: Duke University Press, 1991), pp. 55–67; and Ihab Hassan, "Pluralism in Postmodern Perspective," *Critical Inquiry* 12 (1981): 13–28.

3. Courtney Lehmann, "*Much Ado About Nothing?* Shakespeare, Branagh, and the National-Popular in the Age of Multinational Capital," *Textual Practice* 12, no. 1 (1998): 1–22.

4. Trevor Nunn, *William Shakespeare's Twelfth Night: A Screenplay* (London: Methuen, 1996), p. ii.

5. Boose and Burt, "Totally Clueless?" p. 11.

6. I find *screwball* an unfortunate term for these great comedies. For an understanding of its genesis, see Kristine Karnick, "Commitment and Reaffirmation in Hollywood Romantic Comedy," in Kristine Karnick and Henry Jenkins, eds., *Classical Hollywood Comedy* (New York: Routledge, 1995), pp. 123–46.

7. Branagh, *Much Ado About Nothing: Screenplay*, p. viii.

8. In his interview with me about his performance of Hamlet for the Royal Shakespeare Company in 1992–93, as he was editing his film of *Much Ado*, Branagh remarked, "If I can't make Shakespeare live for a broad audience with all the Hollywood that got packed into the film, then I doubt I will be able to raise the financing for a *Hamlet* film"; see Crowl, interview with Branagh in *Shakespeare Bulletin* 12, no. 4 (1994): 8. For Jackson's remarks, see his "Shakespeare Comedies on Film," in Davies and Wells, *Shakespeare and the Moving Image*, pp. 116–19.

9. Stanley Cavell, *Pursuits of Happiness: The Hollywood Comedy of Remarriage* (Cambridge: Harvard University Press, 1981), pp. 17–18.

10. Ibid., p. 18.

11. Ibid., p. 19.

12. Several essays in Karnick and Jenkins, *Classical Hollywood Comedy*, particularly those by Kristine Karnick and Charles Musser, try to rework Cavell's formulations without significantly improving on them.

13. Beatrice is the most liberated of Shakespeare's comic heroines; she shares

the greatest affinity with Cavell's "new woman" because, unlike Rosalind and Viola, she speaks out of her own voice as a female without having to assume a masculine identity to express an independent, witty perspective on love and romance.

14. Branagh, *Much Ado About Nothing: Screenplay*, p. xi.

15. For instance, C. L. Barber does not include *Much Ado* in his *Shakespeare's Festive Comedy*.

16. Anne Barton, "Shakespeare in the Sun," *New York Review of Books*, May 27, 1993, p. 11.

17. Perhaps spurred by Branagh's film, a recent, highly acclaimed stage production of *Much Ado* by the Cheek by Jowl Company relentlessly underlines the play's class and gender divisions; see Jane Collins's review in *Shakespeare Bulletin* 16, no. 3 (1998): 10–11.

18. Hatchuel, *Films of Kenneth Branagh*, p. 124.

19. See Jorgens, *Shakespeare on Film*, pp. 73–74, for an excellent analysis of the festive comedy atmosphere that pervades Zeffirelli's film.

20. Coursen, *Shakespeare in Production*, p. 116.

21. Branagh, *Much Ado About Nothing: Screenplay*, p. ix. Branagh's film reportedly cost about $12 million to make and has grossed more than $35 million in worldwide sales, not counting television or video rental revenues.

22. Branagh, *Much Ado About Nothing: Screenplay*, pp. ix–x.

23. Branagh's first full-length play, *Public Enemy*, dramatizes the life of a young man coming of age in Belfast in the 1960s through the lens of several Jimmy Cagney films from the 1930s.

24. It is this moment in the film that most troubles Lehmann, who finds it emblematic of Branagh's failure to deliver on his popular and populist impulses. See her "Shakespeare, Branagh, and the National-Popular," pp. 14–16.

25. Maria DiBattista, *Fast-Talking Dames* (New Haven: Yale University Press, 2001), p. 38.

26. With an echo here perhaps of Olivier's more elaborate move from stage to painted sets and to Ireland's Powerscourt (then back again) in his film of *Henry V*. Hatchuel reads this move as the film's artistic credo: "Branagh will make art come to life, as he makes Shakespeare live again from the written pages": *Films of Kenneth Branagh*, p. 124.

27. Ibid., p. 126.

28. Vincent Canby shares my amusement with this opening sequence in his review of the film in the *New York Times* (May 7, 1993), but many viewers have failed to be charmed. A senior colleague in my department who is generally sympathetic to the tastes and habits of the young commented: "I was disappointed with the film. I can literally hear the director shouting 'Come on. Get some life! You over there by the window, show some teeth! Remember Errol Flynn! A little more swash and less buckle!' That opening sequence gave me the Stanford football team on their way to a tryst with a Southern Cal sorority's summer camp."

29. *New Yorker*, May 10, 1993, p. 97.

30. Anne Barton ("Shakespeare in the Sun") notes that Branagh's problem in delivering Benedick's soliloquies comes from "his insistence upon looking everywhere except into the camera." I agree with Barton that had Branagh's Benedick confronted the camera directly he would have given us a less edgy and contorted performance, a version of the more self-assured Benedick we both have come to expect—perhaps a Benedick played with the cool control demonstrated in the film by Denzel Washington. But Branagh clearly wants to stress the insecurity of his Benedick's antiromantic stance. This Benedick is not able to be comfortable with himself or the camera until he has confronted and confessed his affection for Beatrice.

31. Branagh comments on the fountain scene: "Benedick has thrown what he thinks to be a gallant and sexy leg up on the edge of the fountain. He strikes a pose and a tone of voice that reminds one of Tony Curtis as Cary Grant in *Some Like It Hot*. It is a face frozen in a grin that is trying to convey sex, romance, intelligence, wit, and warmth all at once. In short, he looks ridiculous": *Much Ado About Nothing: Screenplay*, p. 47.

32. Branagh admits that Shakespeare's clowns escape him. "In the Dogberry scenes we cut the unfunniest lines. (I realize this is an entirely subjective issue, but having played one of the great unfunny Shakespearean clowns—Touchstone in *As You Like It*—I speak from bitter experience.)" Branagh also acknowledges that, from the beginning, he and Keaton had determined that Dogberry "should be not only a verbal but a physical malaprop": *Much Ado About Nothing: Screenplay*, pp. xiii, xv.

33. Barton, "Shakespeare in the Sun," p. 11.

34. Russell Jackson, the film's textual adviser, comments: "Inserting a scene showing us what Claudio sees to make him think Hero is unfaithful always seemed inevitable to me—one of those moments where the movie audience has the right to see rather than just hear a description": "Working with Shakespeare: Confessions of an Advisor," *Cineaste* 24, no. 1 (1998): 44.

FIVE

1. Nunn left active involvement with the Royal Shakespeare Company in the mid-1980s to work as a freelance director of West End musicals. He returned to the classical repertory theater when he succeeded Richard Eyre as director of the Royal National Theatre in 1998.

2. Trevor Nunn, "Shakespeare in the Cinema: A Film Director's Symposium," *Cineaste* 24, no. 1 (1998): 48.

3. Ann Jennalie Cook, "Off the Book: Extra-textual Effects on Trevor Nunn's *Twelfth Night*," paper presented to the film seminar, World Shakespeare Congress, Valencia, Spain, April 18–23, 2001.

4. See Barber's chapter on the play "Testing Courtesy and Humanity in *Twelfth Night*," in *Shakespeare's Festive Comedy*, pp. 240–61.

5. The finest essay on the musical qualities of the play remains John Hollander's

"The Role of Music in *Twelfth Night*," in *Sound and Poetry: English Institute Essays, 1956* (Cambridge: Cambridge University Press, 1957), pp. 66–82. See also Eric C. Brown's "What's to Come Is Still Unsure: Madness and Deferral in Nunn's *Twelfth Night*," *Colby Quarterly* 37, no. 1 (2001): 15–29, for an intelligent analysis of Nunn's use of Feste's songs to serve the larger interpretive reaches of his film.

6. I am indebted to my graduate students in English 524/724 at Ohio University in spring 1999 for pointing out to me that the storm becomes brutal and perilous at the moment Viola playfully tries to test the reality of her brother's gender identity. Is the storm, for Nunn, nature's response to this subversive gesture?

7. Brown, "Madness and Deferral," p. 17.

8. For a brilliant analysis of Nunn's use of cross-cutting as a means of collapsing these two scenes into a continuous film moment, see Laurie E. Osborne's "Cutting Up Characters in Trevor Nunn's *Twelfth Night*," in Courtney Lehmann and Lisa S. Starks, eds., *Spectacular Shakespeare: Critical Theory and Popular Cinema* (Madison, N.J.: Fairleigh Dickinson University Press, 2002).

9. Rothwell, *History of Shakespeare on Screen*, p. 239.

10. Coursen writes: "Trevor Nunn's *Twelfth Night* is one of the more straightforward translations of a Shakespeare script to film": *Two Traditions*, p. 199.

11. This quotation is from Nunn's screenplay, which uses "I'll" in place of the text's "We'll": *Twelfth Night: A Screenplay*, p. 133.

12. Michael Shurgot, like Nunn, sees that Feste's final song "disables joy." *Stages of Play: Shakespeare's Theatrical Energies in Elizabethan Performance* (Newark: University of Delaware Press, 1998), p. 173.

13. Though they go unmentioned in Nunn's introduction to his screenplay, the poster for the film announced its affinities with these films. See Richard Burt's "New Shakesqueer Cinema," in Boose and Burt, *Shakespeare, The Movie*, pp. 240–68, for a thorough exploration of a queer aesthetic at work in recent Shakespeare films, including Nunn's *Twelfth Night*.

14. Interestingly, Burt ignores the film's treatment of Antonio to concentrate on the Orsino/Cesario relationship: "Orsino's diminished interest in the revealed Viola suggested that he preferred her when she was a he": "New Shakesqueer Cinema," p. 244.

15. Coursen, *Two Traditions*, p. 201.

16. See Laurie E. Osborne, *The Trick of Singularity:* Twelfth Night *and the Performance Editions* (Iowa City: University of Iowa Press, 1996) for a comprehensive stage history of the repositioning of these scenes in performance.

17. For a thorough discussion of "Nature to her bias drew in that" and the centrality of "swerving" implied in that image lifted from the game of bowls, see Stephen Greenblatt's "Fiction and Friction," in his *Shakespearean Negotiations* (Berkeley: University of California Press, 1988), pp. 66–93. Nunn's repositioning of Shakespeare's text also allows him to sustain the film audience's interest in Orsino, who disappears from Shakespeare's play between acts 2 and 5.

18. Valerie Traub, *Desire and Anxiety: Circulations of Sexuality in Shakespearean Drama* (London: Routledge, 1992), p. 136.

19. Brown, "Madness and Deferral," pp. 19–20.

20. It is interesting to remember that Helena Bonham Carter's career as a film actress began when Nunn cast her as the title character in his first film, *Lady Jane* (1985).

21. Orgel, cleverly, sees the issue as more open-ended: "Whatever Viola says about the erotic realities of her inner life, she is not a woman unless she is dressed as one. . . . The costume is the real thing. . . . Clothes make the woman, clothes make the man: the costume is of the essence": Stephen Orgel, *Impersonations: The Performance of Gender in Shakespeare's England* (Cambridge: Cambridge University Press, 1996), p. 104.

22. My students found an interesting subtext for this relationship in the film. In their reading of Staunton's performance, they detected that she has a romantic interest in Feste; she responds to Toby's sloshy command: "Come by and by to my chamber" only after Ben Kingsley's Feste has nodded to her as if to say, "Better take him up on the invitation, I'm not available." If this reading is correct, it makes the union of Maria and Toby even more bitter and melancholy.

23. Twenty years ago, in a production of the play at Canada's Stratford, Brian Bedford's Malvolio appeared in the revels scene in the customary white nightgown but clutching a teddy behind his back. When he began to lecture Sir Toby, the bear inadvertently shot out, held in the scolding hand. This moment got the huge laugh it sought, but like Hawthorne's reading *L'Amour*, it seemed to me out-of-character and sentimental.

24. Coursen, *Two Traditions*, p. 202.

25. Thomas Pendleton is right to see that "the four actors playing the lovers are very appealing; Imogen Stubbs as Viola (even with a mustache) is irresistible; but they and she are so in large part because the prologue provides an emotional base for Viola's sadness, vulnerability, resilience, and hope. The visual images makes her experience powerfully felt; the words make it somewhat clearer": "Shakespeare . . . with Additional Dialog," *Cineaste* 24, no. 1 (1998): 66.

26. Nunn, *Twelfth Night: A Screenplay*, p. ii.

27. Ibid., p. iv.

SIX

1. Parker's film opened in the United States on December 15, 1995; the verdict in the Simpson trial was announced two months earlier (October 3).

2. See Barbara Hodgdon's cultural-studies analysis of the film in her *The Shakespeare Trade: Performances and Appropriations* (Philadelphia: University of Pennsylvania Press, 1998), pp. 64–73, for an inviting attempt to read Parker's *Othello* as a version of the O. J. Simpson/Nicole Brown Simpson story. See also Lisa S.

Starks, "The Veiled (Hot) Bed of Race and Desire: Parker's *Othello* and the Stereotype as Screen Fetish," *Post Script* 17, no. 1 (1997): 64–78.

3. Kenneth S. Rothwell intelligently sees that Parker's opening montage "clarifies the vague pronoun reference, 'this,' in the first line of *Othello* when Roderigo says to Iago '[tush] never tell me! I take it much unkindly / That thou Iago, who hadst my purse / As if the strings were thine, shouldst know of *this*' [Rothwell's italic] (1.1.1). This what? Parker replies in pictures": *History of Shakespeare on Screen*, p. 235.

4. Judith Buchanan, "Virgin and Ape, Venetian and Infidel: Labellings of Otherness in Oliver Parker's *Othello*," in Burnett and Wray, *Shakespeare, Film, Fin de Siècle*, p. 182.

5. Rothwell, I think, misses the repressed homoeroticism that informs Branagh's performance when he comments that "Parker pays no attention to the fashionable vogue for a homoerotic attraction between Iago and Othello": *History of Shakespeare on Screen*, p. 237. Burt, on the other hand, sees Iago's attraction to Othello as being central to Branagh's performance: "Branagh plays Iago in Oliver Parker's 1995 Snoop Doggy-Dog-Style *Othello* as a gay man who loves Othello but cannot admit it and so destroys him and his wife": "New Shakesqueer Cinema," p. 241.

6. Buchanan, "Otherness in Oliver Parker's *Othello*," p. 186.

7. Hodgdon observes, "As Othello, Fishburne is a powerfully controlled, self-possessed figure, radiating a quiet, reserved dignity from a magnificent physical presence": *Shakespeare Trade*, p. 65.

8. Peter Donaldson convincingly argues that, ultimately, it is Branagh's Iago and Fishburne's Othello who are paired as "others" in the film "by their easy fit with US movie star conventions. . . . So I don't read Othello and Desdemona as paired by their otherness, but Iago and Othello, paired by the exoticism of the others, and by their closeness to and appeal for 'us,' the film audience": private correspondence, April 2001.

9. See Lisa S. Starks's analysis of the film's treatment of Fishburne's Othello in her "Veiled (Hot) Bed of Race and Desire," pp. 70–75.

10. Hodgdon, *Shakespeare Trade*, p. 65.

11. Jacob's Desdemona resembles the Miranda-like character she played in Krzysztof Kieslowski's *Red*, the film that brought her to Parker's attention.

12. For Hodgdon, Parker's romantic excess here has led him into troubled waters: she reads this sequence as feeding "a white male viewer's potentially racist fantasies of miscegenation": *Shakespeare Trade*, p. 67. But Buchanan counters by reminding us that "Parker's camera aligns itself intermittently with Desdemona's desirous gaze throughout the film. Othello's body is explicitly eroticized by its visual strategy. On the night of their arrival in Cyprus, it is, for example, his undressing not hers, upon which the camera lingers with the most intimate and detailed appreciation": "Otherness in Oliver Parker's *Othello*," p. 183.

13. Coursen, *Two Traditions*, p. 177.

14. Ibid., p. 177.

15. In an interview with James Lipton, broadcast as part of the *Inside the Actors Studio* series on the Bravo channel, Fishburne remarked that Branagh had sensed his trepidation in approaching Othello and had helpfully commented "I'm from Northern Ireland and I'm not supposed to be able to do this stuff either."

16. The other unusual shot comes in the film's version of 2.1, where Parker's camera gives us a reflection of Desdemona and Cassio in the blade of Iago's knife as he whispers, "With a little web as this I will ensnare as great a fly as Cassio" (2.1.168–69).

17. Buchanan notes that Parker's camera captures Iago here in the film's "only rising, high-angle shot . . . immediately and drastically redefining the camera's relationship with Iago . . . he has now been diminished and objectified. He is now denied the consoling illusion that he is constructing the pictures we see": "Otherness in Oliver Parker's *Othello*," p. 187.

18. Coursen, *Two Traditions*, p. 180.

19. Rothwell writes of this image: "The fetish handkerchief floats aloft as a surrealistic image of its terrible powers": *History of Shakespeare on Screen*, p. 237.

20. *New Yorker*, December 18, 1995, pp. 126–27.

SEVEN

1. See Jonathan Rosenbaum, *This Is Orson Welles* (New York: HarperCollins, 1992), p. 228.

2. Coursen, *Shakespeare in Production: Whose History?* pp. 232–33.

3. Richard Eyre, *Utopia and Other Places* (London: Bloomsbury Press, 1993), p. 157.

4. In his *Richard III: A Screenplay* (London: Doubleday, 1996), McKellen refers, mistakenly I believe, to the bravura physicality of this feat as "cheeky theatricality" well eliminated from his screen performance.

5. Jorgens, *Shakespeare on Film*, p. 136.

6. McKellen, *Richard III: A Screenplay*, p. 13.

7. Eyre, *Utopia and Other Places*, p. 159.

8. James N. Loehlin, "'Top of the World, Ma': Richard III and Cinematic Convention," in Boose and Burt, *Shakespeare, The Movie*, pp. 70–71.

9. McKellen, *Richard III: A Screenplay*, p. 14.

10. Olivier also eliminated Margaret from his film, feeling that the dynastic feud she represents was too removed from a contemporary mass audience. But he did allow his conception of Richard to dominate the film, not only in performance but in film device as well.

11. H. R. Coursen, *Reading Shakespeare on Stage* (Newark: University of Delaware Press, 1995), pp. 9–12.

12. As further evidence of the film's attention to minuscule details, the bandleader bears a striking resemblance to Glenn Miller, and all the music stands are decorated with the intertwining initials *WS*.

13. David Troughton, a recent Richard in England (RSC, 1995–96), also divided the speech in this manner—the first half delivered as a court performance, the second as confessional, directly to the audience.

14. I am quoting from the screenplay where McKellen has transposed lines from Gloucester's soliloquy in 3.2 of *Henry VI*, part 3, into Richard's "Now is the winter. . ." soliloquy; *Richard III: A Screenplay*, pp. 64–65.

15. Ibid. p. 65.

16. Ibid. p. 80.

17. Loehlin, "'Top of the World, Ma,'" p. 71.

18. Howlett also has an analysis of the film that explores its connection to the American gangster film: "Vivid Negativity: Richard Loncraine's *Richard III*," in her *Framing Shakespeare on Film*, pp. 128–48.

19. Loehlin, "'Top of the World, Ma,'" pp. 73–74.

20. Ibid., p. 74.

21. Stephen Holden, "Review of *Richard III*," *New York Times*, December 29, 1995, B1.

22. Stephen M. Buhler has an interesting essay exploring the film's relationship to both camp and the postmodern aesthetic: "Camp *Richard III* and the Burdens of (Stage/Film) History," in Burnett and Wray, *Shakespeare, Film, Fin de Siècle*, pp. 40–57.

23. Linda Charnes, *Notorious Identity* (Cambridge: Harvard University Press, 1993), pp. 32–33.

24. Juan Cobos and Miguel Rubio, "Welles and Falstaff," *Sight and Sound* 35 (autumn 1966): 57.

25. Richard races through the film's depiction of the battle of Bosworth Field in a Jeep; he utters his famous equestrian cry only when the Jeep becomes immobilized after waging battle with several lumbering tanks, thus making a prophet of Terry Hands, the former director of the Royal Shakespeare Company. In a 1990 discussion with several other RSC directors about directing *Twelfth Night*, the conversation turned to the potential dangers of setting the play in a modern context. Hands remarked, "if you set the play on a modern Greek island, then obviously Malvolio would have to come on, not in cross-garters, but in hippy clothes, like a flower child wearing a lot of beads, and there would be a social context you would have to accommodate. The problem is, down that road lies 'A tank, a tank—my kingdom for a tank!'": quoted in Michael Billington, *Approaches to Twelfth Night* (London: Nick Hern Books, 1990), p. 33.

EIGHT

1. The film's title is as slippery as its style. It has been reproduced variously as *William Shakespeare's Romeo + Juliet* (the most common version); as *William Shakespeare's Romeo & Juliet* (used for the published film script); and in two versions that,

for typographical reasons, I will not attempt to reproduce here. The first of those two versions, used in the posters for the film, reproduces the + symbol in the shape of the filigreed cross that frequently appears in the film (in, for example, the tattoo on Friar Lawrence's back and the engraving on Juliet's wedding ring); the second, used on the package for the DVD release of the film, replaces the + symbol with the conventional image for a heart.

2. It must be noted that it did not face stiff competition. It opened alongside such forgettable films as *Mother Night*, an adaptation of Kurt Vonnegut's novel, starring Nick Nolte; *Larger than Life*, with Bill Murray; and something called *Dear God*. These were all $50 million films that quickly disappeared from screens across the country, reminding one again what a major commercial gamble Hollywood films are.

3. For details on the Murdoch connection, see Peter S. Donaldson, "'All which it inherit': Shakespeare, Globes, and Global Media," *Shakespeare Survey* 52 (1999): 198.

4. Rothwell, *History of Shakespeare on Screen*, p. 241.

5. *New York Times*, November 1, 1996, p. B1.

6. Rothwell, *History of Shakespeare on Screen*, pp. 241–44, Coursen, *Two Traditions*, pp. 183–97; Donaldson, "Shakespeare, Globes, and Global Media"; Barbara Hodgdon, "*William Shakespeare's Romeo + Juliet:* Everything's Nice in America?" *Shakespeare Survey* 52 (1999): 88–98; James Loehlin, "These Violent Delights Have Violent Ends": Baz Luhrmann's Millennial Shakespeare," in Burnett and Wray, *Shakespeare, Film, and Fin de Siècle*, pp. 121–36; Courtney Lehmann, "Strictly Shakespeare?" *Shakespeare Quarterly* 52, no. 2 (2001): 189–221; and *Literature/Film Quarterly* 28, no. 2 (2000).

7. Hodgdon, "Everything's Nice in America?" p. 90.

8. Donaldson, "Shakespeare, Globes, and Global Media," p. 198 (italics in the original).

9. Ibid., p. 199.

10. Ibid., p. 200.

11. See Crystal Downing, "Misshapen Chaos of Well-Seeming Form: Baz Luhrmann's *Romeo + Juliet*," *Literature/Film Quarterly* 28, no. 2 (2000): 128.

12. Ibid., p. 128.

13. *William Shakespeare's Romeo & Juliet: The Contemporary Film, the Classic Play* (New York: Bantam, 1996), p. 47.

14. See Hodgdon, "Everything's Nice in America?" p. 90.

15. Ibid., p. 91.

16. Russell Jackson, "Shakespeare, Films, and the Market Place," in Jackson, *Cambridge Companion to Shakespeare on Film*, p. 31.

17. Loehlin, "Baz Luhrmann's Millennial Shakespeare," p. 131.

18. Donaldson, "Shakespeare, Globes, and Global Media," p. 200.

19. Ibid., p. 199.

20. Lehmann, "Strictly Shakespeare?" p. 218.

21. Coursen, *Two Traditions*, p. 186.

22. Quoted in Loehlin, "Baz Luhrmann's Millennial Shakespeare," p. 134.

23. Donaldson, "Shakespeare, Globes, and Global Media," p. 199.

24. Geoffrey O'Brien, "The Ghost at the Feast," *New York Review of Books*, February 6, 1997, p. 13.

25. When the film was shot, DiCaprio was twenty, Danes seventeen. See Hodgdon, "Everything's Nice in America?" for an analysis of the film's incorporation of Afro-Americans, esp. p. 95.

26. Sometimes the ethnic transformations are so convoluted as to be amusing. Paul Sorvino is of Italian descent, here playing an Italian character (Capulet) but transformed in the film into a Hispanic. Where was Edward James Olmos when Luhrmann needed him?

27. See Neil Taylor's "National and Racial Stereotypes in Shakespeare Films," in Jackson, *Cambridge Companion to Shakespeare on Film*, p. 271, for more analysis of this issue in Luhrmann's film.

28. Quoted in Hodgdon, "Everything's Nice in America?" p. 88.

29. Carol Chillington Rutter, "Looking at Shakespeare's Women on Film," in Jackson, *Cambridge Companion to Shakespeare on Film*, p. 258.

30. Downing, "Misshapen Chaos," p. 128.

31. Alec Guinness, *A Positively Final Appearance* (New York: Viking, 1999), p. 16.

32. Coursen, *Two Traditions*, p. 189.

33. See Hodgdon, "Everything's Nice in America?" and Donaldson, "Shakespeare, Globes, and Global Media," for differing readings of the film's final moments.

NINE

1. Harry Keyishian writes compellingly about Branagh's film models, noting that his "*Hamlet* is, to be sure, not reflective of the early epic, which tends to celebrate national values and aspirations, but rather of a later, revisionist kind, full of subversive ironies and demythification": "Shakespeare and Movie Genre," in Jackson, *Cambridge Companion to Shakespeare on Film*, p. 80.

2. Howlett, *Framing Shakespeare*, pp. 178–200, and Emma Smith, "'Either for Tragedy, Comedy': Attitudes to *Hamlet* in Kenneth Branagh's *In the Bleak Midwinter* and *Hamlet*," in Burnett and Wray, *Shakespeare, Film, Fin de Siècle*, pp. 137–46.

3. See Russell Jackson's "Kenneth Branagh's Film of *Hamlet*: The Textual Choices," *Shakespeare Bulletin* 15, no. 2 (1997): 37–38; and Branagh, *Hamlet: Screenplay and Introduction*, p. 174, for discussions of the film's use of F1 and Q2 to construct the film text. There are several uncanny parallels between the worlds of Branagh's *Hamlet* and Welles's *The Lady from Shanghai*, involving revenge, a flirtation with nihilism, a bitter humor, and a fatal blonde.

4. Mark Thornton Burnett, "The Very Cunning of the Scene: Kenneth Branagh's *Hamlet*," *Literature/Film Quarterly* 25, no. 2 (1997): 78–82.

5. Interview with Branagh, March 16, 2001.

6. Ibid.

7. Peter Holland, *English Shakespeares*, pp. 179–80.

8. Kael, *Movie Love*, p. 216.

9. Laurie E. Osborne, "Shakespearean Short Cuts: Fragmentation and Coherence in Branagh's *Hamlet*," p. 1: essay delivered at the 1997 Modern Language Association meeting, Toronto.

10. Holland, *English Shakespeares*, p. 157.

11. See Branagh's introduction to his screenplay for *Much Ado About Nothing*, pp. vii–xvi, for the fullest statement of his aesthetic principles and his desire to make Shakespeare films "that belong to the world."

12. Hatchuel, *Films of Kenneth Branagh*, p. 29.

13. Terrence Rafferty, "Solid Flesh," *New Yorker*, January 13, 1997, p. 80.

14. *Filming Shakespeare's Plays* (Cambridge: Cambridge University Press, 1988), pp. 83–85.

15. *New York Review of Books*, February 6, 1997, p. 12.

16. See, for example, H. R. Coursen's "Words, Words, Words: Searching for Hamlet," paper presented to the New Shakespeare Films seminar, 1997 Shakespeare Association of America meeting, Washington, D.C.

17. Interview, March 16, 2001.

18. Russell Jackson, "Film Diary," in Branagh, *Hamlet: Screenplay and Introduction*, p. 205.

19. See Bernice Kliman's "The Unkindest Cuts: Flashcut Excess in Kenneth Branagh's *Hamlet*," in Deborah Cartmell and Michael Scott, eds., *Talking Shakespeare: Shakespeare into the Millennium* (London, 2001), pp. 151–67.

20. Interview, March 16, 2001.

21. Osborne, "Shakespearean Short Cuts," p. 7.

22. Ibid., p. 7.

23. Donaldson, *Shakespearean Films/Shakespearean Directors*, pp. 31–68.

24. See Burnett, "The Very Cunning" (p. 79) for an analysis of the Branagh-Jacobi, Hamlet-Claudius connections.

25. Robert Willson, "Kenneth Branagh's *Hamlet*, or the Revenge of Fortinbras," *Shakespeare Newsletter* 48, no. 1 (1997): 7 and 9.

26. Ibid, p. 7.

27. Interview, March 16, 2001.

28. Ibid.

29. Ibid.

30. Lisa S. Starks, noting the explicit absence of mother-son oedipal tension in Hamlet's encounter with Gertrude, nevertheless goes on to argue cleverly that "despite its resistance to psychoanalytic interpretation—or perhaps because of this resistance—Branagh's *Hamlet* provides the most "Oedipal" of all filmed *Hamlets*": "The Displaced Body of Desire: Sexuality in Kenneth Branagh's *Hamlet*," in

Christy Desmet and Robert Sawyer, eds., *Shakespeare and Appropriation* (London: Routledge, 2000), p. 160.

31. C. L. Barber and Richard Wheeler, *The Whole Journey: Shakespeare's Power of Development* (Berkeley: University of California Press, 1986), p. 242.

32. Ibid., p. 266.

33. Branagh, interview, March 16, p. 7.

34. See Branagh, *Beginning*, pp. 224–26, for examples of Branagh's relationship with Blessed.

35. Burnett, "The Very Cunning of the Scene," p. 82.

TEN

1. Author interview with Edzard, May 17, 2001, London.

2. Quoted in Amelia Marriette's "Urban Dystopias: Re-approaching Christine Edzard's *As You Like It*," in Burnett and Wray, *Shakespeare, Film, Fin de Siècle*, p. 74.

3. Ibid., p. 73.

4. Interview, May 17, 2001.

5. See Coursen, *Shakespeare in Production*, pp. 101–6.

6. Coursen, *Two Traditions*, p. 201.

7. Ibid., p. 200.

8. Marriette, "Urban Dystopias," p. 79.

9. Hattaway, "The Comedies on Film," p. 95.

10. Coursen, *Two Traditions*, p. 200.

11. Griff Rhys Jones (Touchstone) and Mel Smith (Sir Toby in Nunn's *Twelfth Night*) were comic partners in a popular English television show, *Smith and Jones*. Both Edzard and Nunn were obviously looking to find in contemporary English comedians a modern, fresh, approach to two of Shakespeare's most famous comic characters.

12. Edzard does make a potential connection between the two by dressing them in similar overcoats.

13. Russell Jackson, "Shakespeare's Comedies on Film," in Davies and Wells, *Shakespeare and the Moving Image*, p. 101.

14. The film's initial reviews also said no to its approach to Shakespeare. The film had the unhappy fate of being released in the same week in October 1992 as the reissued, restored print of Welles's *Othello*. Welles's film had, of course, been savaged on its release forty years earlier, but now it was used as the yardstick by which to measure (and find wanting) Edzard's film. I quote from examples of the film's reception (and its comparison with Welles's *Othello*) when it was released in October 1992: "On now to the indestructible Shakespeare; at least he seemed indestructible until Christine Edzard's *As You Like It* . . . can this lifeless film be based on a play that dances with wisdom and wit? There is no chance of thumb-twiddling with Orson Welles's 40-year-old film of *Othello*. . . . This is Shakespeare reinvented for the camera . . . Shakespeare meets celluloid, and a true film is born": *Times*

(London) October 8, 1992; "Christine Edzard's film version of *As You Like It* dons jeans and pin-stripes but signally fails to achieve either objective [contemporary relevance or the 'timelessness' of the script]. Indeed, the effect is not of a revealing incongruity but a drab, self-canceling conflict between text and setting. The contrast with Orson Welles's magnificent monochrome *Othello* . . . could not be more marked. . . . the sheer breadth and grandeur of Welles's cinematic imagination blazes out like a beacon": *Daily Telegraph*, October 9, 1992; "In this misguided and also perversely endearing version [of *As You Like It*], Christine Edzard ultimately proves the Bard's resilience, but she proves it the hard way. Orson Welles in his 1952 *Othello*, now restored, opts for a different blend of liberties and fidelities": *Independent*, October 9, 1992.

15. Interview, May 17, 2001.

16. Michael Apted has made a series of films following the same group of English children from childhood into middle age. He reinterviews the group on camera every seven years. Thus, the titles: *7, 14, 21, 28, 35,* and *42 Up.*

17. In what is no doubt no more than an interesting coincidence, Joy Leslie Gibson, in her book on the boy actor in Shakespeare's age, reports that Queen Elizabeth I provided the Master of the Children of the Queen's Revels sixpence a day for breakfast for his young actors: *Squeaking Cleopatras: The Elizabethan Boy Player* (Stroud: Sutton, 2000), p. 163.

ELEVEN

1. Kline is the exception on this list: he twice played Hamlet at the New York Public Theater, as well as a variety of other Shakespeare roles, including a brilliant Benedick.

2. Metatheatrical elements were at work in many of them, however: there were, for example, Luhrmann's ruined proscenium shell on the beach in his Verona, Hamlet's toy theater in Branagh's film, and the auditorium of the Denmark Corporation in Almereyda's *Hamlet.*

3. Russell Jackson, "Shakespeare at Stratford-upon-Avon, 1996–98; Or the Search for a Policy," *Shakespeare Quarterly* 50, no. 2 (1999): 185.

4. See Jorgens, *Shakespeare on Film,* pp. 7–16.

5. Mark Burnett, "Impressions of Fantasy: Adrian Noble's *A Midsummer Night's Dream*," in Burnett and Wray, *Shakespeare, Film, Fin de Siècle,* p. 92.

6. Ibid., p. 91.

7. Author interview with Noble, May 14, 2001.

8. Ibid.

9. Ibid.

10. See pp. 92–98 of Burnett, "Impressions of Fantasy."

11. Noble's screenplay cuts the sixteen lines at the heart of Helena's early lament about love (1.1.226–48) and a similar passage of fourteen lines from "We, Hermia, like two artificial gods" down through "And will you rent our ancient love

asunder, / To join with men in scorning your poor friend?" In each instance, the confusion and agony men have created in the poignant relationship between Helena and Hermia is lost.

12. Interview, May 14, 2001.

13. Ibid.

14. Bergman's *Magic Flute* was first broadcast on Swedish television on January 1, 1975, as a New Year's present to the nation. Bergman wanted his film of Mozart's opera to appeal to the entire family, from children to grandparents. He incorporated into his treatment three cherubic boys who serve as guardian spirits over the action; his camera also repeatedly pans the audience watching the performance, frequently lingering on the enraptured face of a young girl. Noble's film was released in England in late November 1996; I think he wished to follow in Bergman's footsteps in offering a greatly loved work from the English classical repertory as a Christmas box for the entire family. Unlike Bergman's offering, his package had a hard time, not only being slashed by savage reviews but disappointing also because of its own shortcomings. The film might have had a more welcome reception if, like Bergman's, it had initially been shown on television as a holiday treat. When, in fact, the film was televised a year later, the response, according to Noble, was more positive.

15. Here is a sample of the dismissive responses to Noble's film from the British newspaper reviewers: "Adrian Noble's *A Midsummer Night's Dream* . . . proves so lacking in screen presence that it puts the Bard's cause back a hundred years": *Times*, November 28, 1996; "The combination of Adrian Noble, the Arts Council, Channel 4 films and William Shakespeare is enough to strike fear into the hearts of all true Philistines. But relax. Noble's adaptation is no arty nightmare. On the contrary, it's more Muppets Christmas Special. I presume you all know the plot. I didn't and got lost within 60 seconds": *Sunday Times*, December 1, 1996; "*A Midsummer Night's Dream*, the gifted Adrian Noble's first venture into the cinema, is an unmitigated disaster . . . the fairies are dressed in the coarse, garishly colored material once favored for nasty bath mats and lavatory seat covers": *Observer*, December 1, 1996; "Adapted this way [as a child's dream], so that Shakespeare's text becomes a blueprint for the producer's imagination, the risks are considerable. Only half of them come off": *Guardian*, November 29, 1996.

16. Hoffman, introduction to *William Shakespeare's A Midsummer Night's Dream: A Screenplay* (New York: HarperEntertainment, 1999), p. ix.

17. H. R. Coursen, "Hoffman's *A Midsummer Night's Dream* and the Misuses of History," *Shakespeare and the Classroom* 7, no. 2 (1999): 54.

18. David Denby, "Bottom's Up," *New Yorker*, May 17, 1999, p. 97.

19. Ibid.

20. Russell Jackson, "A Shooting Script for the Reinhardt-Dieterle *Dream*: The War with the Amazons, Bottom's Wife, and other Missing Scenes," *Shakespeare Bulletin* 16, no. 4 (1998): 39–41.

21. Coursen, "Misuses of History," p. 54.

22. I am indebted to Peter S. Donaldson for the idea about the phonograph and the transforming cultural powers of technology in the twentieth century.

23. Coursen, "Misuses of History," p. 52.

24. Stanley Kauffmann, "Dream Time," *New Republic*, May 31, 1999, p. 32.

25. Ibid., p. 32.

26. Denby, "Bottom's Up," p. 97.

27. I am indebted to Aidan Kelleher Crowl for reminding me that Pooh is visiting Rabbit when he overindulges and gets stuck.

TWELVE

1. Michael Almereyda, *William Shakespeare's Hamlet: A Screenplay Adaptation* (London: Faber and Faber, 2000), p. xi.

2. See Rothwell, *History of Shakespeare on Screen*, pp. 241–44, for an analysis of the myriad cinematic sources for Luhrmann's film.

3. Almereyda, *William Shakespeare's Hamlet*, p. vii.

4. Ibid., p. ix.

5. Ibid., p. x.

6. Ibid., p. xii.

7. *New York Times*, May 12, 2000, p. B1.

8. Ibid., p. B18.

9. Ibid., p. B1.

10. "Flesh and Blood," *New Yorker*, May 15, 2000, p. 105.

11. Almereyda, *William Shakespeare's Hamlet*, p. 140.

12. Wiring Ophelia was Ethan Hawke's suggestion (inspired evidently by Linda Tripp). It is worth noting that the device also had been used several years before the Clinton incident by Henson Keys in his stage production of *Hamlet* at Ohio University in 1994.

13. Almereyda, *William Shakespeare's Hamlet*, p. ix.

14. Ibid., pp. 141–42.

15. The idea to begin with Hamlet rather than the ghost came after the first test screenings of the completed film by Miramax. Almereyda reports that they received "the second worst scores in the company's history." The director felt that part of the problem was that "Hamlet's first appearance in the film came too late and felt flat," so he devised, with Hawke, a new opening, using video-diary excerpts from the "What a piece of work is a man" speech to jump-start the movie, "giving the prince a series of intimate close-ups and a private (pixelated) language": Almereyda, *William Shakespeare's Hamlet*, p. 135. The film became the surprise Shakespeare film success of 2000, outgrossing both Taymor's *Titus* and Branagh's *Love's Labour's Lost*.

16. Ibid., p. 143.

17. Matthew Warchus, in his stage production of Hamlet starring Alex Jennings for the Royal Shakespeare Company in 1998, used film to show a flashback home-movie sequence of the Hamlet family ice skating—evidently for both directors an image of a happy family at play. Warchus's production was not well received, largely because of his compression and rearrangement of the text. At the time, I thought he had fashioned a Hamlet more interesting as a filmscript than play text, something equally true of Peter Brook's more famous stage production of the play in Paris in 2000 and 2001.

18. The filmscript (p. 136) tells us that it is Ophelia's birthday. The film gives us a montage of Hawke's struggle to write this poem, perhaps a sly reference to the relative difficulties of writing and videoing.

19. Almereyda, *William Shakespeare's Hamlet*, p. xiv.

20. *O*, directed by Tim Blake Nelson, was completed in 1999, before Almereyda's *Hamlet*. Its release, however, was postponed until August 2001 because of the Columbine High School shootings.

21. This effective cut was another editing-room necessity when plans to film Hamlet's famous soliloquy in three different locations, including Bill Viola's video installation "Slowly Turning Narrative" at the Whitney Museum, went awry because of Hawke's impromptu marriage to Uma Thurman. Viola's installation had moved on to Amsterdam by the time Hawke returned to work.

22. Shepard's family plays are famous for being dominated by strange, eccentric fathers. I had not realized, until watching his performance as the ghost, how importantly Hamlet's father figures as a compelling literary source for the power of those characters.

23. Almereyda reports that this idea came from reading Andrei Tarkovsky's notes for his stage production of *Hamlet*: *William Shakespeare's Hamlet*, p. 133.

24. See ibid., pp. 140–41.

THIRTEEN

1. Appropriately, Olivier was the narrator of the BBC's monumental retelling of World War II, *The World at War*, thought by many to be the best historical documentary ever made for television. When Ted Turner determined to make a similar twenty-episode account of the cold war, he recruited the man who had made *The World at War*, Jeremy Isaacs, to do the job. Isaacs then selected Branagh to narrate the series for CNN.

2. See Lawrence F. Kaplan's "Fall Guys," *New Republic*, June 26, 2000, pp. 22–25.

3. Taymor has commented: "The reason the story [*The Lion King*] works is that it's a classic coming-of-age tale. It touches on the timeless themes that can be found in all great literature and in ritual theater: the death of the father, the dark rite of

passage of a young man before he can return home, the competition for power in a family, and the balance of nature with man": *New York Times*, Sunday, April 16, 2000, pp. 18–19.

4. Adrian Noble used a similar device, and the same actor, as the frame for his film of *A Midsummer Night's Dream*.

5. *New Republic*, January 24, 2000, p. 30.

6. The most recent version of which, in Sam Mendes's film *American Beauty*, does not improve upon Shakespeare's example.

7. Miranda Johnson-Haddad, "A Time for *Titus:* An Interview with Julie Taymor," *Shakespeare Bulletin* 18, no. 4 (2000). 35.

8. See Barber and Wheeler, *Whole Journey: Shakespeare's Power of Development*, pp. 125–57.

9. This is Shakespeare's invention. Blood sacrifice was not a Roman ritual, and there is no mention of the practice in the scanty sources we have for *Titus Andronicus*.

10. See Rothwell, *History of Shakespeare on Screen*, p. 3.

11. *Titus: Production Notes* (press packet for the film), p. 10.

12. "Film Reviews: Three by H. R. Coursen," *Shakespeare and the Classroom* 8, no. 1 (2000): 40.

13. Ibid., p. 40.

14. Johnson-Haddad, "A Time for *Titus*," p. 36.

15. Kathy M. Howlett makes an intelligent parallel between this reflecting pool and the earlier pit that swallowed Bassanius and Titus's sons. See her "Antipodal Anxieties in Julie Taymor's *Titus*," presented at the Seventh World Shakespeare Congress, Valencia, Spain, April 19, 2001, p. 6.

16. For a thorough discussion of the way several modern stage productions, particularly those by Peter Brook (1955), Trevor Nunn (1972), and Deborah Warner (1989), have dealt with Shakespeare's heady mixture of styles in the play, see Alan Dessen's *Titus Andronicus*, Shakespeare in Performance series (Manchester: Manchester University Press, 1989).

17. *Titus Andronicus*, ed. Jonathan Bate, The Arden Shakespeare (London: Routledge, 1995), p. 90.

18. Taymor notes that she intended for her film to hint at the animal imagery that provides a subtext for Chiron and Demetrius's encounter with Lavinia: "Within this very gritty drama there is a constant referencing to Latin and Greek mythology as well as to animal and nature's symbolism. We see the teeth of cruelty and then hear that 'Rome is but a wilderness of tigers.' . . . Lavinia . . . is often referred to as a doe. . . . The image of Lavinia, the doe, being ravished by Chiron and Demetrius, at once the sons of Tamora and ferocious tigers, had to be realized": *Production Notes* press packet, p. 10. Unfortunately, nothing in the film's depiction of Chiron and Demetrius gives us that sense of their animal savagery.

19. *Titus Andronicus*, pp. 11–12.

20. This is another instance of Taymor's creation of young Lucius as a compassionate reflector of her own humane values: "And this child . . . his first act is to try and help his aunt. He gives her that box, and she opens it, and the wooden hands are there. It's one of my favorite additions to the script": Johnson-Haddad, "A Time for *Titus*," p. 35.

21. The film's distinguished cinematographer, Luciano Tovoli, was justifiably proud of the way in which his camera and lighting captured this moment:

> I like the look of that scene very much . . . the place where we shot it was
> very small, so we placed the camera outside the door and used a very wide-
> angle lens. I didn't have much room for lights, so I placed a tower outside
> the room, and aimed an 18K HMI through the small window in the shot.
> I also added a small, warm, slightly different 1K Fresnel light on the right-
> hand side of the room for Anthony Hopkins' face, along with a bit of
> smoke to enhance the look of steam from the bath. I also bounced another
> small 1K to add a bit of warmth to the wall. It was a simple but elegant
> look, a bit like a painting.

Stephan Pizzello, "A Timeless Tale of Revenge," *American Cinematographer*, February 2000, p. 62.

FOURTEEN

1. Stanley Plumly, "Field," in *The Marriage in the Trees* (Hopewell, N.J.: Ecco Press, 1997), p. 60.

2. Coursen, *Two Traditions*, p. 240.

3. James Agee, "Henry V," reprinted in Charles W. Eckert, ed., *Focus on Shakespearean Films*, p. 54.

4. Boose and Burt, "Totally Clueless?" p. 19.

5. "Shakespeare's Cinematic Offshoots," in Jackson, *Cambridge Companion to Shakespeare on Film*, p. 310.

Index